# Using
# CompuServe®
## Third Edition

# Using

# CompuServe®

## Third Edition

*Michael Miller*

# Using CompuServe, Third Edition

Screen reproductions in this book were created using Collage Plus from Inner Media, Inc., Hollis, NH.

# Credits

**President**
Roland Elgey

**Publishing Manager**
Lynn E. Zingraf

**Editorial Services Director**
Elizabeth Keaffaber

**Managing Editor**
Michael Cunningham

**Director of Marketing**
Lynn E. Zingraf

**Acquisitions Editor**
Martha O'Sullivan

**Product Development Specialist**
John Gosney

**Production Editor**
Audra Gable

**Copy Editor**
Tom Lamoureux

**Strategic Marketing Manager**
Barry Pruett

**Technical Editor**
Herb Feltner

**Technical Support Specialist**
Nadeem Muhammed

**Software Relations Coordinator**
Patty Brooks

**Book Designer**
Ruth Harvey

**Cover Designer**
Dan Armstrong

**Production Team**
Linda Cox
Erin M. Danielson
Dimonique Ford
Trey Frank
Kay Hoskin
Daryl Kessler
Michelle Lee
Kaylene Riemen

**Indexer**
Craig Small

Composed in *ITC Century, ITC Highlander,* and *MCPdigital* by Que Corporation.

*To Sherry, who is happily back in my life after far too many years away.*

# About the Author

**Michael Miller** is Vice President of Business Strategy for Macmillan Publishing and has been active in the publishing industry for almost a decade. He is the author of more than a dozen computer books, including Que's *Using Prodigy, Easy Internet, OOPS! What to Do When Things Go Wrong,* and the previous edition of *Using CompuServe.* He writes the monthly column "Miller's View" for the Macmillan Information SuperLibrary newsletter, and he has his own Web pages at **http://www.mcp.com/people/miller/**. His e-mail address is **mmiller@mcp.com**, and his CompuServe ID is **73207,2013**.

# Acknowledgments

Thanks to everyone at Que for their hard work and cooperation on this project.

# We'd Like to Hear from You!

As part of our continuing effort to produce books of the highest possible quality, Que would like to hear your comments. To stay competitive, we *really* want you, as a computer book reader and user, to let us know what you like or dislike most about this book or other Que products.

You can mail comments, ideas, or suggestions for improving future editions to the address below, or send us a fax at (317) 581-4663. For the online inclined, Macmillan Computer Publishing has a forum on CompuServe (type **GO QUEBOOKS** at any prompt) through which our staff and authors are available for questions and comments. The address of our Internet site is **http://www.mcp.com/que** (World Wide Web).

In addition to exploring our forum, please feel free to contact me personally to discuss your opinions of this book: I'm **104436,2300** on CompuServe, and I'm **jgosney@que.mcp.com** on the Internet.

Thanks in advance—your comments will help us to continue publishing the best books available on computer topics in today's market.

John Gosney
Product Development Specialist
Que Corporation
201 W. 103rd Street
Indianapolis, Indiana 46290
USA

# Contents at a Glance

## Surfing the Internet from CompuServe 239

## Que CompuServe Directory 313

## Index 427

# Table of Contents

## 7 The Heart of CompuServe: Fun with Forums

## 8 Talk Is Cheap: CompuServe's Chat Services

## 9 Finding and Downloading Files

## Part III: Getting More out of CompuServe

## 10 Making Your Sessions Automatic with CompuServe Navigator

## 11 Other Ways to Automate Your Sessions

## 12 Going Global

## 13 Going Traveling

## Part IV: Surfing the Internet from CompuServe

## 22 Forums on the Internet: USENET Newsgroups

## 23 Finding and Downloading Files on the Internet

# Introduction

If experience is the best teacher, I must know a lot about CompuServe. At least that's the impression you'd get if you saw my monthly CompuServe bills. Let's hope I can help you become a CompuServe expert without causing you to rack up monthly bills like mine.

## What is CompuServe?

CompuServe is a commercial online service that competes with other services such as America Online, Prodigy, and The Microsoft Network. You dial into CompuServe using your computer and a modem, and CompuServe charges you for the privilege.

CompuServe is like an electronic small town. You wander down the virtual main street and find all sorts of shops—large and small, general and esoteric. And as you walk, you run into all sorts of interesting people to talk with. All manner of social interaction can be yours, just for the asking.

Want up-to-the-minute news and stock reports? A large collection of newspaper and magazine articles? A place to share your opinions on issues of the day? Some help using your computer hardware and software? A forum to share your hobbies and special interests? A collection of stores that offers a variety of quality merchandise? Well, CompuServe has all of that—and more. In short, you can find just about anything you want on CompuServe.

## What is the Internet?

If CompuServe is an electronic small town, the Internet is the electronic *world*—with hundreds of millions of global citizens. CompuServe 3.0 provides you with a direct connection to the Internet, where you can use such Internet services as e-mail, USENET newsgroups, and the World Wide Web.

The Web is, in my opinion, the neatest thing you can find online. On the Web, you'll find a mind-boggling array of sites covering just about every topic imaginable, all linked to one another via the use of a hot new technology called **hypertext**.

Fortunately, CompuServe 3.0 includes a built-in Web browser that lets you view Web pages the same way you access CompuServe's proprietary services. In fact, with CompuServe 3.0, it's hard to tell where CompuServe ends and the Internet begins!

# Why would you use CompuServe?

Of course, just about everything you can do with CompuServe, you can also do by walking down the main street of your town. But with CompuServe, you don't have to lace up your shoes, put on your jacket, and do the walking. All you have to do is pull a chair up to your computer and punch a few keys. Nobody cares how you're dressed or if you've washed your hair today. In fact, no one will even notice you're there unless you want them to.

It's just more convenient to do all that stuff in one place. And what place could be more convenient than your own home? No matter what you want to do, you can do it on CompuServe. Why wouldn't you use it?

# Why should you read this book?

If you're reading this book—while at home, at work, or at the bookstore—you're probably already connected to CompuServe (or you want to be). You will use this book for at least one of these purposes:

- You're new to CompuServe, and you want to learn the ropes.

- You've used an older version of CompuServe, but you want to learn about CompuServe 3.0.

- You know your way around CompuServe, but you want to expand your horizons.

- You already use CompuServe a lot, and you want to cut your online expenditures.

- You have some sort of a problem with CompuServe and need to find a solution for it.

Whatever the case, you've come to the right place. This book can help you do whatever it is you want to do with CompuServe.

# What will you find in this book?

Let's take a quick look at the 5 major parts of *Using CompuServe, Third Edition* and see how they can help you become a better CompuServe user.

- **Part I: Getting Around: CompuServe Basics**. Learn how to get up and running and explore some basic features of CompuServe 3.0.

- **Part II: Communications and Communities**. Learn all about - CompuServe e-mail, forums, files, and chat services.

- **Part III: Getting More out of CompuServe**. Learn all about CompuServe's features and services—including third-party programs that help you use CompuServe more quickly and more effectively.

- **Part IV: Surfing the Internet from CompuServe**. Learn how to explore the wide, wide world of the Internet from within CompuServe.

- **Que CompuServe Directory**. An A-to-Z directory of CompuServe services and related services on the Internet.

This book was designed to be used for reference, so feel free to jump directly to those sections that interest you the most. You don't have to read the book from cover to cover to find out what you need to know.

# What's new with this edition?

This third edition of *Using CompuServe* has been completely updated and rewritten to focus on the new features of CompuServe 3.0, such as the redesigned interface and automatic links to Internet-based resources. In addition, this book covers all the newest (and updated) CompuServe forums and services.

This book focuses on CompuServe 3.0 for Windows 95. The Windows 95 version of CompuServe is functionally identical to the Windows NT version, and it's very similar to the Windows 3.X and Macintosh versions. You should be able to use this book no matter which version of CompuServe you're using; however, you might have to do some slight interpolating if you're not running Windows 95.

If you've read the previous edition of this book, no doubt you've already noticed the newest feature of this book: the Que CompuServe Directory. In the directory, you'll find information on all of CompuServe's services and forums—as well as related Internet-based resources—listed alphabetically by topic.

# Conventions used in this book

The conventions used in this book have been established to help you learn to use CompuServe quickly and easily. Here are some of those conventions:

- Text you are instructed to type appears in **bold type**.

- An underline marks the letter that's underlined in CompuServe's menu names and dialog box choices; you can use the underlined letter to access commands from the keyboard.

- Screen messages and on-screen results appear in a `special typeface`.

- Key combinations use a plus sign (+) to separate the keys (Ctrl+S, for example). This means to press and hold the first key, press the next key, and then release both keys at once.

- Special commands, called GO commands, contain all uppercase characters (GO IQUEST, for example).

- Tips and cautions give time-saving shortcuts, additional information, and warnings about potential problems.

- Question & answer sections present some common problems and help you solve them.

# Part I: Getting Around: CompuServe Basics

# 1

# Getting Started with CompuServe

● **In this chapter:**

- **CompuServe's membership requirements**

- **How much does it cost?**

- **How do I sign up?**

- **Finding the right access number**

- **Changing your user options**

*CompuServe is as easy to use as pointing and clicking your mouse—providing you know what to point at!* . . . . . . . . ➤

**T**his chapter is for first-time CompuServe users. If you're already registered with CompuServe and are cruising along just fine, you can probably skip ahead. If you're new to all of this, however, or if you're just thinking about signing up, this chapter is for you.

Becoming a CompuServe member is really quite easy. And after you sign up, you will see that CompuServe offers several services specifically designed for new users. So, if you're ready, let's move ahead and learn how you, too, can become a CompuServe member.

# Are you ready to sign up?

You've decided you want to become a CompuServe member, but you're not sure what that really entails. Just what do you need to join and access CompuServe?

- A personal computer. Just about any PC will do. However, this book specifically deals with the Windows 95 version of CompuServe, so to get the most out of this book, you'll want a PC capable of running Windows 95.

- A modem—the faster the better! A 14,400 baud modem is the bare minimum for acceptable performance; 28,800 is recommended.

- A phone line. Your normal phone line will do; you don't need a separate line to use CompuServe.

- A CompuServe access number. (See the section "Finding the right number," later in this chapter.)

- A form of payment for fees. These are generally charged to a credit card, but you can arrange direct-billing options.

# The privileges—and costs—of membership

I hate to remind you, but CompuServe isn't free. As soon as you sign up, you start paying for the privilege of being a CompuServe member.

CompuServe has two basic membership plans: the Standard Plan and the SuperValue Plan. The Standard Plan gives you five hours a month for $9.95

and bills you $2.95/hour for additional hours. The SuperValue Plan gives you twenty hours a month for $24.95 and bills you $1.95/hour for additional hours.

 **TIP** **Some services on CompuServe carry additional charges above the** standard billing rates. These Premium Services are identified by a ($) next to the service name.

# All about modem speeds

You connect to CompuServe (and other online services) via a modem; this is a piece of equipment that lets your computer communicate with other computers via standard phone lines. There are different types of modems, which operate at different connection speeds.

The most popular modems today are based on a standard that was set by the Hayes brand modems; such modems are referred to as *Hayes-compatible*. Chances are, no matter which company makes your modem (it might be U.S. Robotics, Supra, or Motorola, for example), your modem is probably Hayes-compatible.

Modems transmit data at varying rates; the faster the transmission rate, the faster your CompuServe sessions go. Transmission speed is measured in *bauds*. A 28.8K baud modem, for example, is roughly twice as fast as a 14.4K baud modem.

If you're a heavy online user, you want the fastest modem you can afford, which is a 28.8K model. You can connect to CompuServe at lower speeds, but it will take longer to cruise the service and download files and messages. And, if you venture out onto the Internet via CompuServe, you'll find

that a slower modem can be painfully frustrating. In fact, for most users, I'd say that a 14.4K baud modem is the bare minimum for acceptable access times; I recommend that you spend the bucks for a 28.8K baud model.

There are ways to connect to CompuServe other than by plain phone lines, however. If you have a direct Internet connection—like a T1 line at your place of business—you don't have to use a modem to connect to CompuServe; you can connect directly from your fast Internet connection. Similarly, if you have an ISDN connection, all you have to do is select the proper ISDN modem in the Modem Control Settings dialog box, and select the fastest available speed in the Port speed box. (Leave the Access network box in the default CompuServe position.) If you have problems with either of these types of connections, don't hesitate to call CompuServe technical support at 1-800-848-8199.

In the not too distant future, you'll also see high-speed connections via cable modems and digital satellite systems. Until then, however, most of us will be limited to 28.8K baud modems.

# Joining CompuServe via the CompuServe Membership Kit

The easiest way to sign up with CompuServe is to purchase a CompuServe Membership Kit. You can find these kits everywhere software is sold and even in some bookstores.

**Q&A** *How can I obtain a CompuServe Membership Kit if I can't find one locally?*

If you can't find a CompuServe Membership Kit locally, you can order one directly from CompuServe by calling 1–800–524–3388. You can also order a CompuServe Membership Kit directly from CompuServe's Web site, located at **http://www.compuserve.com/**.

The CompuServe Membership Kit includes a copy of the CompuServe 3.0 software, instructions for setting up your account, a manual of CompuServe information, and an offer for free connect time. You'll probably pay from $10 to $35 for the Membership Kit, depending on where you buy it. However, because installation entitles you to free connect time, the Kit virtually pays for itself!

**TIP** The CompuServe Membership Kit gives you other software as well. At the time of this writing, the Membership Kit CD-ROM set contained Adobe Acrobat, Xing/Streamworks, Cyber Patrol, WorldsAway, and Home Page Wizard—all programs that you would otherwise have to download from CompuServe separately.

# Installing CompuServe 3.0

Before you can sign up with CompuServe, you first have to install the CompuServe software that came with your Membership Kit.

CompuServe 3.0's interface features a combination of pull-down menus, toolbar buttons, and desktop icons to help you navigate through CompuServe. All services are accessible with the click of your mouse, so all you have to do is point and click to go in the general direction you want to go.

To install CompuServe, you simply insert the CD-ROM in your CD-ROM drive and follow the on-screen instructions after the CD-ROM automatically launches. CompuServe's Setup Wizard leads you step by step through the installation procedure.

 **CAUTION** **If the CompuServe CD-ROM *doesn't* automatically start, click the** Windows 95 Start button, select Run, and launch the SETUP.EXE file on the CD-ROM.

## Signing up with CompuServe

After the CompuServe software is installed, you're ready to sign up for a CompuServe membership. (Actually, you were asked if you wanted to sign up for membership during the software installation. If you answered yes, you're already where you need to be.)

When the sign-up procedure starts, you're presented with a series of dialog boxes that ask you how you want to be billed. You can elect to be billed via credit card or via a direct debit from your checking account. Whichever option you choose, you need to have your account information handy.

**CAUTION** **You also need to enter the Agreement Number and Serial Number** that came with your CompuServe Membership Kit.

When the sign-up program has all the information it needs, it automatically calls CompuServe and signs you up. At this time, CompuServe assigns you a permanent User ID number and a temporary password. You can use this password for limited CompuServe access until you receive your permanent password in the mail (the regular U.S. Postal Service mail, not e-mail). Generally, it arrives in two weeks or so.

 **Q&A** ***I try to connect to CompuServe, but all I get is an error*** ***message that says*** `Could not initialize port.` ***What*** ***should I do?***

This error message appears when CompuServe is not configured properly for your computer. You need to change CompuServe's session settings to better fit your PC.

Begin by pulling down the Access menu, choosing Preferences, and selecting the Connection tab. Look at the COM Port displayed in the Port box. Chances are, this is not the right port for your computer. If you know which port your modem is connected to, change the setting to that port. If you're not sure, simply select another port, click OK, and try connecting. If you still get the error message, repeat the procedure and change to yet another port. When you find the right port, CompuServe should connect properly.

If changing the port doesn't get you connected, you may need to do something more complicated. From the Connection tab, click the Define Modem button. When the Modem Control Settings dialog box appears, check the Modem list and make sure you have the right modem selected. If the modem selected is not the modem installed on your system, pull down the list and select the proper modem.

Because CompuServe uses Windows 95's built-in Dial-Up Networking by default, many of these settings are "hard-wired" from the settings determined by Windows 95. To edit the Dial-Up Networking connection, click the Configure Phone button to display the CS3 Connection dialog box. From here you can change your connection phone number, select a new modem, and (by clicking the Configure button) change the communications port and connection speed. (Other options are available via both the Configure and Server Type buttons, but you generally don't have to bother with them.)

If the problems persist, you may need to call someone more technically proficient to reconfigure the Initialize setting in the Modem Control Settings dialog box.

### *I entered my temporary password incorrectly during the sign-up procedure. What do I do now?*

First, don't panic. You have two more attempts to enter the correct temporary password. If you don't get it right by the end of the last attempt, CompuServe thinks you're up to no good and shuts down the sign-up process. If this happens to you, call CompuServe (1-800-524-3388) to explain your situation and get a new temporary password.

### *I entered some of my membership information wrong. How do I change it?*

This is discussed in detail later in this chapter. For now, just note that you have to click the Main Menu button, select the Member Assistance tab, and select the Account Information icon.

# Finding the right number

Now that you have subscribed, you need to find the best way to dial into CompuServe.

If you purchased a CompuServe Membership Kit, you should have the list of access numbers included in the kit's instructions. (CompuServe has an entire network of local numbers you can call to access its service; this way you don't have to dial a central long-distance number to log on.) If, for some reason, you can't find the instruction booklet, you can call 1-800-848-8199 and use CompuServe's automated voice mail system to obtain a local access number.

In case you can't find a local number to dial, CompuServe does offer a toll-free 800-line access number you can use. There are four of these numbers, each of which corresponds to a specific modem speed. Of course, using an 800 number costs a bit more than dialing a local number—$6 per hour, to be precise.

| Modem Speed | Number |
|---|---|
| 300, 1200, or 2400 baud | 1-800-848-4480 |
| 9600 or 14,400 baud | 1-800-331-7166 |
| 28,800 baud | 1-800-454-8327 |
| 57,600 baud | 1-800-473-6282 |

The best way to use an 800 number for access is to initially connect via the 800 number, and then search CompuServe for a local access number. It takes only a few minutes to find a local number, and when you do, you can disconnect and then reconnect using the lower-priced local number.

Once you're connected to CompuServe, it's easy to search for access numbers. Just click the Main Menu button on the left side of the Home Desktop, select the Member Assistance tab, and click the Access Phones icon. Here you can search for phone numbers by city or by area code.

**Q&A** *How do I change my modem speed?*

Well, you can't change the speed of the modem itself. But if CompuServe isn't connecting at the speed you want, you can change CompuServe's setting for modem speed (up to the maximum speed of your modem, of course.). Pull down the Access menu, choose Preferences, and select the Connection tab. Pull down the Port Speed list and select the proper speed for your modem. (For example, if you have a 28,800 baud modem, select 28,800 from this list.) Click OK to confirm the configuration. (If you're using Windows 95's Dial-Up Networking, click the Configure Phone button. In the CS3 dialog box, click the Configure button to change the connection speed.)

*I want to change the phone number I use to connect to CompuServe. How do I do that?*

Begin by pulling down the Access menu, choosing Preferences, and selecting the Connection tab. Enter the new phone number in the Access phone field and click OK. (If you're using Window's 95 Dial-Up Networking, click the Configure Phone button. In the CS3 dialog box, you can change the access number.)

*Can I connect to CompuServe through a separate Internet connection?*

If you're using another dial-up PPP connection, follow these connections to use your current connection instead of CompuServe's default connection. Begin by pulling down the Access menu, selecting Preferences, and choosing the Connection tab. Under Winsock Connection Type, select the connection you wish to use (normally, this is Dial-Up Networking, using the Windows 95 dialer). You may wish to choose Default WINSOCK to use a previously installed Internet connection. It's also possible that you still want to use Dial-Up Networking, but you simply need to choose a different provider; if so, leave Dial-Up Networking as the Winsock Connection Type and choose a different provider under Dial-Up Networking.

If you have a direct connection to the Internet (like a T-1 or T-3 line), you can use this ultra-fast connection to log onto CompuServe. To do so, pull down the Access menu, select Preferences, and choose the Connection tab. Under Winsock Connection Type, select Default WINSOCK. Under Access network, choose Internet. And under Dial type, choose Direct. Then connect to the Internet as you do normally and start CompuServe. You should connect automatically.

# Welcome to the Welcome Center

CompuServe now features a special section just for new users: the New Member Welcome Center. To access the Welcome Center, pull down the Access menu, select Go, and type **WELCOME** in the dialog box. (See Chapter 3 to learn more about the GO command.)

Using the Welcome Center is free. Because you don't pay connect-time charges, it's a good place to learn the CompuServe ropes. You can use it to read helpful tips, discover CompuServe services that match your interests, and get an idea of what CompuServe is all about.

You also can use the Welcome Center to access CompuServe's Customer Service. This is the place

to go if you have problems; the Welcome Center has staff on hand to help new users through a variety of problems.

When you enter the Welcome Center, you see the screen shown here. You're presented with numerous options; I recommend that you click the Help Station button and, on the following screen, check out the Tips and Highlights sections. If you want to practice using CompuServe, click the Welcome Forum button; if you need personal assistance, click the Help Station button and, on the following screen, select the Help Desk.

CompuServe's Welcome Center is a good place to learn how to use and navigate CompuServe.

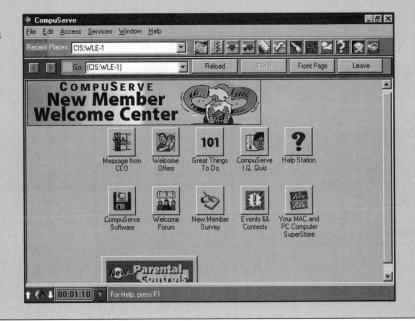

**Q&A** ***I'm trying to connect to CompuServe through a hotel switchboard that requires me to dial 9 before the number. How do I change my setup to allow for this?***

As with the previous problem, pull down the <u>A</u>ccess menu, choose <u>P</u>references, and select the Connection tab. Then type a **9** in front of the number in the Access phone field and click OK. (You may also want to add a comma (,) after the 9; the comma instructs CompuServe to make a slight pause after dialing the 9, which is necessary with some switchboards.) Note that you may need to change this in Windows 95's Dial-Up Networking; edit "CS3 Connection" as appropriate.

# Getting the latest and greatest version of CompuServe

You probably obtained your version of CompuServe from the CompuServe Membership Kit. However, CompuServe constantly upgrades and improves its software. So there may be a newer version available, with more features than the version you use.

To find out which version of CompuServe you have, pull down the <u>H</u>elp menu and choose <u>A</u>bout CompuServe for Windows. This displays the About CompuServe for Windows dialog box, which tells (among other things) which version you're running.

At the time of this writing, the most recent version of CompuServe is version 3.0. If you have an older version, you definitely need to upgrade. You need the latest version in order to take advantage of some of the newest features.

Fortunately, CompuServe makes it easy to obtain new versions of their software. Pull down the <u>A</u>ccess menu, select <u>G</u>o, and enter **CISSOFT**. From here you can order the latest version of CompuServe on CD-ROM, to be delivered via the U.S. Postal Service.

Now that you're properly connected and set up, it is time to learn what's available on CompuServe and how to navigate the service. This means, of course, that you need to advance to Chapters 2 and 3.

# A Preflight Check: Configuring and Using CompuServe 3.0

● **In this chapter:**

- **What are the major changes in CompuServe 3.0?**

- **Configure CompuServe for your own personal needs**

- **Find your way around CompuServe**

- **Making the CompuServe connection**

*Discover how to use the latest version of CompuServe . . . .*❯

f you've used prior versions of CompuServe, CompuServe 3.0 is sure to seem a little unfamiliar to you. This is the most significant change in the CompuServe interface since the CompuServe Information Manager (CIM) was first introduced. (Prior to the first CIM—which was available for DOS PCs—you had to access CompuServe in a text-only mode.)

The previous version of CompuServe (through the CIM software) used a series of buttons and menus to move you around the CompuServe service. Once you got used to it, you could use it to go wherever you wanted. However, it wasn't terribly straightforward, it confused a lot of new users, and it wasn't competitive with the interface from CompuServe's chief competitor, America Online.

So the folks at CompuServe changed their interface. Completely. Radically. Utterly.

# The new CompuServe for old users

If you've used CompuServe for awhile, you're probably familiar with the screen in Fig. 2.1, which is the screen from CIM version 2.0 for Windows.

**Fig. 2.1**
This is what the previous version of CompuServe looked like.

When you compare this interface to the new interface of CompuServe 3.0, you'll see a world of difference. If you're a new CompuServe user, I'm sure that you'll prefer the new interface. It's straightforward, attractive, easy to use, and versatile.

If you're an old CompuServe user, however, you'll probably complain a little about the new interface. After all, in the online world you're an old dog, and you know what they say about old dogs and new tricks. But when you finish complaining, you'll no doubt find that this new interface is actually easier to use than the old WinCIM interface. Yes, it's different—and you *will* have to relearn a few things—but you will get used to it and learn to like it.

What's different in CompuServe 3.0? A lot. Some of the more important changes in CompuServe 3.0 are detailed in Table 2.1. The main screen is totally different, and you now have more direct access (via the left-side buttons and across-the-top tabs) to more services. The main window also serves as the Web browser and the window to CompuServe's forums, so you'll now do just about everything in this main window.

Because the Web browser is integrated into CompuServe 3.0, CompuServe has taken the opportunity to more fully integrate Web-based services into the core CompuServe service. Many screens are actually HTML-based Web pages, and many forums and other areas include links to services on the Web.

Some things, fortunately, stayed the same. You can still use the GO command to go directly to specific services, and the FIND command to search for specific subjects. CompuServe Mail still works the same, and—even though the interface is different—CompuServe forums are more or less still CompuServe forums. And rest assured, your Favorite Places list stays exactly the same.

**Table 2.1    Differences between CompuServe 2.0 and 3.0**

| CompuServe 2.0 | CompuServe 3.0 |
| --- | --- |
| Chat services are called CompuServe CB. | Chat services are called CompuServe Chat. |
| Connect command is on File menu. | Connect command is on Access menu. |

continues

**Table 2.1   Continued**

| CompuServe 2.0 | CompuServe 3.0 |
| --- | --- |
| Filing cabinet uses 2.0 format. | Filing cabinet uses new 3.0 format with search functions. Old filing cabinets have to be converted to new format (using the new Filing Cabinet Utility). |
| Go and Find commands are on the Services menu. | Go and Find commands are on the Access menu. |
| Interface is called CompuServe Information Manager (CIM) | Interface is simply called CompuServe; no more CIMs. |
| Internal dialer. | Uses CompuServe Dialer for a PPP connection. |
| Has limited file viewing capabilities. | Use of Inside Out viewer to view most common text and graphics formats. |
| Preferences, Connection Info, and Terminal are commands on the Special menu. | Preferences, Connection Status, and Terminal Emulator commands are on the Access menu. |
| Session Settings are on the Special menu. | Session Settings are in the Preferences section of the Access menu. |
| Enables you to view old forum messages by resetting the High Message Number. | Enables you to view old forum messages by selecting the See More Messages command on the Forum menu. |
| Web browser supports HTML 1.0 format. | Web browser supports HTML 2.1 format. |
| Web connection via external Mosaic program. | Web connection via internal browser (based on Internet Explorer) or via separate external browser. |

# Configuring CompuServe for your personal information

The first time you install CompuServe, you need to set some configuration information. You do this by pulling down the Access menu and selecting the Preferences option. This displays the Preferences dialog box shown in Fig. 2.2. From this dialog box, you can configure the following settings, or you can live with the default settings—as most users do.

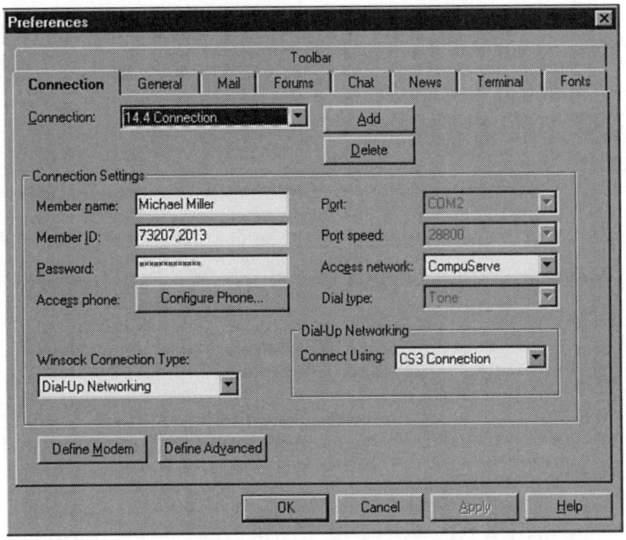

**Fig. 2.2**

Setting Connection settings in CompuServe's Preferences dialog box.

On the Connection tab, you can set up the following options:

- **Connection.** You can create any number of different connections (each with different settings) for use in different situations. For example, you can set up one version of CompuServe with multiple users, each of whom has his or her own separate connection information. Or, if you travel a lot, you might want to create different configurations for different cities.

- **Member name.** Fill in your name.

- **Member ID.** Fill in your CompuServe ID.

- **Password.** Enter your CompuServe password.

*CAUTION* **The Password field displays asterisks instead of the actual characters you type so that no one can read your password over your shoulder.**

- **Access phone.** Enter the number you dial to access CompuServe. (If you're connecting via Windows 95's Dial-Up Networking, click the Configure Phone button and edit the connection labelled "CS3 Connection."

- **Port.** Indicate which communications port your modem uses. (If you're connecting via Windows 95's Dial-Up Networking, this is filled in automatically.)

- **Port speed.** Select the maximum speed you can connect at. (If you're connecting via Windows 95's Dial-Up Networking, this is filled in automatically.)

- **Access network.** Tell how you connect to CompuServe (most members use the default "CompuServe").

- **Dial type.** Indicate whether you have a tone or pulse phone line. (If you're connecting via Windows 95's Dial-Up Networking, this is filled in automatically.)

- **Winsock Connection Type.** This lets you determine if you want to connect via Windows 95's Dial-Up Networking (the default, and recommended method) or via another Winsock previously installed on your PC.

- **Dial-Up Networking.** If you choose this option, you can select which dial-up connection you want to use to connect to CompuServe. The default (and recommended) connection is labeled "CS3 Connection."

In addition, there are buttons that let you define and set up your particular modem, as well as buttons that define various advanced settings (such as which language you use and which country you live in; English and the United States are the defaults).

You can use the options on the General tab to do any of the following things:

- Select an Internet Browser. If you choose to use a browser other than CompuServe's internal browser (which is based on Microsoft's Internet Explorer), type the path and filename of the browser here.

- Prompt to save opened graphics. This instructs CompuServe to ask if you want to save any graphics you're viewing to your hard disk. This option is normally selected.

- Retrieve graphic versions of menus. This option is also normally selected.

- Display Confirmation Messages. Click the button to activate this option.

- Set Directories. Click the button to select directories for various types of files used by CompuServe. (CompuServe sets its own default directories if you don't select any.)

On the Mail tab, you can choose from the following options:

- Keep a copy of all sent mail in: *foldername*, where you replace *foldername* with the name of the folder in which you want to save the mail messages.

- Immediately show recipient dialog when you're composing a new message.

- View mail online before retrieving. (It's generally selected.)

- Delete mail from online mailbox when retrieved. (If you don't select this, you have to do it manually.)

Under the Forums tab, you'll see these options:

- Automatically file sent messages. You select the folder.

- Set Conferencing Preferences. Here you can set various options for in-forum conferences (not to be confused with Chat preferences).

- Retrieve Forum Logos. Displays the graphic logos of every forum you visit.

- Forums visited. Lists the last forums you've visited. You have the option of deleting items from this list.

- Name to use within the forum. It doesn't have to be your real name.

- Name to use while conferencing.

On the Chat tab, you'll find these options:

- Nickname. The name you use when participating in Chat; it doesn't have to be your real name.

- Display all private chats in one window. Otherwise, you get a separate window for each private chat session.

- Add prohibited members to list. Here you can leave instructions to ignore certain members Permanently, For today only, or at your option (Ask me).

- Record chat text (in a log file).

- Add new text to the room's log file. (If you don't select this, you create a new log file.)

- Ignore invitations for Private chats or Group chats.

- Retrieve Graphics files, Sound files, or Save all retrieved files.

On the News tab, you have the following choices:

- Show Public Folders and/or Personal Folders.

- Delete all retrieved articles. (If this is not selected, they keep accumulating.)

The Terminal tab contains these options:

- Size of scrollback buffer. Terminal mode consists of scrolling text, so you can select how much text you can scroll back through.

- Strip High Bit. This is necessary to properly view most terminal screens.

With the options on the Fonts tab, you can change the fonts used for CompuServe's Body Text, Fixed Body Text, Terminal text, Printer text, and Printer Fixed text. Or you can just use the default fonts.

Finally, the Toolbar tab lets you change the buttons you see on CompuServe's toolbar. Just select a function in the left-hand list, and click the Insert button to add it to the right-hand list.

After you configure everything to your satisfaction, click OK to register the configuration. With all the configurations set, you should be ready to dial CompuServe.

# Changing your user options

After you've signed onto and configured CompuServe, you're set for life, right? That could be, but it's likely that you'll want to change one or more of your user options at a later time. For example, you might want to add the executive option or change your password.

How do you change your personal CompuServe setup? To change your membership settings, click the Main Menu button on the Home Desktop, select the Membership Assistance tab, and click the Account Information icon. This takes you to the Account/Billing Information window (see Fig. 2.3). From here, you can change your billing address, billing option, password, and other important options. This menu also includes information on CompuServe's pricing plans and the ZDNet service. And you can even use this menu to cancel your CompuServe membership.

**Fig. 2.3**
Changing your membership information in CompuServe's Account/Billing Information area.

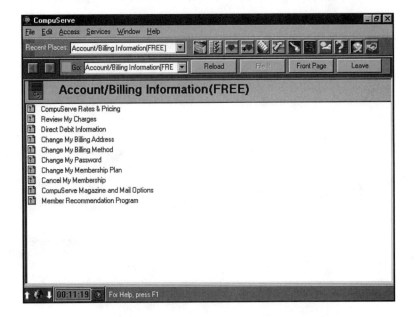

When you select an option from this menu, you're presented with instructions specific to that option. Follow the instructions to make your changes, and then return to the main menu to make any additional changes.

 **CAUTION**   **CompuServe won't let you change your password until you** correctly enter your current password.

# The grand tour of CompuServe

After you have CompuServe installed, you can start it by clicking the Windows 95 Start button, pointing to Programs, pointing to CompuServe, and then clicking the CompuServe 3.0 icon. (There should be a CompuServe 3.0 icon installed on your main Windows 95 desktop; you can also click that icon to launch CompuServe.) CompuServe launches and displays the Home Desktop.

You access all of CompuServe service areas from the Home Desktop or from CompuServe's menus and toolbar. The Home Desktop consists of combinations of buttons (along the left side of the screen), tabs (which differ according to which button is selected), and icons (which vary from tab to tab). Here's what you can do from each of the Home Desktop's six buttons:

- **Main Menu.** From the Main Menu (shown in Fig. 2.4), you can go to CompuServe's What's New, Table of Contents, Internet area, Chat rooms, and Forums & Communities. In addition, you can click on the Member Assistance tab to access phone, account, and member information.

**Fig. 2.4**
Starting with
CompuServe's Main
Menu.

- **Go.** Click the Go... button on the left to access the Go tab, the Favorite Places tab, and the Parental Controls tab. The Go tab (see Fig. 2.5) lets you revisit recently visited services, select areas from the CompuServe Directory, or use the GO command to visit specific services. The Favorite Places tab displays your Favorite Places list. The Parental Controls tab contains options you can use to control your family members' access to specific areas. (See Chapter 4 for more information on parental controls.)

**Fig. 2.5**
Going directly to
CompuServe areas via
the Go window.

## 66 *Plain English, please!*

The CompuServe Directory is a listing of all the forums and services available
on CompuServe. 99

- **Find.** Click the Find button on the left to access the Services, Files,
  and Members tabs (see Fig. 2.6). The Services tab lets you search
  CompuServe services by subject; the Files tab lets you search forums
  for specific files; and the Members tab lets you search the CompuServe
  member base for specific individuals.

- **Mail Center.** Click this button to access CompuServe's e-mail services
  (see Fig. 2.7). The Read tab lets you read waiting e-mail; the Create tab
  lets you create new e-mail; the Address Book tab displays your personal
  list of e-mail addresses; and the Search tab lets you search for specific
  e-mail messages.

**Fig. 2.6**

Searching for specific services from the Find window.

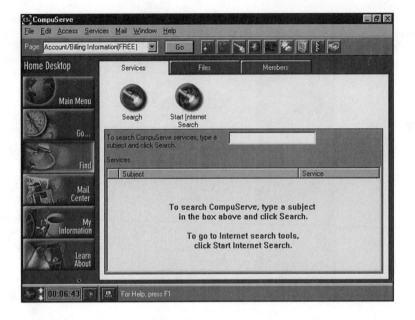

**Fig. 2.7**

Checking e-mail messages in the Mail Center window.

- **My Information.** Clicking this button gives you access to the Filing Cabinet and To-Do List tabs (see Fig. 2.8). The Filing Cabinet tab lets you manage your filing cabinet; the To-Do List tab lets you process any waiting actions.

**Fig. 2.8**
Confirming account information in the My Information window.

- **Learn About.** Click this button to learn more about CompuServe's services (see Fig. 2.9). The CompuServe tab displays Help information about e-mail, forums & communities, chat, news, and the CompuServe Directory; the Mail tab displays Help about CompuServe's e-mail services; the Services tab displays Help about navigating the CompuServe service; and The Internet tab displays Help about CompuServe's Internet services.

The Home Desktop changes according to the services you enter. For example, if you select Forums and Communities from CompuServe's Main Menu, the desktop changes to the one shown in Fig. 2.10. (See Chapter 7 for more details on CompuServe's forums.) And if you choose to go to a site on the World Wide Web, the entire desktop changes into a Web browser. (See Chapter 25 for more details on CompuServe's Web browser.)

**Fig. 2.9**
The Learn About
window.

**Fig. 2.10**
Choosing from
CompuServe's forums
and communities.

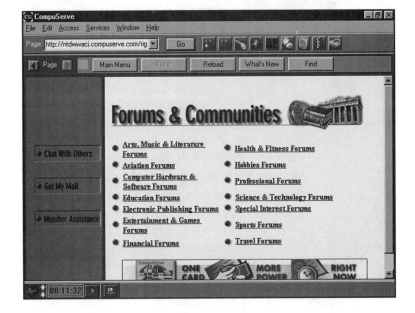

# Pushing the right buttons

CompuServe includes a "button bar" across the top of the screen. The buttons listed in Table 2.2 let you access many CompuServe services.

## Table 2.2 CompuServe services buttons

| Icon | Name | Description |
|------|------|-------------|
| Go | Go | Uses the GO command to take you directly to services and forums. |
| | Add to Favorite Places | Lets you add a service to your Favorite Places list. |
| | Favorite Places | Displays a list of favorite services you've designated. |
| | Search | Uses the Search command to find specific services and forums. |
| | Browse the Internet | Opens the integrated Web browser to access the World Wide Web. |
| | Quotes | Lets you access stock quotes. |
| | Weather | Lets you obtain an up-to-date weather forecast for your area. |
| | Filing Cabinet | Displays folders you can use to store documents and forum messages. |
| | To Do List | Displays any pending tasks such as files to download or messages to retrieve. |
| | Connect or Disconnect | Affects your connections to CompuServe (and closes CompuServe on the way out). |

To the left of the button bar is a List of Recent Places. Pull down this list to see where (on CompuServe and on the Web) you've recently visited; click any of the places listed to revisit a specific service.

# Making the connection

Now it's time to connect to CompuServe, a task which is pretty easy. You can click the Connect button, and you are connected automatically. Or you can select a service (via the GO command, the Search command, the Favorite Places list, or various other areas), and you'll automatically be connected to CompuServe and taken to that particular service.

 **TIP** **If you have a multimedia PC hookup, CompuServe "talks" to you** during certain operations. For example, every time you connect to the service, a voice says, "Welcome to CompuServe."

CompuServe 3.0 actually uses another program to make the connection. By default, CompuServe sets up a connection (labeled "C3 Connection") in Windows 95's Dial-Up Networking. This connection enables you to use all the settings previously configured by Windows 95, without having to install a new connection program. Dial-Up Networking automatically connects to

## CompuServe 3.0: Internet Savvy!

Here's something else new about CompuServe 3.0: much of it resides on the Internet! More specifically, many new CompuServe services are being written in HTML so that they can be accessed via a Web browser. (HTML is the language of the World Wide Web, which allows "hyperlinks" between selected text/graphics and additional pages or areas.)

Fortunately, CompuServe 3.0 includes an integrated Web browser (a version of Microsoft's Internet Explorer). That means that CompuServe can display both normal CompuServe services *and* pages from the Web. In fact, it does this rather seamlessly, so it's hard to tell whether you're viewing a CompuServe-specific service or a CompuServe-created Web page.

For example, CompuServe's Home Desktop is a CompuServe-specific window, while the Table of Contents is actually a Web page. Because CompuServe displays both types of screens flawlessly, it's hard to tell which is which—and it really doesn't matter. CompuServe can go directly to either type of screen and lets you add either screen to your Favorite Places list.

Because of this seamless integration of HTML pages to the CompuServe service, you need CompuServe 3.0 to take full advantage of all that's there. If you're trying to use an older version of CompuServe, you simply won't be able to access all of the services now available on CompuServe.

CompuServe and logs on whenever you choose to connect; you don't have to do anything else except select where you want to go. (In other words, Dial-Up Networking remembers your member ID and password, so you don't have to enter them manually.)

**Q&A** ***I have trouble connecting to CompuServe. What's wrong?***

You may need to reset CompuServe's configuration options. Pull down the Access menu, choose Preferences, and click the Connection tab. Make sure you have the right phone number entered and the right COM port selected. Then click the Define Modem button to display the Modem Control Settings dialog box. Select your correct Modem type from the modems listed; this automatically configures the other settings in the dialog box. If your modem isn't listed, enter the various settings manually. (Consult your modem manual for this information.)

If you're using Windows 95's Dial-Up Networking to connect to CompuServe, many of these settings are already configured for you. To edit the Dial-Up Networking connection, click the Configure Phone button. In the CS3 Connection dialog box, you can change your connection phone number, select a new modem, and (by clicking the Configure button) change the communications port and the connection speed. (Other options are available via the Configure and Server Type buttons, but you generally don't have to bother with them.)

If you still have trouble, you may want to call CompuServe's main voice number: 1-800-848-8990.

***I've connected to CompuServe, but it seems to be locked up. What's wrong?***

Several things can cause your CompuServe session to go awry. First, line noise on your telephone line can garble information, which freezes CompuServe and ultimately disconnects you from CompuServe. Second, if you run low on Windows memory or disk space, it freezes CompuServe, and you have to reboot your computer. Third (and most commonly), when CompuServe gets extremely busy, access sometimes slows to a crawl. This makes it appear as if your system is frozen. If the access becomes too slow, your CompuServe software itself "times out," disconnecting you from CompuServe.

When this happens, there are two things you can try—one simple and one drastic. For the simple solution, place your cursor over the "globe" button in the lower-left corner of the Home Desktop. "Shift-click" (press and hold the Shift key and click the left mouse button) in this area to manually disconnect from CompuServe. If this doesn't disconnect you, the only other option is the drastic one. You'll have to force a shut down of CompuServe by pressing Ctrl+Alt+Del and choosing the End Task option. Once you've disconnected from CompuServe, you can reconnect and then restart whatever it was you were doing when things locked up.

# Calling it quits

Believe it or not, disconnecting from CompuServe is easy. Simply click the Disconnect button. You're automatically logged off the service, and Dial-Up Networking disconnects you from the service. The CompuServe software remains open on your desktop for any offline work you may want to do. To exit the software completely, pull down the File menu and select Exit.

# 3

# The CompuServe Road Map

● **In this chapter:**

● **How is CompuServe organized?**

● **What are the basic parts of CompuServe?**

● **Getting around on CompuServe**

● **Searching for topics of interest**

● **What Internet services are available to CompuServe members?**

*You need a road map to find your way around CompuServe—and this chapter is that road map!* . . . . . . . . . . . . . . . . ▶

CompuServe offers a variety of services for all types of users. There are forums and databases galore. Some are for computer junkies; some are for business people; some are for serious researchers; others are for fun-loving hobbyists.

Whatever your tastes, you can find something (or many somethings) of interest on CompuServe. The key is to figure out how to find what you want and how to get there.

Fortunately, it's easy to get around on CompuServe, where there are lots of ways to get to any one place. You can click an icon on CompuServe's Home Desktop, you can go directly to a service via the GO command, or you can search for a specific service using the FIND command. Just be sure to check out all the places you can go before you decide.

# What CompuServe is made of

Before we talk about how CompuServe is organized, you need to understand the basic types of services offered by CompuServe. Those services include:

- **E-mail.** The popular way to send correspondence to other CompuServe members—or anyone online—via the Internet. (See Chapter 6 for more details.)

- **Forums**. These are like "communities" that are organized by topic, where members with similar interests gather to exchange messages and share files. (See Chapter 7.)

- **Chat**. This is a way for members to engage in real-time communications with other members. (See Chapter 8.)

- **Reservation services**. A great way to book airline, hotel, and automobile reservations. (See Chapter 13.)

- **Online periodicals**. Some of your favorite newspapers and magazines are also available in electronic format. (See Chapter 14.)

- **News services**. Up-to-the-minute news, including weather, sports, and stock quotes. (See Chapters 14 and 16.)

- **Databases**. These are large repositories of information that are ideal for research. (See Chapter 15.)

- **Shopping services**. Where you can shop for goods and services while you're online. (See Chapter 18.)

# How CompuServe is organized

Because CompuServe provides so many options, you're probably wondering how you make sense of everything. How do all these services fit together?

## Exploring CompuServe's main services

When you click the Main Menu button and the Main Menu tab on CompuServe's Home Desktop, you have the option of heading in any of five directions within CompuServe (see Fig. 3.1).

**Fig 3.1**
CompuServe makes it easy for you to access five main areas of the service.

The following list describes each of the options shown in Fig 3.1.

- **What's New** shows you what's new on CompuServe each day.

- **Table of Contents** enables you to explore CompuServe's different services by topic area.

- **Internet** gives you access to services on the Internet.

- **Chat** takes you to the area where you can take part in real-time conversation with other CompuServe members.

- **Forums & Communities** takes you to an area where you can correspond with other members interested in specific topics.

Unless you have a specific area you want to visit, I recommend that you check out What's New to get the latest updates, and then go to the Table of Contents, where you can browse through the various topics offered by CompuServe.

## Exploring by topic

CompuServe has thousands of different services in all. If you click the Table of Contents button, you'll find these services organized into a dozen different topics, which you can see in Fig. 3.2.

**Fig. 3.2**
Use CompuServe's Table of Contents to access different topic areas.

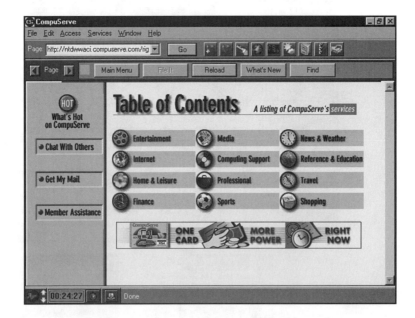

When you click one of these buttons, you go to a new window where you're presented with a variety of services related to the main topic. These services range from message forums to file libraries and chat rooms. In many cases, they include related services on the Internet.

# Getting there with GO commands

If you know exactly what service you want, the quickest way to get there is through the GO command. You activate the command by clicking the Go button on the toolbar, or by pulling down the <u>A</u>ccess menu and choosing <u>G</u>o. The Go... dialog box appears, in which you type the name of the desired forum or service in the Service text box (see Fig. 3.3). When you click OK, you're automatically transported to where you want to go.

**Fig. 3.3**
The Go... dialog box.

For example, the GO word for the Macmillan Computer Publishing Forum is MACMILLAN. So, to go directly to this forum (where you can talk to Que), type **MACMILLAN** in the Go... dialog box. This direct action is often written in condensed form as "GO MACMILLAN." Therefore, if you should go to the IQuest database, you might be told to "GO IQUEST." To do so, use any method for accessing the Go... dialog box, and then type **IQUEST**.

You can also use the GO command to go to sites on the World Wide Web. Just enter the URL (the Uniform Resource Locator, which is an address on the Web) in the Go... text box, and CompuServe takes you to that specific Web site. (See Chapter 25 for more information on the World Wide Web.)

As an example, the URL for Macmillan's Information SuperLibrary Web site is **http:/www.mcp.com**. If you type that URL into the Go... dialog box and click OK, CompuServe's internal Web browser displays the home page for the appropriate Web site.

**Q&A** ***I entered a GO command and received a message that the service was unrecognized. What does that mean?***

This generally means that you typed a GO command that doesn't exist. Typing errors are the problem for most commands that are unrecognized. Type the command again and double-check it for accuracy. If your command is accurate and you still get the unrecognized command message, it might mean that the GO command has changed. Use the Search command (discussed next) to locate the new GO command for a specific service.

# Searching for things you can't find

What do you do if you don't know the GO command for a given service? Fortunately, you can find commands by using CompuServe's Search command.

When you click the Search button (the one that looks like a flashlight) on the main toolbar, your computer displays the Services Search dialog box (see Fig 3.4). Type what you're looking for (in general terms), and click Search or press Enter. CompuServe returns a list of services that most closely match what you're looking for. To access one of these services, select it from the list and click the Go button. Voilà! You've accessed the service you were looking for.

**Fig. 3.4**
Use the Services Search dialog box to find a particular subject.

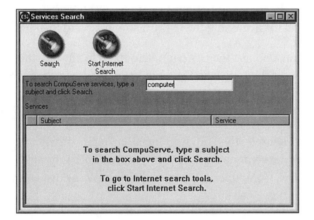

**TIP** **The Search command is also called the Find command and is** available in the Access menu.

**Q&A** *I used the Search command, and it didn't return any matches. How do I find the service I want?*

There can be numerous reasons for "no finds." First, you may have typed something wrong. Second, you may have conducted too narrow a search. (Try changing your search parameters to something more general.) Third, there may not be any services that deal with what you're looking for (unlikely, but possible). You may want to use the CompuServe Directory (pull down the <u>H</u>elp menu and choose CompuServe <u>D</u>irectory) to see if there really are any services that fit the bill.

# Cruising the Internet from CompuServe

In addition to the normal proprietary parts of CompuServe, you also have access to sites and services on the Internet. This means that virtually all of the online world (except the parts controlled by competing online services such as America Online and Prodigy) are available to you through your CompuServe connection.

Chapter 21 goes into great detail explaining the various parts of the Internet, but we'll do a quick overview of the Net while we're here. On the Internet you can find the following services:

- E-mail (like CompuServe Mail)

- World Wide Web, the coolest and most popular part of the Net

- USENET Newsgroups (kind of like CompuServe forum message boards)

- FTP, for downloading software files

- Telnet, for communicating with older computers

In addition to the main CompuServe features (forums, e-mail, chat, etc.) you can use CompuServe to access all of these features on the Internet—effectively doubling the content available to you as a CompuServe subscriber!

# Cruising CompuServe's most popular areas

Because CompuServe has literally thousands of separate areas, even this book can't describe them all. In the following sections, however, I would like to point out some of the more popular areas of the service. So fasten your seat belts, and let's go for a quick cruise on the CompuServe highway.

## Your favorite places

A neat feature of CompuServe is the Favorite Places list. This list contains those services to which you go most often. Of course, CompuServe isn't smart enough to figure out which services you use the most, so you have to add items to the list yourself.

To add a new service to the list, click the Add To Favorite Places button. When the Define Favorite Place dialog box appears, enter a Name for the service in the first box, the GO command in the Location box, and the Priority level of this location. Click OK to add the new entry to your Favorite Places list.

## The best way to navigate CompuServe

Actually, there's no "best way" to navigate CompuServe, but there is *my* way, and I'll share it with you. When I log on—which I do every other day or so—here's what I do (in order):

1 Check my e-mail messages by clicking the Mail Center button, selecting the Read tab, and clicking the Get Mail icon.

2 Find out what's new on CompuServe by clicking the Main Menu button, selecting the Main Menu tab, and clicking the What's New icon.

3 Check today's news with the GO NEWS command.

4 Check today's weather by clicking the Weather button on the button bar.

5 Go directly to my Favorite Places list by clicking the Favorite Places button on the button bar. Then I click through my list of favorite places (mostly forums), systematically.

6 If I have time, I like to cruise the Web, which I do by clicking the Browse the Internet button on the button bar and then entering the URLs of the sites I want to visit.

This procedure might not be for everyone, but it works for me.

**TIP** **If you're in a forum or service when you click the Add to Favorite** Places button, the name and GO command for that service will automatically be displayed in the Define Favorite Place dialog box.

To access a service on your Favorite Places list, highlight the item and click the Go button. You're automatically connected to CompuServe and taken to the selected service.

The Favorite Places list is a great way to store the forums and services you go to frequently; it's easier to pick them off the list than it is to use the GO command each time.

## Getting (stocks) quoted

With CompuServe, it's easy to get updated stock reports from CompuServe. Just click the Quotes button to display the Stock Quotes dialog box. This dialog box lists all of your favorite stocks and lets you obtain quotes and performance charts for any and all of the listed stocks.

To obtain stock quotes for a given folder, open the folder and answer No to the question Do you want to work offline?. If you've been working offline, you can click the Update button to go online and obtain quotes. (See Chapter 16 for more information about stock-related features on CompuServe.)

You can also get an "instant quote" by typing a stock's symbol in the box at the bottom of the dialog box and clicking the Get Quote button.

## Weather reports on the button

Getting the most recent weather report for your area is as easy as clicking a button. When you click the Weather button, you see the Weather dialog box. From this box, you can obtain your local weather report by clicking the Get Weather button. If you want to see a weather map, click the View Maps button and choose from a variety of real-time maps.

## Doing the e-mail thing

Getting new mail is pretty simple with CompuServe. When you connect to CompuServe, the mailbox icon in the lower-left corner indicates whether you have new mail, and if so, how many new messages you have. Just click this button to retrieve your waiting e-mail and to display the Online Mail window. (You can also access this area by clicking the Mail Center button on the

Home Desktop, selecting the Read tab, and clicking the <u>G</u>et Mail button.) To read a piece of e-mail, highlight it and click the <u>O</u>pen button.

To create your own e-mail message, go to the Mail Center, select the Create tab, and click the New button. This opens the Create Mail window (Fig. 3.5). Click the <u>R</u>ecipients button and enter the e-mail addresses of your recipients, or click the Address <u>B</u>ook button to select recipients from the list in your address book. Click OK to confirm the recipients.

**Fig. 3.5**
Creating a new e-mail message.

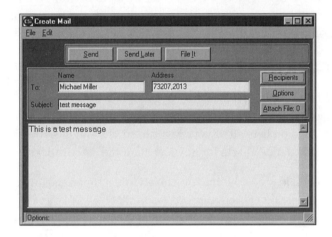

In the Create Mail window, you now see the name and address of the recipient. Fill-in the Subject of the message and type your message in the bottom part of the window. When you're done, click <u>S</u>end to log on and send the message immediately. (Or, you can click the Send <u>L</u>ater button to file the message for a future transfer to CompuServe. This enables you to compose mail offline and mail it at a later time when you connect to CompuServe.)

**TIP** **Many of the button-based services are also available on the** <u>A</u>ccess menu.

# Making CompuServe Safe for Children

● In this chapter:

● **Using CompuServe's Parental Controls Center**

● **Limiting access to certain types of content on CompuServe**

● **Using Cyber Patrol to limit access on the Internet**

*Use Parental Controls to limit access to CompuServe's more adult areas* . . . . . . . . . . . . . . . . . . . . . . . . . . . .⊘

C ompuServe is a service for everybody—but that doesn't mean that everybody should have access to all areas of CompuServe. There are some parts of CompuServe and some parts of the Internet that you might want to keep your kids away from. Fortunately, CompuServe offers Parental Controls that you can use to make your CompuServe service "kid safe."

# All about CompuServe's parental controls

You get to CompuServe's Parental Controls Center from the Home Desktop by clicking the Go... button, selecting the Parental Controls tab, and clicking the Parental Controls icon. (Alternately, you can GO CONTROLS.) As you can see in Fig. 4.1, the Parental Controls Center lets you set controls for both the CompuServe service and CompuServe's Internet services. In addition, the Talk About It button takes you to a special Parental Controls Forum.

**Fig. 4.1**
CompuServe's Parental
Controls Center.

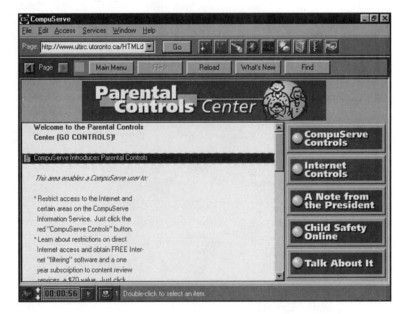

# Setting CompuServe limits

Click the CompuServe Controls button to access the CompuServe Controls area (shown in Fig. 4.2). In this area, you can enable and disable access to selected areas on CompuServe and to Internet services that you go to directly from CompuServe, such as newsgroups and FTP sites.

**Fig. 4.2**
The CompuServe
Controls area.

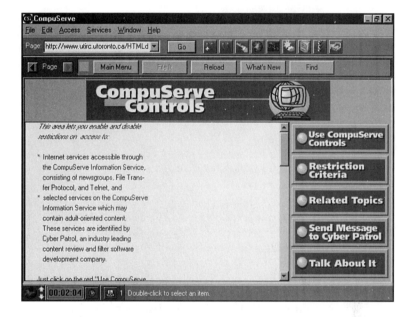

When you click the Use CompuServe Controls button, you're prompted to enter a password. This password protection prevents others from changing the access settings. On your first visit, you're also asked to enter a question. Enter any personal question that only you can answer. (This is in case you forget your password at some later date; you'll be asked the personal question instead.)

The next screen lets you restrict access to either CompuServe (CIS) or Internet services, either for the current session or permanently. After you make your choices, click OK, and the restrictions will be put into effect.

These restrictions are based on a "CyberNOT" list maintained by a third party contracted by CompuServe. The restricted content on the CyberNOT list includes:

- Alcohol and tobacco

- Drugs and drug culture

- Gambling

- Gross depictions (pictures or text that are vulgar or improper)

- Intolerance (advocating prejudice or discrimination)

- Militant /extremist

- Nudity

- Profanity

- Questionable/illegal activities

- Satanic/cult

- Sex education

- Sexual acts

- Violence

According to CompuServe, these criteria are determined by a panel of parents and teachers hired by MicroSystems, Inc., the developer of the software. Members of the panel supposedly come from the Parent-Teachers Association, the American Civil Liberties Union, the clergy, the media, and the psychology profession. The panel's decisions are based on the impact an area's content could have on a typical 12-year-old child.

Note that evaluation of these topics is made for you; you cannot pick and choose among restricted sites. You can only deactivate the controls completely.

# Setting Internet limits

When you click the Internet Controls button, you're taken to the Internet Controls area (GO PATROL) shown in Fig. 4.3. For controlling access to areas of the Internet, CompuServe uses a software program called Cyber Patrol.

With Cyber Patrol, you can restrict access during certain times of the day; you can limit the total amount of time spent online; you can block access to sites featuring topics on the CyberNOT list; and you can block access to particular resources and sites you select.

**TIP**   **The CyberNOT list is maintained by MicroSystems Software, Inc.,** the developers of Cyber Patrol. Normally, a twelve-month subscription to this list costs $70; CompuServe gives you one year free when you download the Cyber Patrol software.

**Fig. 4.3**
CompuServe's Internet Controls area.

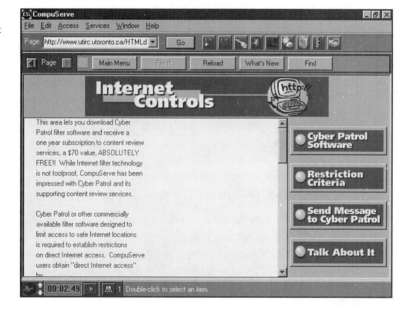

To use Cyber Patrol, you must download it from CompuServe and install it separately from the CompuServe software. To download Cyber Patrol, click the Download Cyber Patrol button and select Download Cyber Patrol for Windows. This downloads the CP-SETUP.EXE file into your c:\cserve\ download directory. Click the Windows 95 Start button, select Run, and choose the c:\cserve\download\cp-setup.exe file. When the installation starts, you'll be prompted to select the Tamper-Resistance Level. The options are "High Security" (recommended) and "Low Security." (See Chapter 9 for more information on downloading files.)

Once the installation is complete, you'll be prompted to restart your system. After restarting, you'll see a message stating `You must be online to register Cyber Patrol`. When you start CompuServe, you'll see a new Cyber Patrol button on the toolbar. Click this button to connect to CompuServe.

You'll be prompted to register your copy of Cyber Patrol; you'll need to fill out the registration information to receive a password. While you're in Cyber Patrol Headquarters, you should identify the types of controls you want to establish: the type of content that can be accessed, the amount of time that can be spent, and the services that can be used.

When Cyber Patrol is up and running, you can use your password to access any Internet sites you want, but your kids will be denied access to the types of sites you specified during installation. It's a good way to keep the Internet safe for all members of your family.

**TIP** **Even though these controls do a decent job of filtering unsavory** sites, they don't catch everything; it's still good to monitor your kids' sessions yourself. A little parental supervision never hurt.

**Q&A** *What do I do if I forget my parental control password?*

For one, you'll be asked the "backup" question you provided when you first set up the parental control service. If you flub the answer to that question, you'll need to call CompuServe Support (1-800-848-8990) for the CompuServe Controls, or Cyber Patrol Technical Support (508-879-9000) for the Internet Cyber Patrol software.

### I don't want to use Cyber Patrol anymore; how can I delete the software?

WARNING: Do not delete the Cyber Patrol files manually; this could make areas of CompuServe permanently unavailable to you! Instead, use the Uninstall option from the Icon or HQ File menu; this will properly shut down the software and delete the proper files.

# Protection vs. censorship

There is a lot of online debate about censorship. Do you want access to everything available online, or do you want it "filtered" according to someone else's morals and tastes? When does limiting access to certain types of information become censorship?

The Online Issues Forum (GO OLISSU) tackles this and other tricky issues of the online world on a daily basis. If you monitor the threads on this forum, you'll quickly see why it's important to balance the need to protect children from improper content with the need to protect first amendment rights. It's tempting to go too far one way or the other. Even the government is getting its hands in the issue by sponsoring legislation intended to eliminate "indecent" material online.

CompuServe itself was embroiled in controversy concerning this issue early in 1996. The German government forced CompuServe to stop access to a variety of Internet newsgroups. Because CompuServe (at the time) did not have the technology to cut off access to members in a single country, they had to deny these newsgroups to all members. This caused a great uproar, and CompuServe ultimately restored access to all newsgroups, but not before proving just how volatile the censorship issue really is.

Personally, I like the compromise solution—giving users access to everything, but providing control software so that each user can decide whether to block access to specific areas. This is the online equivalent of changing the channel on your television when you see something you don't like; you protect your family without imposing your views on others.

# 5

# Finding Help Online

## ● In this chapter:

- **Three ways to get help**

- **Services in the CompuServe Directory**

- **Selecting the Home Desktop's Learn About button**

- **Go to CompuServe's various online help and member services**

- **Contacting CompuServe directly by phone or mail**

*CompuServe offers so much help online, you might not need to consult this book if you get into trouble!* . . . . . . . . . . ➤

There are many ways to find help on CompuServe. Both the CompuServe service itself and the CompuServe software offer very comprehensive help systems. This chapter will show you how to find the help you need when you run into problems with CompuServe.

# Getting the form of help you need

The fastest way to get help with a particular area is to press the F1 key. The F1 key brings up a **context-sensitive** Help window; this means that the Help information displayed is directly related to what you were doing when you pressed the button.

You can choose what type of Help you want by pulling down the Help menu. The Help menu gives you the following options to choose from:

- Contents: the main place for help. It lists *everything*!

- Search for Help on…: the quickest way to review particular topics.

- How to Use Help: Help about using Help!

- Upgrading to 3.0 from CIM: basic upgrading info.

- What's New in 3.0: a list of new features of CompuServe 3.0.

- CompuServe Directory: a comprehensive list of CompuServe's services, areas, and forums.

- About CompuServe for Windows: tells which version of CompuServe you're using.

The Contents and Search options are probably the most useful sources for general help. They each display pretty much the same information; Contents is arranged alphabetically, while Search lets you search for specific words and phrases.

The CompuServe Directory is a very useful utility. It lists just about everything that's available on CompuServe by topic. Within each topic, particular areas are listed. If you click one of those areas, CompuServe displays a short description of what you'll find there, and displays the GO word in blue. Fig. 5.1 shows a screen of information in the CompuServe Directory. The GO command (EDRIVE) is blue; clicking on the GO command takes you directly to that area.

**Fig. 5.1**
A typical listing in the CompuServe Directory; the GO command for the service appears in blue.

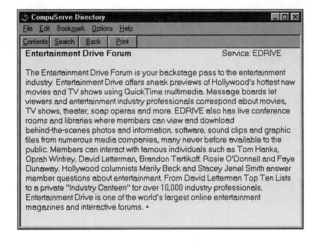

# Learning about CompuServe on the Home Desktop

When you click the Learn About button on the Home Desktop, you can get basic information about all of CompuServe's core services (e-mail, forums, chat, and news). Similarly, when you click the CompuServe Directory icon, you're taken directly to the CompuServe Directory (described in the previous section).

# Getting Help online

In addition to the Help utilities you just learned about, CompuServe offers a variety of other member support services online. These services are all free, and you can go directly to them by using the GO commands shown in Table 5.1. Most of these services are also available from the main Member Services area (GO HELP) shown in Fig. 5.2.

**Fig. 5.2**
CompuServe's Member Services area gives you access to a number of online support services.

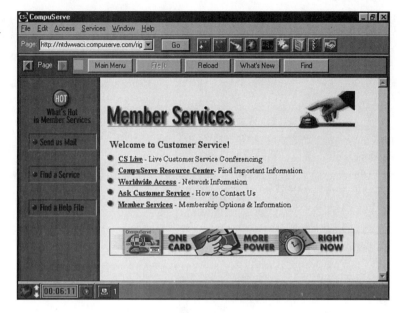

## Table 5.1    CompuServe's customer support forums

| Service | GO Command |
| --- | --- |
| Access phone numbers | PHONES |
| Billing information | BILLING |
| Change your password | PASSWORD |
| Change your phone number or address | ADDRESS |
| Command summary | COMMAND |
| Common questions | QUESTIONS |
| CompuServe Applications Forum | CSAPPS |
| CompuServe Community Center | CISCENTER |
| CompuServe Help forum | HELPFORUM |
| CompuServe Navigator information | CSNAV |
| CompuServe software | CISSOFT |
| Customer Help Database | CSHELP |
| Feedback to CompuServe | FEEDBACK |

| Service | GO Command |
| --- | --- |
| GO commands | QUICK |
| Index of services | INDEX |
| Logon instructions | LOGON |
| Membership directory | DIRECTORY |
| New Member Welcome Center | WELCOME |
| Online questions and answers | QUESTIONS |
| Online settings | PROFILE |
| Online tour of CompuServe | TOUR |
| Practice forum | PRACTICE |
| Rates information | RATES |
| Review charges | CHARGES |
| Service terms and rules | RULES |
| Subject index | INDEX |
| Summary of commands | COMMAND |
| What's New articles | NEW |
| WinCIM General Support Forum | WCIMGE |
| WinCIM Support | WCIMSUPPORT |
| WinCIM Technical Support Forum | WCIMTE |

One other way to get help online is to go to CompuServe's Convention Center area ( pull down the Access menu, select Go, and enter **CONVENTION** ). Once you're in the Convention Center, you have access to live online customer service. To talk live with CompuServe's Customer Service personnel, select Enter Customer Service Live Area from the introductory Convention Center screen.

**CAUTION**   **Never give your password to anyone online—even if he or she** claims to be from CompuServe. CompuServe employees will never ask for your password online.

# Contacting CompuServe offline

If you can't find the answer to your problems in any of the areas detailed in this chapter, you can always contact CompuServe directly.

**U.S. MAIL:**
CompuServe
PO Box 20212
5000 Arlington Centre Blvd.
Columbus, OH  43220

**E-MAIL:**
postmaster@compuserve.com

**WORLD WIDE WEB:**
http://www.compuserve.com

**VOICE PHONE:**
800-848-8990
614-529-1340

**FAX:**
614-529-1611

# Part II: Communications and Communities

# 6

# Pushing the Virtual Envelope: Sending and Receiving CompuServe E-Mail

● **In this chapter:**

● **How much does CompuServe Mail cost?**

● **How soon does a person receive a message after it's sent?**

● **The components of an e-mail message**

● **How do you find an address you don't know?**

● **Using CompuServe Navigator to manage your e-mail**

*Use CompuServe Mail to communicate with your friends— even if they're not on CompuServe!* . . . . . . . . . . . . . . . ●

E-mail (short for electronic mail) is quickly replacing the U.S. Postal Service as the preferred medium for written communication. E-mail is faster than U.S. mail, and it generally costs less per message. In addition, e-mail is more versatile: you can use e-mail to send computer files as well as text messages. If you're not using e-mail yet, you probably will be soon. After you get into the habit, you'll loathe the snail-like pace of the stamped envelope crowd.

Because you're connected to CompuServe, sending and receiving e-mail is fairly easy. And most of your e-mail needs are covered under CompuServe's standard pricing plan, so you don't pay additional fees. Well, then, what's stopping you? It's time to wean yourself from "snail mail" and get on the e-mail bandwagon!

# A little background on CompuServe Mail

You can think of CompuServe as a big electronic post office, through which you send your electronic letters to other users (even users served by other post offices). Of course, with CompuServe, you don't get to see an electronic mailman at your door once a day. But, oh well....

CompuServe's e-mail is called CompuServe Mail, and it is handled through the Mail Center. With CompuServe Mail, you can communicate electronically with other CompuServe members and with online users who have e-mail through other services (such as the Internet, America Online, Prodigy, The Microsoft Network, MCI Mail, and so on). You also can use CompuServe Mail to send regular U.S. mail, telexes, and faxes.

You can use CompuServe Mail to send all sorts of files to other users. You can send spreadsheet files, word processing documents, and graphics files— all in their regular formats—via e-mail.

With CompuServe Mail, you can send your messages normally or tag them "receipt requested." When you do the latter, you get a notification in your (electronic) mailbox when the message is retrieved by the recipient.

Despite all these options, CompuServe Mail is really easy to use—especially with CompuServe 3.0.

# How much does it cost?

The only charges for sending or receiving standard CompuServe Mail are your normal connect-time charges. However, some special forms of e-mail carry additional charges. Table 6.1 contains the details.

**Table 6.1  CompuServe Mail pricing menu**

| Service | Charge |
| --- | --- |
| Send and receive normal CompuServe Mail | No charge |
| Send and receive e-mail via the Internet | No charge |
| Send CandidateGram | $1.50 |
| Send CongressGram | $1.00 |
| Send CupidGram | $2.00 |
| Send fax messages (European destination) | $0.90 per 1,000 characters |
| Send fax message (outside U.S. & Europe) | Varies by destination; GO MAILRATES for a complete listing. |
| Send fax messages (U.S. destination) | $0.75 for first 1,000 characters in a message<br>$0.25 for each additional 1,000 characters |
| Send letter via U.S. mail (International destination) | $2.50 for first page<br>$0.20 for each additional page |
| Send letter via U.S. mail (U.S. destination) | $1.50 for first page<br>$0.20 for each additional page |
| Send SantaGram | $2.00 |
| Send telex and TWX messages | Varies by destination; GO MAILRATES for a complete listing. |

# How long does it take?

CompuServe e-mail is fast—much faster than normal "snail mail," but it isn't instantaneous. Most messages sent between two CompuServe users reach their recipients in a matter of minutes. Messages transferred to other services (such as the Internet or MCI Mail) are normally delivered in fewer than four hours.

**TIP** **All e-mail messages are automatically deleted from the** CompuServe system after 30 days, whether or not they have been read.

## What is my e-mail address?

Your CompuServe membership number is your e-mail address. Therefore, if your address is 12345,1234, another CompuServe member who wants to send you e-mail simply addresses it to 12345,1234. However, if someone from the Internet or another online service wants to send you e-mail, that person must replace the comma with a "dot" and add **@compuserve.com** to the end. So your address would look like this: **12345.1234@compuserve.com**.

While your member ID is your standard e-mail address (and you'll always receive e-mail sent to this address), CompuServe does let you change your e-mail address to something that's easier to remember. To create what CompuServe calls a **Personal Address**, GO MAILCENTER to enter CompuServe's main Mail Center, click the Mail Manager button, and select Pre-Register Personal Address from the next screen. Read the instructions there and click the Proceed button. Follow the instructions to create your own Personal Address, and you're ready to go.

**TIP** **Your Personal Address must contain at least 2 but no more than** 32 characters, which can include uppercase and lowercase letters, numbers, and the underscore character. Your address must contain at least one letter, and it cannot contain the same character more than four times in a row. Personal Addresses are limited; if someone else has already claimed the address you want, you'll have to choose another one.

Once you have a Personal Address, you can receive mail addressed to either your Personal Address or your original CompuServe member ID e-mail address.

## Dissecting an e-mail message

Take a look at the e-mail message in Fig. 6.1. You see the following components:

- The sender's name and address (member ID number); note that a single message can be addressed to multiple recipients.

- The date and time the message was sent

- The recipient's name

- The subject of the message

- The body of the message

- Notification of whether the message has files attached

**Fig. 6.1**
A CompuServe Mail message contains information about the sender, the recipient, and the message itself.

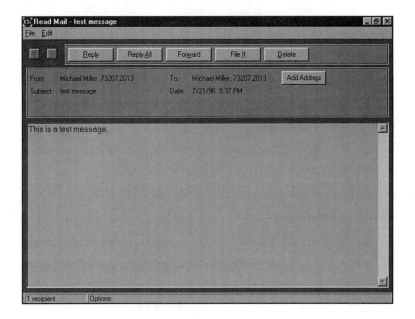

# Doing basic e-mail stuff

With CompuServe 3.0, it's easy to send and receive e-mail. You can do anything you need to do from within the Mail Center.

## Receiving and sending e-mail

The basics of receiving e-mail are pretty simple with CompuServe. Just click the Mail Center button on the Home Desktop, select the Read tab, and click the Get Mail icon. CompuServe lists all waiting messages in the Online Messages list (see Fig. 6.2). In addition to new messages you've received, this list includes any old e-mail messages that you have read but haven't deleted yet.

**Fig. 6.2**
Getting new mail.

To read an e-mail, highlight the listing and click the Open button. When you see the message window, you can reply to the message at hand by clicking the Reply button, or you can store a copy of the message on your hard drive by clicking the File It button. Of course, you can also delete the message by clicking the Delete button.

Creating an e-mail message with CompuServe is just as simple. Click the Mail Center button, select the Create tab, and click the New icon. This opens a Create Mail window like the one in Fig. 6.3. Enter the name of the recipient in the To box, and then enter the CompuServe address of the recipient in the Address box. (You can also click the Recipients button if you want to add multiple recipients, or choose recipients from your Address Book.) After you enter the Subject of the message, type your message in the bottom part of the window. When you're done, click Send to send the message immediately.

**TIP** If you'd rather send this message at a later time, click the Send Later button. This message then appears in your To-Do List. To send messages in the To-Do List, click the To-Do List button on the toolbar and select Process Next.

**Fig. 6.3**
Creating a new
message.

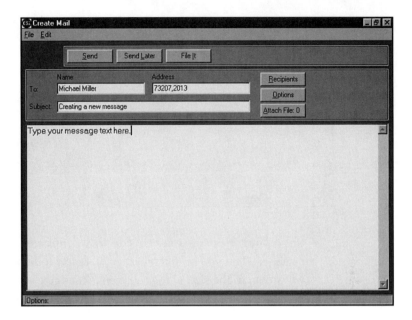

## More things you should know about CompuServe and e-mail

You can use several additional options when creating e-mail messages with CompuServe. The following are just a few:

- **Send a single message to a list of people.** The easiest way to add multiple recipients is to click the Recipients button to display the Message Recipients dialog box (see Fig. 6.4). Fill in the name and address for each recipient and click Add To List. When the list at the bottom of the dialog box is complete, click OK.

**TIP** When you start typing a recipient's name in the Name box, if the name is in your Address Book (described in the next section), the program automatically fills in the Address box before you finish typing the name.

- **Select multiple recipients from your Address Book list.** From the Message Recipients dialog box, click the Address Book button. Select the name(s) you want to add and click the OK button. (To select multiple names, hold down the Ctrl button while you click the names.)

**Fig. 6.4**
Adding multiple
recipients to your
message.

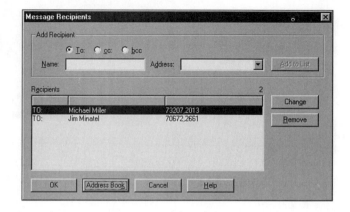

- **Send your message exactly the way it appears on your screen.**
  Usually, when you send a message, it's okay to let the words wrap
  according to the size of the recipient's message window. However,
  if you're sending information in a list or table, you'll probably want it
  to retain the formatting you have on your screen. To do so, click the
  Options button to display the Set Mail Options dialog box (see Fig. 6.5).
  Select the Send exactly as shown option and click OK.

**Fig. 6.5**
Changing e-mail
options in the Set Mail
Options dialog box.

- **Flag your message as urgent.** Click the Options button to display the
  Set Mail Options dialog box. Select the Indicate message is urgent
  option and click OK.

- **Request a return receipt.** Click the Options button to display the Set
  Mail Options dialog box. Select the Notify me when message is received
  option and click OK. You will be notified (via e-mail) when the recipient
  receives your message.

# Using CompuServe's Address Book

CompuServe includes a feature called the Address Book that lets you store frequently used e-mail addresses. To access the Address Book, click the Mail Center button and select the Address Book tab. The Address Book, shown in Fig. 6.6, appears.

**Fig. 6.6**
Use CompuServe's Address Book to store the names of people to whom you often send e-mail.

As you can see, the Address Book is a simple list of names and e-mail addresses. You can add names to the list, delete names from the list, and change existing names. Better yet, you can use the Address Book to quickly add recipients to your e-mail messages.

To add a name to the Address Book, click the Add Entry button, confirm that you're adding an Individual Address, and when the Define Address Book Entry dialog box appears, enter a name and CompuServe User ID (see Fig. 6.7). If you're adding the address of a non-CompuServe recipient, pull down the Address type list and select from the types listed: Internet, America Online, Prodigy, MCI Mail, SprintMail, Advantis, AT&T Mail 400, AT&T Easy Link, Fax, Microsoft Network, WOW!, or other. You can also enter comments about this recipient. Click OK when you're done, and the name and address are automatically added to your list.

**Fig. 6.7**
Adding names to your
Address Book.

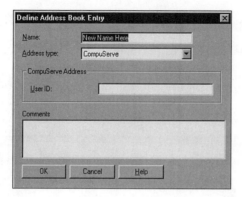

To delete a name, select the name and click the Delete button. To edit a name and address, select the name and click the Open button. When the Change an Address Book Entry dialog box appears, make any necessary changes.

When you create an e-mail message, you can easily look up a name in the Address Book and add it to the list of recipients for your message. When you're creating a new message, click the Recipients button, and then the Address Book button. The Select Recipients dialog box appears, complete with a list of all the entries in your Address Book. Click the name(s) you want to add, and then click OK when you're done.

**TIP** You can also create mailing lists—collections of recipients—in your Address Book. Just select Group Mailing List in the Define Address Type dialog box, and create a list of names/addresses in the Define Mailing List window. Give the list a name and click OK, and the list name appears in your Address Book. When you select the list name as a recipient, every addressee in the list receives an identical e-mail.

## The problem of unknown addresses

Even if you can't remember the CompuServe address of someone to whom you are sending mail, there is hope. CompuServe lets you search its membership lists to find the member(s) you want.

To search for recipients while you're creating a new e-mail message, click the Recipients button and then the Address Book button. When the Select Recipients dialog box appears, click the Search Members button to display the Member Search dialog box (see Fig. 6.8).

**Fig. 6.8**
Searching for members
in CompuServe's
database.

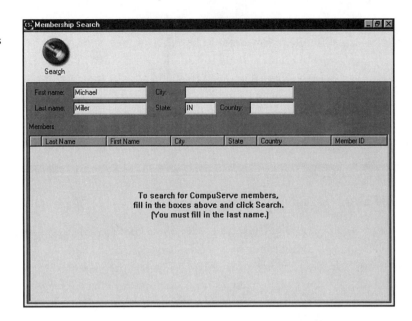

 **TIP** You can also search for members by clicking the Find button on the Home Desktop and selecting the Members tab.

Enter as many parameters as you know (first name, last name, city, state, country), and then click the Search button. CompuServe returns a list of names and corresponding CompuServe addresses that match your search parameters. You can find more information about anyone on the list by clicking the Open button, or you can add them to your Address Book by clicking the Add to Address Book button.

 **CAUTION** You can use this feature only to search for users with CompuServe accounts. This service does not search for users on the Internet or on other online services.

## E-mail etiquette

Electronic correspondence—whether in the form of e-mail, CompuServe forum messages, or USENET newsgroup articles—is much, much different from normal written or verbal correspondence. What is acceptable in verbal communication can be unacceptable in an electronic message, if for no other reason than that you lack the benefit of body language while online.

So when you're communicating electronically, you need to do some things differently. You want to use shorter messages, write less formally, and find a way to communicate the subtleties of voice inflection and body language on-screen. There's no need to spend a lot of time making sure you're using the most correct grammar; no one will care much as long as what you're saying is clear and understandable.

# Emoticons and smileys

There are times when you can shorten your messages by abbreviating certain words and phrases. In fact, the society of online communications has constructed a core group of acronyms for common phrases. Feel free to use any of those acronyms listed here. You'll save space, everyone will know what you're talking about, and you'll look like a pro, IMHO.

AKA = also known as
ASAP = as soon as possible
BTW = by the way
CIS = CompuServe Information Service
FWIW = for what it's worth
FYI = for your information
GD&R = grinning, ducking, and running
IMHO = in my humble opinion
IOW = in other words
LOL = laughing out loud
OTOH = on the other hand
PMJI = pardon me for jumping in
ROFL = rolling on the floor laughing
TLA = three letter acronym
TTFN = ta ta for now!

In addition to these abbreviations, many experienced online users use *emoticons* (also called "smileys") to denote emotion in their messages.

Emoticons are little figures created by normal keyboard characters that, when looked at sideways (tilt your head to the left), convey an emotion or tone.

For example, the most common smiley is :-) . When you look at this emoticon sideways, you see a grinning face. Online users often put this smiley at the end of a sentence that shouldn't be taken too seriously. It communicates the writer's light-hearted tone to the reader. My advice is that you use smileys sparingly and only in situations where you're likely to be misunderstood.

Here are just a few of the emoticons I've encountered over the past few years. Some of them are practical, and some totally useless (but funny!).

| Smiley | Meaning |
| --- | --- |
| :-) | Grinning |
| :-( | Frowning |
| :-o | Surprised |
| ;-) | Winking |
| :-/ | Skeptical |
| :-)' | Drooling |
| :-)8 | Well-dressed (see the bow tie?) |
| 8-) | Wearing glasses |
| *<|:-) | Santa Claus (see the hat?) |

All that said, understand that the nature of e-mail dictates a kind of "formalized informality" in language usage. Use short sentences, and abbreviate long or common words whenever possible. Try to "write for the screen," keeping messages to a length that can be read in a single screen without having to use the scroll bars.

 **CAUTION** **Unfortunately, misunderstandings can sometimes provoke rude** behavior from other online users. When you see a particularly virulent response to a message, chances are you're seeing what is called a **flame**. A flame is a nasty, generally uncalled-for response to what someone considered a dumb or insulting message.

Most users don't appreciate flames, which are often misdirected and overwrought. More often than not, flamers end up looking worse than the original message sender. So avoid sending flames; it's better not to send a response at all than to send a flame.

One more thing you need to know is how to compose a proper reply to another message. You'll see many replies that begin with a recap of the original message. Usually, this "quote" from the original message is set off with angle brackets, and it helps readers remember what the original message was all about. When you reply, you type your message normally after the quote from the original message.

# Using CSNav to send and receive e-mail

Creating an e-mail message with CompuServe Navigator for Windows is quite similar to creating one with the regular CompuServe software. (For more information on CompuServe Navigator, see Chapter 10, "Making Your Sessions Automatic with CompuServe Navigator.")

To send e-mail in CSNav, you must make the CompuServe Mail item part of your script. Click the arrow button next to Create Mail Message or Send File, and you see the CSNav version of the Create Mail window (see Fig. 6.9). The buttons in this window are a little different from those in regular CompuServe, but they perform similar functions.

**Fig. 6.9**
Creating a new
message with CSNav.

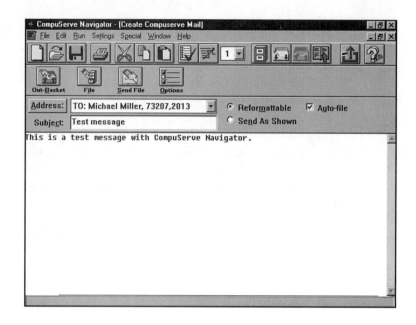

To make sure your e-mail is sent on the next CSNav pass, click the Out-Basket button when you finish. This queues up the message for transmittal the next time CSNav is online.

# Sending files via e-mail

CompuServe also lets you send non-mail files to other users. These files can be of any type, from .DOC files created in Microsoft Word to .GIF graphics files. Sending files via e-mail is much easier than using Federal Express to send disks across the country.

**TIP** In CSNav, you can attach a file to a normal e-mail message by clicking the Send File button in the Create CompuServe Mail window.

Begin by creating a new e-mail message. When you click the Attach File button, you'll see a File Open dialog box. Select the file you want to attach and click Open.

**CAUTION** Don't confuse the Attach File button with the File It button, which sends a copy of the message to your filing cabinet.

Next, you'll see the Attach Files dialog box, shown in Fig. 6.10. If you're attaching only this one file, click OK. If you want to attach additional files, click the Add To List button and repeat the procedure.

**Fig. 6.10**
Attaching files to a message.

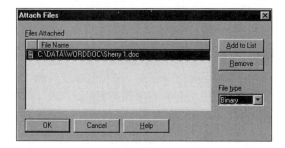

The file type should automatically appear in the File type box. If the type shown is not correct, pull down the list and choose the appropriate type of file as described here:

- Binary: program and document files

- GIF: graphics files

- JPEG: graphics files

- Text: files that contain only ASCII text

**TIP**  **Anything that isn't a text file, or a GIF or JPEG graphics file,** should be sent as a binary file. All program files (.EXE and .COM extensions), word processing files (.DOC, .SAM, and .WRI extensions), spreadsheet files (.WK* and .XL* extensions), database files (.DBF extensions), and other graphics files (.PCX and .TIF extensions) are binary files. In fact, if you're not sure what kind of file you have, send it as binary.

# E-mailing outside of CompuServe

There are many other networks that manage e-mail, and each and every one uses a different addressing scheme. Fortunately, you normally don't have to do anything special in order to receive e-mail from other networks; you do, however, have to learn some new addressing schemes in order to send mail from CompuServe.

In most cases, about all you have to do differently when e-mailing outside of CompuServe is to make sure you have the right address. Because every network and online service uses a different addressing scheme, this isn't as easy as it sounds. This chapter shows you the proper way to address mail to users who aren't on CompuServe.

# Sending mail to other online services

CompuServe isn't the only commercial online service in the U.S., and none of the other commercial services talk directly to each other. Fortunately, we have the Internet to act as a go-between for messages sent between services.

To send mail to a user of another service, you need to know the person's user ID (which should be similar to your CompuServe user ID). This is, in effect, the person's e-mail address. To send him or her mail, type the user ID, followed by an @ sign, followed by the Internet domain name for the service he or she uses.

I'll talk about sending Internet e-mail later in this chapter. For now, learn the addressing schemes for the popular commercial services listed in Table 6.2.

**Table 6.2    E-mail addresses for other commercial online services**

| Service | Address Format |
| --- | --- |
| America Online | INTERNET:*userid*@aol.com |
| BIX | INTERNET:*userid*@bix.com |
| CIX | INTERNET:*userid*@cix.compulink.co.uk |
| GEnie | INTERNET:*userid*@genie.geis.com |
| GNN | INTERNET:*userid*@gnn.com |
| The Microsoft Network | INTERNET:*userid*@msn.com |
| Prodigy | INTERNET:*userid*@prodigy.com |
| WOW! | INTERNET:*userid*@wow.com |

# Sending and receiving mail via the Internet

Having read the preceding section, you should have an understanding of how Internet e-mail is addressed. In general, to send e-mail from CompuServe to someone on the Internet, use the following address form:

**INTERNET:*ADDRESS***

By adding INTERNET: before the Internet address, you instruct CompuServe Mail to send this message out to the Internet and then to the address specified.

If you want to get more specific, however, an Internet address is really comprised of three specific parts:

*username@organization.domain*

Each part of the address has a specific function.

- *username* is the recipient's Internet username. (For example, my Internet username is mmiller, which happens to be my first initial and my last name run together.)

- @ separates the username from the domain address.

## Receiving messages from the Internet and other commercial services

To receive mail from someone on the Internet, you should instruct senders to address their messages to you as follows:

**userID@compuserve.com**

Note that you must replace the comma in your ID number with a period. Therefore, because my CompuServe user ID is 73207,2013, my mail should be addressed as follows:

**73206.2013@compuserve.com**

Also note that this format must be used when a member of another online service (America Online, Prodigy, and so on) sends mail to you on CompuServe. Remember, the commercial services don't talk directly to one another and must use the Internet as a go-between.

- *organization.domain* is referred to as the domain address. Typically, the domain address identifies the user's Internet service providers. (For example, my Internet service is provided through my employer, Macmillan Computer Publishing—MCP, for short—and its domain address is mcp.com.) A domain address can have more than two parts and more than one period. For example, the domain address for the CIX service is **cix.compulink.co.uk**.

Using my Internet address as an example, to send an e-mail message from CompuServe to me on the Net, you would use the following address:

**INTERNET: mmiller@mcp.com**

In practice, you'll have your recipient's entire Internet address in front of you, and you really won't need to worry about which part is the username and which is the domain address. Just add INTERNET: to the front of the Internet address, and CompuServe Mail does the rest.

## Sending mail to other networks

When you're sending e-mail from CompuServe to another network such as MCI Mail or AT&T Mail, just add the prefix listed in Table 6.3 to the front of the recipient's e-mail address, and everything should work just fine. In almost all cases, it doesn't matter whether you type the address in lowercase or uppercase letters. However, to ensure accuracy, you probably want to duplicate exactly the form you see in this chapter.

**Table 6.3   E-mail prefixes for popular commercial networks**

| Network | Prefix | Example | Comments |
|---|---|---|---|
| Advantis | X400 | X400: *ADDRESS* | Advantis is a network operated jointly by IBM and Sears. |
| AT&T EasyLink | X400 | X400: *ADDRESS* | This service was formerly called Western Union 400. |
| AT&T Mail | X400 | X400: *ADDRESS* | |
| Deustche Bundesposte (DBP) | X400 | X400: *ADDRESS* | DBP is Germany's private e-mail system. |

| Network | Prefix | Example | Comments |
|---|---|---|---|
| Infonet | X400 | X400: *ADDRESS* | |
| MCI Mail | MCI MAIL | MCIMAIL: *ADDRESS* | This works with the basic MCI Mail service only. For recipients on MCI XChange 400, see that specific entry. |
| MCI Mail XChange 400 | X400 | X400: *ADDRESS* | This works only with MCI Mail XChange 400; for normal MCI Mail, see that specific entry. |
| NIFTY-Serve | X400 | X400: *ADDRESS* | NIFTY-Serve is the Japanese sister service to CompuServe. |
| SprintMail | X400 | X400: *ADDRESS* | |

**Q&A**

### When I try to send an e-mail message, I receive a reply that the delivery fails. What's going wrong?

Many things can cause an e-mail to go undelivered. The most common cause is an incorrect address. If e-mail sent to an x.400 address is undeliverable, you'll receive a Delivery Report that lists a reason for the delivery failure. If possible, use the information in that report to correct your message and send it again.

# Receiving mail via x.400 connections

Normally, you don't have to do much of anything to receive e-mail from another service. However, if someone on a remote mail system is trying to reach you via an x.400 connection (which is a common communications protocol used by Sprint and other commercial e-mail systems), he or she has to know the following information to properly address the e-mail:

Country = US
ADMD = CompuServe
PRMD = csmail
DDA Type = id
DDA Value = *youruserID* (with a period instead of a comma)

# Sending mail in other formats

If sending mail electronically isn't enough, you can use CompuServe Mail to send e-mail where e-mail generally can't go—such as to the U.S. Postal Service and fax machines. Of course, these services cost a little more than normal e-mail.

 **TIP** **When you use CompuServe Mail to send regular printed** messages—such as U.S. mail—CompuServe simply prints a copy of your message and has it placed in an envelope, has postage affixed, and has it mailed. Likewise, when you use CompuServe Mail to transmit a fax, CompuServe sends an electronic copy of your message over normal phone lines to your recipient.

To send an e-mail message to a fax machine, all you have to do is replace your recipient's normal address (the user ID number) with the following:

**FAX:phonenumber**

Fax messages sent via CompuServe Mail cannot exceed 50,000 characters. CompuServe automatically generates a confirmation message when your fax message is delivered.

Sending an e-mail message to a telex machine is similar to sending a fax, except that you substitute "TLX:" for "FAX:" in the Address field like this:

**TLX:phonenumber**

As with fax messages, telex messages cannot exceed 50,000 characters.

To send an e-mail letter via the U.S. Postal Service, you have to compose the letter in a special CompuServe Mail facility. CompuServe prints the message on a laser printer, sticks a stamp on it, and posts it for you. Here's what you need to do:

**1** GO ASCIIMAIL.

**2** When the Terminal Emulation window appears, type **compose** at the Mail! prompt and press Enter.

**3** Compose your message.

*CAUTION*   **There is no line wrap in the Terminal Emulation mode. You have**
to make sure that you press the Enter key at the end of each line, and that
no line exceeds 80 characters. Also make sure that your message does not
exceed 219 lines.

**4** When you finish typing your message, type **/exit** by itself on the last
line.

**5** At the Send To (Name or User ID): prompt, type **POSTAL**.

**6** When prompted, enter the recipient's name and U.S. Mail address.

**7** When prompted, enter your U.S. Mail return address.

**8** Confirm that you want to send the message, and then either press the
Enter key to leave asciimail or click the Disconnect button to exit
CompuServe.

If you send your electronic message before 4:30 p.m. EST Monday through
Friday, your letter is delivered to the post office that same day. If you send it
after 4:30, it is delivered the next day. If you send your message on a week-
end, it doesn't reach the post office until Monday.

 *CAUTION*   **Using CompuServe to send snail mail costs much more than an**
envelope and a stamp. CompuServe letters cost $1.50 for the first page and
20 cents for each additional page.

In addition to the mail operations presented so far, there is another class of
messages you ought to know about. I call this class ExtraGrams because
all of the messages end with "gram": CongressGrams, CandidateGrams,
SantaGrams, and CupidGrams. As you might guess, some ExtraGrams are
seasonal. For example, SantaGrams are available only during the Christmas
season, and CupidGrams are available only around Valentine's Day.

ExtraGrams cost extra, too—anywhere from $1.00 to $2.00, depending on the
service. But, hey, if that's what you're into, it's worth the price.

To order an ExtraGram, GO GRAMS and select from the ExtraGrams available. CompuServe then processes your message, prints it out on paper, tucks
it in an envelope, places a stamp on it, and drops it in the nearest mailbox.
(Saves you a lot of effort, doesn't it?)

# Subscribing to Internet mailing lists

Just as you can receive mail from the Internet, you can also receive mail from **Internet mailing lists**. An Internet mailing list is similar to a CompuServe forum, in that people of similar interests get together electronically to exchange messages. On the Internet, subscribers to a mailing list send messages to a central address; periodically, the manager of the mailing list compiles all the messages and sends them to all of the list's subscribers.

At last count, the Internet could boast more than ten thousand mailing lists, covering topics as diverse as teeny bopper fan clubs to nuclear physics. To obtain a list of mailing lists, follow these instructions:

**1** Compose a CompuServe mail message to **INTERNET:mail-server@rtfm.mit.edu**.

**2** For the subject of the message, type **LIST**.

**3** In the body of the message, type the following lines exactly as they are shown:

**size 0**

**send usenet/news.answers/mail/mailing-lists/***

Soon you should receive a file (a *big* file!) listing all of the mailing lists currently available. Attached to this "list of lists," you should receive general directions for subscribing to specific lists. In most cases, it's as simple as sending an e-mail to the address with the word **subscribe** as both the subject and the body text.

# 7

# The Heart of CompuServe: Fun with Forums

● **In this chapter:**

● **What is a forum?**

● **How are forums organized?**

● **Reading and sending forum messages**

● **Finding and downloading forum files**

● **How to talk with forum members**

*Find others who share your interests in CompuServe forums.* . . . . . . . . . . . . . . . . . . . . . . . . . . . . . .

**D**espite all of CompuServe's variety, one part of CompuServe undoubtedly gets more use than any other: the forums. You can find forums on almost any topic, from scuba diving to Java programming, for example. Whether you want to become a true CompuServe expert or just a competent user, you need to know how to use the forums.

Using forums is pretty simple once you get the hang of it. All forums have a message board (where members send messages to each other) and a file library (where forum files are stored). Each of these parts is divided by topic into additional sections. So, for example, if you want to find a file relating to a specific topic, you would just go to the part of the library section that covers your topic of interest.

# What is a forum, anyway?

A forum is like one of those after-school clubs you belonged to in high school. It's where people with the same interests get together to talk and exchange information. Once you enter a forum, you're confronted with a variety of options (covered in more detail later in this chapter):

- You can move to a more focused section of the forum; most forums have at least ten distinct sections targeting different subinterests.

- You can read the messages of other forum members, and you can reply to those messages if you want.

- You can search through the forum libraries for files. When you find a file you want, you can download it directly to your computer.

- If other members are visiting the forum when you're online, you can "chat" with them.

- From time to time, you can participate in special conferences that incorporate a number of other forum members.

CompuServe offers many types of forums, such as professional forums and hobbyist forums. You'll also find narrow-interest forums and general-interest forums, as well as forums run by eager amateurs and forums run by large companies. In short, CompuServe forums come in just about every shape and size.

**TIP** **CompuServe forums were initially called SIGs (short for Special** Interest Groups). Because of this, some older forums still use SIG in their names or descriptions.

# Joining a forum

If you want to participate in a forum regularly, you should become a member of that forum. You do that by "joining" the forum. Remember, you don't have to join the forum to look around; it's perfectly okay to browse forums without joining them.

It doesn't cost anything to join a forum. But some forums send monthly notices (via e-mail) to their forum members. If you would like to receive these notices, you'll want to join some forums.

How do you join, then? When you enter a forum for the first time, you're presented with a dialog box that asks whether you want to join (see Fig. 7.1). At this point, you can choose to leave without looking around, to look around but not join, or to join.

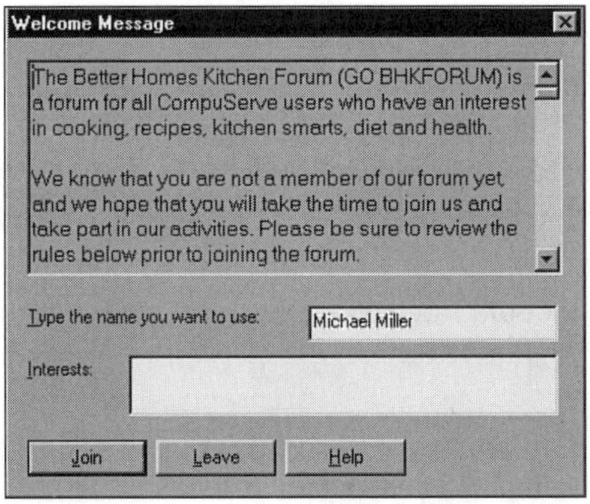

**Fig. 7.1**
Joining a CompuServe forum.

> **Welcome Message**
>
> The Better Homes Kitchen Forum (GO BHKFORUM) is a forum for all CompuServe users who have an interest in cooking, recipes, kitchen smarts, diet and health.
>
> We know that you are not a member of our forum yet, and we hope that you will take the time to join us and take part in our activities. Please be sure to review the rules below prior to joining the forum.
>
> Type the name you want to use:  Michael Miller
>
> Interests:
>
> Join   Leave   Help

My recommendation: Go ahead and join. There's no harm done, and it doesn't cost anything (except the time it takes to read notices sent via e-mail). And don't worry about "un-joining." Even though you can't "un-join" a forum, forum membership doesn't really come with any obligations. The only reason you have to join is so forum management can register your CompuServe ID, and count you as a member in the reports that measure such things. (Of course, if you *don't* join, you can't use the forum.)

**CAUTION**    **Many forums request that you use your real name instead of a** nickname or pseudonym. You may get kicked out of a forum if you don't adhere to this rule!

# Parts is parts: forum organization

Every forum consists of three main areas:

- Message boards (similar to electronic bulletin boards), where forum members exchange messages with each other.

- File libraries, where forum files are stored.

- Forum conferences, where forum members talk to one another in real time via their keyboards.

All of these sections are made up of multiple topic sections. And each of those sections, in turn, represents a more focused area of interest within the main forum topic. For example, the Florida Forum has sections for Ft. Lauderdale, Tampa, St. Petersburg, and other locations.

In many forums, the sections constantly change. You can log on to a forum today and find ten sections, but you might log on next week and find twelve. This is because forum **SysOps** (System Operators, the people who run these things) are always trying to keep their forums up-to-date. They add new sections that may be of greater interest to their members, and delete sections that see little or no traffic. So when you see sections mentioned in this book, be aware that they could have changed between the time I wrote the book and the time you read it.

# Navigating through forums

When you enter a forum, the Home Desktop changes dramatically. All of the buttons and tabs change, and the screen looks something like what you see in Fig. 7.2.

**Fig. 7.2**
The Forum Desktop.
Click the buttons on
the left side of the
screen to go wherever
you want to go.

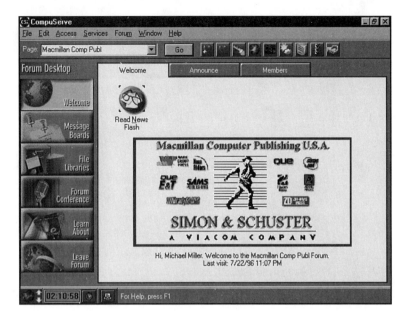

# Browsing through forum messages

The very first thing I do when I enter a forum is browse through the messages. You can find lively discourse on a variety of topics related to the forum's main area of interest (well, most of the time they're related).

When you click the Message Boards button, you have the option of reading, sending, or searching through messages (select the corresponding tab). To read messages, click the Read tab. You'll see the Message Sections list shown in Fig. 7.3.

Double-click a specific message section (or highlight the section and click the Open icon), and all the message topics for that section appear. Note that message topics are displayed only for those messages that have been posted since you last visited this forum. Double-click a message topic (or highlight the topic and click the Open icon), and the first message in that topic **thread** is displayed (see Fig. 7.4).

**66** *Plain English, please!*

A *thread* is a series of related messages on the same topic. **99**

**Fig. 7.3**
Listing sections in a forum.

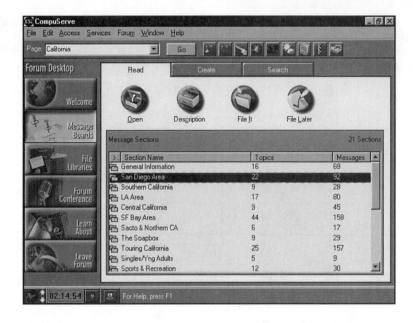

**Fig. 7.4**
Reading a forum message.

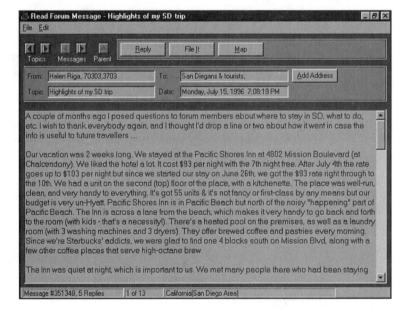

The buttons at the top of the window are the tools you use to move around. From this first listing, you can do several things:

- Read the message.

- Move to the next message in the topic (click the right-pointing arrow button above Messages).

- Move to the previous message in the topic (click the left-pointing arrow button above Messages).

- Move to the first message in the next topic (click the right-pointing arrow button above Topics).

- Move to the first message in the previous topic (click the left-pointing arrow button above Topics).

- Move to the "parent" message to this particular thread (click the up arrow button above Parent).

- View a "map" of all messages in this topic (click the Map button).

- Reply to this message (click the Reply button).

- File the message in your filing cabinet.

- Add the author of the message to your address book.

- Close this window and return to the message topics list (click the Windows Cancel button).

**TIP** If a particular arrow is "grayed-out," that means you're at either the end or the beginning of a message thread; you can't go any further in that direction!

# Printing, saving, filing, copying, and sending forum messages

Reading and replying to messages is fine, but sometimes you want to save a message for future reference. CompuServe gives you several ways to do this.

If you want to keep a hard copy version of any message, make sure you have the message window open, pull down the File menu, and select Print. When the Print dialog box appears, click OK, and CompuServe sends a copy of this message directly to your printer.

If you would prefer to save a copy of a message on your hard disk, just open the message, pull down the File menu, and select Save As. The Save As dialog box opens. Select a name and location for the message file and click Save.

# Dealing with message overload

The only problem I have with forum messages is that you can spend a lot of online time (and money) reading them. This gets especially bad in a busy forum that you haven't visited in awhile. It's tough to sort through literally thousands of messages in hundreds of topics.

To help deal with this message overload, I follow a specific routine when I visit busy forums. First, I resist the temptation to "browse" through the messages. It's just too easy to get caught up in extraneous message threads; before you know it, you've spent an hour in a single forum and still haven't found what you came for!

What works best for me is to sort the message threads by date (by clicking the bar above the file icons in the message list). This way I can skip past older message threads and go straight to the new stuff. (Chances are, older threads contain only lagging responses to the original message, anyway; and nine times out of ten, it's the original message and its immediate replies that contain the "meat" you're interested in.)

Then I scroll through all the message headers before I start reading specific messages. This gives me an idea of what's there for the reading, and I can (in my mind) prioritize certain threads for immediate reading. If I read the most important threads first, I feel better if I have to cut a session short; any unread threads are the less important ones that I'm less likely to miss.

Finally, when I decide to start reading a specific message thread, I try to limit myself to only the first half-dozen messages or so. As replies start piling up on top of replies, the content level starts getting pretty thin; it's good to develop the discipline to get out while the getting is good.

Another way to deal with message overload is with an autopilot program such as CompuServe Navigator (discussed in Chapter 10). CSNav and other autopilot programs (see Chapter 11) let you download specific messages to read offline on your own time—ultimately reducing the money you spend plowing through a mass of messages while online.

Of course, you might simply choose to avoid certain forums during particularly busy times. For example, some people avoid software-related forums right after the release of a new software product. After new products are released, these forums are typically inundated with all sorts of messages about installation problems and bugs. If you aren't having any problems yourself, you may want to avoid this message overload. Then again, if you're having problems, you'll need to browse the forum's message board. If this is the case, make sure you check in *daily*; if there are too many messages each day, old messages *scroll off* the board (and are deleted).

Another place to avoid is the Star Trek section in the Science Fiction and Fantasy Media forum (GO SFMEDIA1) at the start of a new television season. Unless you're a hard-core Trekkie, the number of messages posted there can be overwhelming. (Of course, the same situation occurs in other forums devoted to new television shows and movies.)

You can file a copy of any message to your File Cabinet. To do so, open the message, pull down the File menu, and select File It. When the File Item dialog box appears, select the folder you want and click the File It button.

You can also copy parts of a message to another file. Use your cursor to highlight the part of the message you want to copy. Then pull down the Edit menu and select Copy. To paste this text into another application, go to that application, position your cursor where you want the text inserted, pull down the Edit menu, and select Paste. CompuServe copies the selected text into the second application.

Finally, you can send a copy of any message directly to another CompuServe member. With the message open, pull down the File menu and select Send To. Determine whether you want to send this via CompuServe Mail, a forum message, or regular (non-CompuServe) e-mail. Enter the name and address of the recipient just as you would if you were sending any other e-mail or message. Then click the Send button to launch the message on its way.

# Searching for specific messages

If you don't want to browse through all the messages in a forum, you can search for a specific message or for messages on a specific topic. Click the Search tab and fill in the search criteria you want CompuServe to use when searching for the message(s). You can use any of these criteria:

**Topic**  Select "whose topic contains" from the center drop-down list, and then enter the topic you want to search for in the text box to the right.

**Sender's name**  Select "whose sender's name contains" from the center drop-down list, and then enter the name of the sender in the text box to the right.

**Sender's Member ID**  Select "whose sender's Member ID is" from the center drop-down list, and then enter the ID number you want to search for in the text box to the right.

**Recipient's name**  Select "whose recipient's name contains" from the center drop-down list, and then enter the name of the recipient in the text box to the right.

**Recipient's Member ID**  Select "whose recipient's Member ID is" from the center drop-down list, and then enter the ID number to search for in the text box to the right.

**Message number** Select "whose message number is" from the second drop-down list, and then enter the message number in the text box to the right.

**Other** Select "using another search method" from the center drop-down list. When you select this option, the screen changes so you can search by date or in specific message sections. (Clicking the More icon also displays this additional search criteria.) Fill in the appropriate criteria to tell CompuServe what you want to search for.

When you finish selecting your search criteria, click the Search icon. CompuServe runs the search and displays all matches in a separate Topic list. You can then choose or decline to read each one.

# Replying to messages

When you finish reading a message, you might want to reply to what you've just read. All you have to do is click the Reply button, and you will be whisked off to a new window where you can compose your reply (see Fig. 7.5).

**Fig. 7.5**
Replying to a forum message.

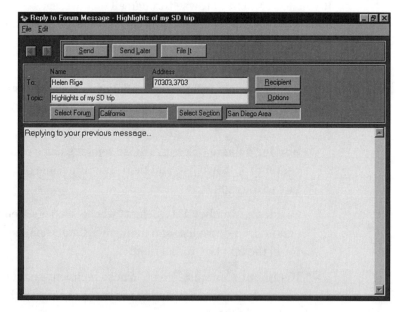

 **TIP** **People who only read messages and never reply are called lurkers.** Being a lurker isn't a bad thing—but it is considered a bit antisocial.

Note that your reply is already addressed; all you have to worry about is the text of the message itself. When you're done writing your reply message, click the Send button to send it. If you do nothing else, the message is posted publicly. If you prefer to post the message privately or send it via e-mail (instead of as a forum message), click the Options button and select the appropriate check boxes.

# Creating new messages

Replying to messages is fun, but if that's all you do, you're missing out on some of CompuServe's community spirit. To be more proactive, you can start your own message thread by creating an original message.

To create a new message, select the Create tab and click the New icon. The Create Forum Message window shown in Fig. 7.6 appears.

In the Create Forum Message window, enter the following data for your new message.

- In the To boxes, indicate to whom you wish to post the message; you can enter a specific member name and address or just enter **All** to reach everybody in the selected section.

- Enter a topic in the Topic text box.

- Click the Select Forum button and choose the forum to which you want to post your message.

## Don't get emotional

If you've done any forum browsing at all, you've probably noticed that some members tend to respond to messages in an overly emotional manner. This isn't a polite thing to do—in fact, it's downright impolite and immature. These emotional messages are often referred to as *flames.*

When you send a flame to another member, you are flaming that member. Flaming is not proper CompuServe etiquette. In fact, you often see flamers getting flamed themselves by other members who are upset by their ranting and raving.

Be a good CompuServe citizen. Keep your head, and don't let untempered emotions turn you into a flamer. Your online friends will thank you for it.

- Click the Select Se<u>c</u>tion button and choose the section of the forum you want to post your message to.

- Click the <u>O</u>ptions button to send the message as <u>P</u>rivate or via CompuServe e-mail (rather than as a public forum message).

**Fig. 7.6**
Creating a new forum message.

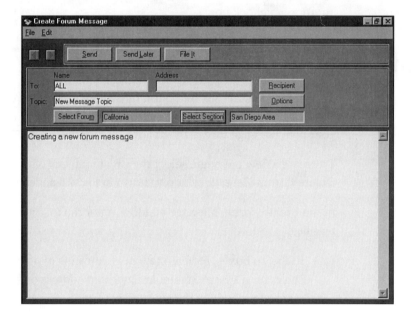

**TIP**   **All forum messages are available for other members to read—**
unless they're marked "private." If they're marked as private, they go directly to the respondent and are not posted publicly. You can also elect to send a message through e-mail; see Chapter 6, "Pushing the Virtual Envelope: Sending and Receiving CompuServe E-Mail" to learn more.

After you fill in all of the information at the top of the window, enter the text of your message in the big area at the bottom of the window. When you finish, send the message by clicking the <u>S</u>end button

**Q&A**   *I'm looking for a particular message, but it doesn't appear in the message lists. Am I out of luck?*

Unless the message is so old that it has scrolled off the board, there is a way to view it. You see, CompuServe assumes that each time you visit a forum, you view all of the messages that are displayed. Therefore, the next time you visit that forum, CompuServe shows you only those messages that have been posted since your last visit.

If you want to see old messages, you need to reset this parameter. Pull down the Foru<u>m</u> menu and select <u>S</u>ee More Messages. Select a new range of dates or messages and click OK. This displays the older messages held in the message sections.

**Q&A** *How do I change my name in a forum?*

When you first join a forum, you specify the name you want to use. To change that name, pull down the Foru<u>m</u> menu and select Change <u>N</u>ick-name. Type your new nickname in the box and click OK. Remember, though, to use your real name if the forum requires it.

# Finding forum files

Forums are also great places to find all types of files. Depending on the forum you're visiting, you can find:

- Text files that archive important message threads
- Reviews of computer software or hardware, of consumer electronics, or of the latest movies and TV shows
- Graphics files, icons, and Windows wallpaper
- Freeware and shareware software programs and utilities
- Travel tips
- Song lyrics
- Other bits and pieces of advice stored in text files

How do you find the files you want in a forum? Well, to begin with, a forum's files are arranged in sections, just like forum messages. You can click the File Libraries button and select the Read tab to browse through all the libraries. However, a better way to find files is to click the Search tab. When you do this, a new screen appears. Click the More icon to expand the search criteria and view the options show in Fig. 7.7

You can elect to search for files that match what you specify for any of the following criteria:

- Filename or keywords
- Date the file was submitted

- Forum sections that may contain the file

- Members that contributed to the file

- File extensions

**Fig. 7.7**
Searching for forum
files.

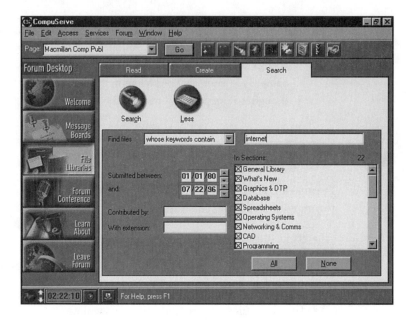

When you click the Search icon, CompuServe scans the forum's libraries for any and all files that match your search criteria. It displays the matching files in the File Search Result list.

If you want to see a more complete description of a file, click the Description icon. If you want to view a text file online, click the Open button. If you want to download the file to your computer, click the Retrieve button, enter a name for and specify a directory for the file you're about to download, and click OK. The file is downloaded automatically to your hard disk.

**TIP** **You can also choose to download a file at a later time. To do that,** select the file and click the Retrieve Later icon. You'll be asked where to save the file, and then you're allowed to go about your business. When you eventually want to download the file, click the To-Do List button on the main toolbar, and then click the Process Next button. This is a great way to use your online time efficiently, and you won't get stuck in the forum downloading a file.

**Q&A** ***I want to view a file online, but the View button is unavailable. What gives?***

Only text or graphics files can be viewed online. You're probably trying to view a program file, which is composed of indecipherable programming code.

# Conversing in a forum conference

Reading messages and files is fun, but that can sometimes be a little impersonal. If you crave real contact with an actual human being, you can use CompuServe's conference feature to talk with other forum members. Click the Forum Conference button to enter the conference area shown in Fig. 7.8.

**Fig. 7.8**
CompuServe's Forum Conference area.

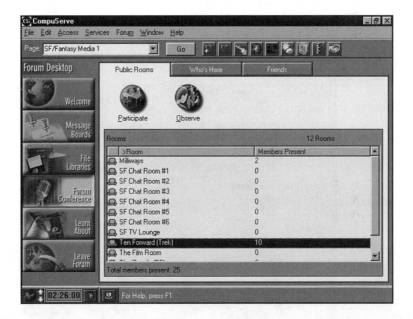

## Another kind of conference

Actually, you'll find two types of conferences in forums. Informal person-to-person conferences (like the one mentioned here) pop up spontaneously. But you can also have organized, large group conferences. These organized conferences are kind of like town meetings, where as many members as possible join together to discuss a common topic. Very often these planned conferences feature special guests who answer members' questions. Watch your forum notices to find out if and when group conferences are scheduled.

Before you initiate a new conference (or enter an existing one), find out who's available. Click the Who's Here tab, and you'll see a list of all members currently in the forum. From this box you can access a detailed Member Profile or initiate a private session with a selected user (click the Start Private Chat icon).

You can also select members to include on a special "friends" list (click the Make Friend icon). Then you can check the Show friends only box to display only those members on your friends list. To view your entire friends list, select the Friends tab.

If you want to enter an existing conference, click the Public Rooms tab, select a room from the list, and click the Participate icon. When you choose to enter a conference, you see a Chat Room Database window that displays the ongoing chat among forum members (see Fig. 7.9). Notice that the other members' conversation is in the upper part of the window; you type your comments in the lower part.

**Fig. 7.9**
Participating in a forum conference.

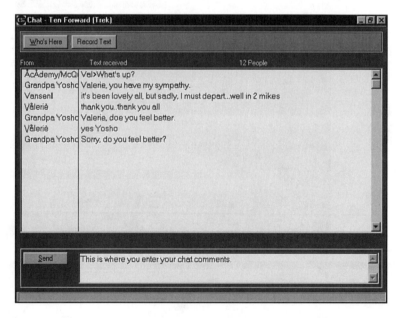

Chatting in a conference takes a little getting used to. There's a time lag involved in these online conversations, partly because most people think faster than they type. In addition, there will be some overlapping of conversations at times, but you'll get used to it.

**TIP** **A forum conference is a lot like CompuServe's Chat service. See** Chapter 8, "Talk Is Cheap: CompuServe's Chat Services," for more information on CompuServe Chat—including detailed instructions for chatting to other users in a forum conference.

# Proper conference conduct

Because it's so easy to get confused when carrying on multiple conversations, here are some simple DOs and DON'Ts you can follow when you're participating in a large public conference.

- DO take the time to learn a little about other members in the conference. From the Who's Here tab you can click the Member Profile icon to read a profile about any highlighted member.

- DON'T jump right into the conversation. Wait a bit, and get the flavor of the conversation before you make your first comments. (In fact, you may want to click the Observe icon in the Public Rooms tab to eavesdrop on a forum before you actually enter the room.)

- DO respond when other members talk to you. It's just darned rude to ignore other members when they're talking to you!

- DON'T use a public conference for long private conversations. If you want to talk privately to another member, go to the Who's Here tab and start a private chat session.

- DO address your comments to a specific user by prefacing your comments with the user's name.
  (For example, if you were talking to a guy named Fred, your comment might be: "FRED: How long have you been a member?")

- DON'T waste other members' time. Track the conversation to make sure your question hasn't been asked by another member. And try not to ask questions that have no relevance to the conversation at hand.

# 8

# Talk Is Cheap: CompuServe's Chat Services

● **In this chapter:**

● **What is Chat?**

● **Starting a Chat session**

● **Can I have one-on-one chats with other members?**

● **Participating in CompuServe conferences**

*Talk to online members with CompuServe Chat. . . . . . . .*

I n Chapter 7, you learned to join real-time discussions with fellow CompuServe members through forum conferences. Although forum conferences are fine, it can be difficult to find people with whom you want to talk (or who want to talk with you). If you're serious about doing some online chatting, there's a better place to hang out: CompuServe Chat.

# All about CompuServe Chat

CompuServe Chat is kind of like one of those 900-telephone chat lines— except you use your keyboard instead of a telephone, and you won't run up a large bill. You can just listen to conversations, or you can join in yourself. You don't have to use your real name (unlike in most forums), and you can assign a nickname for yourself.

## Areas and rooms

CompuServe Chat has three main areas: a General area and two Adult areas. An area is nothing more than a collection of "rooms." Each area has 36 different rooms, and each room has its own focus and atmosphere. To chat with the members in a particular room, you have to enter the room. Once you're in, you can observe the conversation in a room without actually participating.

## Do you fit the profile?

Every Chat user must assign himself a "handle," which will be his online nickname. (This is shorter and easier than using your Member ID number.) You can change your handle anytime you want, so if you want to be "Big Mike" on one channel and "Little Bruce" on another, that's okay. Note that your handle should be socially acceptable because users of all areas— including the General area—can read it.

When you're talking in Chat, you might find that you want to learn more about the person you're talking to. Fortunately, every member is asked to fill in a **profile** containing some very basic personal information. As you'll learn later in this chapter, you can easily access this information when you're in a chat session.

**TIP**    **Unfortunately, not every user fills in the Chat Profile. It's not**
uncommon to see a profile that contains only the user's CompuServe ID
number and Chat handle. It's proper form, however, to fill in a complete
profile so that other users can find out a little bit about you before they
engage in conversation with you. Be a good Chat citizen and fill in all your
information!

# Using CompuServe Chat

You can enter the Chat section with the GO CHAT command. From the
screen shown in Fig. 8.1, choose the area you want to access.

**Fig. 8.1**
The introductory
Chat screen.

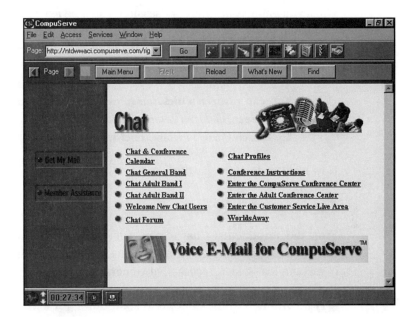

## Getting started

Before you enter a Chat area for the first time, you should complete your
Chat profile. Click Chat Profiles and select Enter/Change Your Profile. Fill in
the following information:

- Date of birth
- City/State

- Machine/Computer
- Occupation
- Interests

Click the Submit button to register this information.

 **TIP**  **Click the CompuServe Chat Guidelines button to read some**
DOs and DON'Ts that pertain to chatting online.

## Choosing a nickname

When you enter your first Chat session, you'll be asked to pick your Chat
nickname. If you later decide to change (*not* reserve) your nickname, pull
down the Chat menu and select Change Nickname. Type your new nickname
in the Define Nickname dialog box and click OK.

 **TIP**  **You can reserve a nickname for future use. From the introductory**
Chat screen, click the Reserve a Chat Handle button. You will be charged
$5.00 each time you reserve or change a nickname.

Now it's time to start chatting.

## Going chatting

From the introductory Chat screen, select the area you want to visit. Because
this book isn't authorized for an R rating, we'll stick to the General area for
our examples. Select Access Chat General Band.

 **CAUTION**  **The two Adult Chat areas sometimes get a little racy and often**
contain explicit language; they're not for shy or easily embarrassed
CompuServers. They are, however, more popular than the non-adult area.

As you can see in Fig. 8.2, the look of the Chat Desktop differs from that of
the Home Desktop. There are four buttons to the left of the desktop:

- Welcome, where you'll find announcements and messages.
- Chat, where all the action takes place.

- Learn About, which gives you access to a simple help section.

- Leave Chat, which should be the last button you click.

Let's get right to it; click the Chat button.

**Fig. 8.2**
The Chat Desktop.

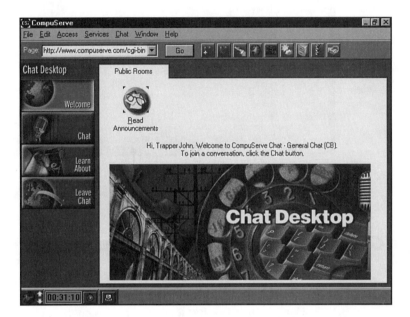

After you click the Chat button, you'll see four tabs along the top. The Public Rooms tab lets you enter specific chat rooms; Who's Here gives you information about other members currently chatting; Invitations enables you to answer invitations to private chat sessions; and Friends displays your list of chat "friends."

The next thing to do is to select a room to chat in. Scroll down the Room list and select a room. Then click the Participate icon. (If you just want to watch, click the Observe icon.) As you can see in Fig. 8.3, the Chat Room window consists of two main parts. The upper part of the window displays the ongoing conversation; the lower part is where you type your contributions. Type your dialog and click the Send button to send your message to the other members in this room.

It's as simple as that. You'll find CompuServe Chat easy to use and highly addictive. All you have to do is type and click, and soon you'll be making friends from all over the country!

**Fig. 8.3**
Chatting on
CompuServe.

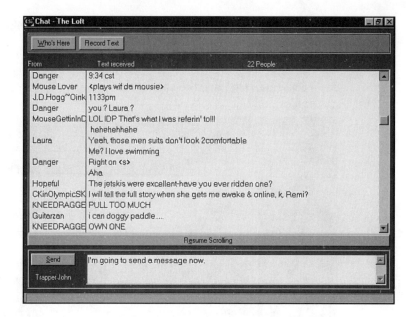

 **CAUTION** **CompuServe Chat is not the same thing as Internet Relay Chat (IRC).** CompuServe Chat lets you chat only with other CompuServe members; IRC lets you talk to anyone on the Internet. Unfortunately, CompuServe does not offer access to IRC at this time. However, that might be for the best; IRC is much harder to use than CompuServe Chat is.

## Chat tips

Chatting can be a lot of fun, but here are some tips that will ensure you have an enjoyable Chat experience.

- Don't assume that you really are talking to the person you think you're talking to. After all, it's pretty easy to hide behind a nickname and create a totally different persona; that buxom blonde femme fatale you're chatting with could truly be a fat old guy.

- Don't give out your real name, address, or phone number unless you really, truly know who you're chatting with. Until your fellow Chatmate shares his/her CompuServe ID and real name, you never really know who you're talking to online. You should know your Chatmate very well before you exchange personal information, and you should know someone extremely well before you meet him or her in person.

- Never give your CompuServe password to *anybody* online—not even someone purporting to be a member of CompuServe support!

- Although a lot of romances that started online have actually been consummated in the real world, you need to be careful and realistic. You never know what might happen.

- If you do get personal online, do it privately. No one in the middle of a multimember Chat session should be made to hear a two-way personal conversation; create a Private Chat session for your one-on-one conversations.

- Feel free to use Group Chat for non-personal business. Group Chat is a great way to conduct short cross-country business sessions.

- Watch your kids in Chat areas. Certain rooms are specifically geared towards children and teenagers, and those rooms are good places for them to hang out. But the online world is part of the real world, and unsavory types sometimes harass youngsters online. Make sure that your kids are well informed, that they use good judgment, and that they never, *ever* arrange to meet a Chatmate without your supervision. (See Chapter 4, "Making CompuServe Safe for Children," for ways to shield your kids from any bad stuff online.)

- Spelling and grammar really don't count for much in Chat rooms, but try to at least keep your messages understandable. And try to avoid indecent language, especially in the General areas.

- It's okay to abbreviate in Chat sessions. Acronyms (like FYI and ROFL) work just fine here, IMHO. See Chapter 6 for more information on acronyms and other online abbreviations.

## Who's who?

If you want to find out who's talking on Chat at any given moment, click the Who's Here button. This displays the Who's Here box (see Fig. 8.4), which lists all the members of a particular room. You can then click the Member Profile button in the Who's Here box to learn more about specific members.

**Fig. 8.4**
Checking Who's Here
in a Chat session.

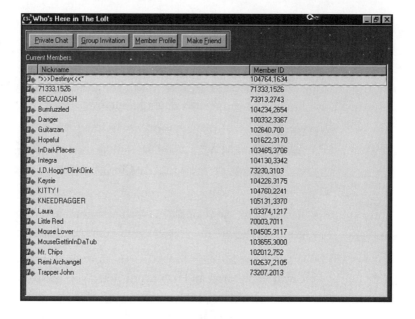

## Talking privately

While CompuServe Chat is great for holding group conversations, you can also opt to talk privately to other users. Just display the Who's Here dialog box, select a user, and click the Private Chat button. This displays a Private Chat window, where you can carry on your private conversation with your fellow Chatter. (Private chat sessions run simultaneously with public chat sessions.) Of course, the person you page is not obligated to respond to you. You might be rejected—just like real life.

**TIP**    **If you want to permanently screen out chat from a specific**
member, click the Prohibit button in the Private Chat window.

## Doing the group thing

You can add multiple members to a Private Chat, which then creates a Group Chat. From the Who's Here box, select the members you want to chat with, and click the Group Invitation button. This opens a new Group Chat window (that looks just like the regular chat window) for your private Group Chat session.

## Making friends

If you find someone online with whom you'd like to continue a correspondence, add them to your Friends List. The Friends List is your own private list of chat users. To add someone to your Friends List, select the Friends tab on the Chat desktop, click the New icon, and select a name from the list. (You can also add a friend from the Who's Here box by selecting a member and clicking the Make Friend button.)

What can you do with your Friends List? Well, not much, I'm afraid. Probably the best use is for abbreviating the number of members displayed in the Who's Here list. When you click the Who's Here tab, you can check the Show friends only option, and only members of your Friends List will be listed.

# Visual chat with WorldsAway

If you're tired of chatting on-screen, it's time to enter the fantasy world of WorldsAway. WorldsAway is a cross between CompuServe Chat and a visual multiplayer adventure game.

As you can see in Fig. 8.5, the typical WorldsAway environment looks a little bit like a cartoon. When you're in WorldsAway, you pick an on-screen character (called an *avatar*) to represent you, and then you interact visually with other avatars. For example, you (through your avatar) actually "walk" down the street and enter different buildings, using your mouse for navigation. You can stop at a bar and talk to other avatars, or you can just meander around the area, eavesdropping on conversations if you want. While it's difficult to express emotion in a normal Chat session, your avatar can actually display different facial expressions.

While WorldsAway is found on CompuServe, it requires its own software. You can download that software from the main WorldsAway menu (GO AWAY; I *love* that command!). From there, you can get more information on WorldsAway or view a WorldsAway demo. You can also view sample screens in the WorldsAway Gallery, visit the WorldsAway forum, download the WorldsAway software, or enter the WorldsAway area (called The Dreamscape). Note that no more than six avatars can be in any area at any one time; if the limit has been reached, your avatar appears as a "ghost" until someone leaves and some room is freed up.

**Fig. 8.5**
Some visual chatting in
WorldsAway.

# Big-time chat: CompuServe conferences and the Conference Center

CompuServe also allows you to attend virtual group conferences. Hundreds of members often attend these meetings in order to hear a guest speaker answer questions from the assembled CompuServe audience.

There are two types of conferences: Round Table and Moderated. In a Round Table conference, all attendees can speak at any time. A Moderated conference is run by a moderator, who decides which of the submitted questions will be presented to the guests. Most larger conferences are moderated, and some may require reservations in advance.

CompuServe Conferences often feature some big names. As I write this section, upcoming conferences include TV celebrity Leeza Gibbons, science fiction author Larry Niven, Senator Bill First, stock expert Alvin Hall, and comic strip character Dilbert (talking about business issues). To see what's coming up, select Current Conference Schedule from the main Convention screen.

You can enter the Conference Center from the main Chat screen (GO CHAT). Note that there are two Conference areas—regular and adult. Click on the Conference Center you want. You'll then be asked to "join" the area as you would a forum. Once you join, CompuServe displays the Conference Center desktop shown in Fig. 8.6. Click the Conference Rooms button to see a list of conferences in progress. Then you can click the Participate icon to jump right into a conference, or you can click the Observe button to lurk.

**Fig. 8.6**
From CompuServe's Conference Center desktop, click the Conference Rooms button to check schedules or enter conferences.

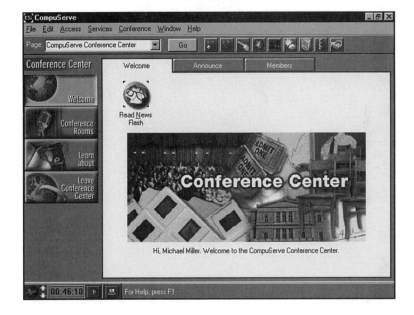

**TIP** **One unique feature of CompuServe Conferences is live customer** service. Select Enter Customer Service Live Area from the introductory Conference Center screen to talk live with CompuServe's Customer Service personnel.

From here, a CompuServe Conference works pretty much like a Chat session, with a few important exceptions. First, in a moderated conference, you follow a routine when submitting a question. You click the Ask button, type your question, and click the Submit button. Your question is then placed into a queue, and the Moderator may (or may not) choose to submit it to the conference guest.

**TIP** **You can withdraw a question before it's been presented by** clicking the Ask button and then the Withdraw button. You can also change a question by clicking the Ask button, changing the question, and then clicking the Resubmit button.

Second, in some conferences, the Moderator might ask the audience to vote on a particular question. When that happens, you are presented with a Vote box, containing either a Yes/No selection or a series of responses. Select your response and click the Cast Vote button. When the vote is over, you'll automatically see the results. You can also check the results at any time by clicking the Tally button.

# 9

# Finding and Downloading Files

● **In this chapter:**

- **Search forum libraries for software**

- **Use CompuServe's File Finders to find specific software**

- **How do I download software from CompuServe?**

- **Is finding and downloading software from the Internet the same?**

- **How to decompress files after downloading**

*Downloading a file from CompuServe is easy—providing you can find the one you're looking for!* . . . . . . . . . . . . . . . . ⟩

C ompuServe contains a lot of pretty neat software programs that can be yours at your simple request. All you have to do is find them and download them to your personal computer. Of course, finding the files is one thing, and downloading them is another—and neither is particularly straightforward. But that's where this chapter comes in handy.

# Where to find files on CompuServe

You can find interesting files in just about any CompuServe forum library. Some libraries, however, have more and better files than others.

## Surfing for software

Table 9.1 lists some of the best places to look for cool software. Remember, though, that you can find good software in just about any forum. You just have to look for it!

**Table 9.1   Good places to find software on CompuServe**

| Area | GO Command | Comments |
| --- | --- | --- |
| Berkeley Systems | GO ADWIN | User-developed After Dark screen savers (in the Berkeley Systems section of the file libraries) |
| Desktop Publishing Forum | GO DTPFORUM | Fonts, clip art, and DTP utilities |
| Epic Megagames Forum | GO EPICFORUM | Action-packed shareware games |
| Hot Games Download Area | GO HOTGAMES | The hottest PC games available for downloading |
| IBM Applications Forum | GO IBMAPP | Shareware and freeware programs |
| IBM Communications Forum | GO IBMCOM | Communications programs and utilities |
| IBM New Users Forum | GO IBMNEW | "Starter" and entertainment files and programs |
| IBM Systems/Utilities Forum | GO IBMSYS | Utilities for operating systems |
| Internet Resources Forum | GO INETRES | Tools and software for Internet users |

| Area | GO Command | Comments |
|------|-----------|----------|
| Mac Applications Forum | GO MACAPP | Lots of different Macintosh programs and utilities |
| Mac Entertainment Forum | GO MACFUN | Macintosh games |
| Macmillan Computer Publishing Forum | GO MACMILLAN | Shareware files and program codes from Que (and other) computer books |
| Microsoft Software Library | GO MSL | Official software Microsoft drivers and utilities |
| MIDI/Music Forum | GO MIDIFORUM | Song files, synthesizer patches, and so on |
| PC World Online | GO PCWORLD | Shareware and freeware from PC World magazine |
| Rush Limbaugh's Download Area | GO RUSHDL | Files of interest to Dittoheads |
| Science/Math Education Forum | GO SCIENCE | Educational software |
| Sigh and Sound Forum | GO SSFORUM | MIDI song files, WAV files, and hardware drivers |
| Space/Astronomy Forum | GO SPACE | Space shuttle status reports, launch schedules, and so on |
| UK Shareware Forum | GO UKSHARE | The best shareware programs from England |
| Web Central | GO WEBCENTRAL | The place to find Web browsers like Netscape, as well as other Web-related software |
| Windows Fun Forum | GO WINFUN | Games, icons, bitmaps, and desktop themes |
| Windows Shareware Forum | GO WINSHARE | Windows utilities and small applications |
| Windows Vendor Forums | GO WINAPP | Seven different forums with files from third-party Windows software vendors |

# Grazing for graphics

CompuServe has dozens of libraries and forums that specialize in graphics files that you can either view online or download to your PC. Of course, you might be asking what you can do with it once you've got it. Well, in addition to just looking at them, you can import CompuServe graphics into your own graphics program or even into your word processor or page layout program.

Because most graphics forums specialize in specific types of graphics, it's simply a matter of finding the forum that carries the type of pictures you're looking for. For example, if you're looking for current news photos, try Reuter NewsPictures Forum (GO NEWSPI). On the other hand, if you're looking for sexy models, try the Glamour Graphics Forum (GO GLAMOUR). You get the picture.

 **TIP** **CompuServe offers an online tutorial to help you learn about** graphics and CompuServe's graphics forums. GO GRAPHICS to access this tutorial from the main Graphics menu.

The majority of CompuServe's graphics resources are centralized in the Go Graphics area (GO GRAPHICS). As you can see in Fig. 9.1, Go Graphics lists all the major graphics-related forums, points out monthly highlights, and even

# Freeware, shareware, and commercial software

The software you find on CompuServe is not quite the same type of software you find in your local computer software store. For one thing, it's free... kind of.

There are typically two kinds of software available on CompuServe. The first is called **freeware** because you can download it completely free of charge. You don't have to pay anybody anything to use this software. Most of these programs are developed by interested users; out of the good- ness of their hearts, they make them available through CompuServe at no charge.

Some freeware is also public domain software. That means that, because the copyright is public property, you can copy and modify the program freely. However, the copyright for other freeware programs remains with the developer; in those cases, you are not free to modify the program without the consent of the developer.

Another type of program that's available on CompuServe is classified as **shareware**. This type of program is freely distributed for evaluation purposes only. If you like and decide to use the program, you are supposed to send the developer a registration fee. Naturally, there's no way to monitor you, but some shareware programs quit working after a specified length of time if they're not officially registered.

The kind of software you find at retail stores, normal **commercial software**, is generally unavailable on CompuServe and other online services because there is no way to collect money when software is distributed online. So if you want the latest version of Word or Excel, CompuServe isn't the place to look. You'll have to go to your local shopping center!

has a "featured image" for your viewing pleasure. Go Graphics is probably the best place to start your graphics voyage through CompuServe.

**Fig. 9.1**

"Home base" for CompuServe's graphics files: Go Graphics

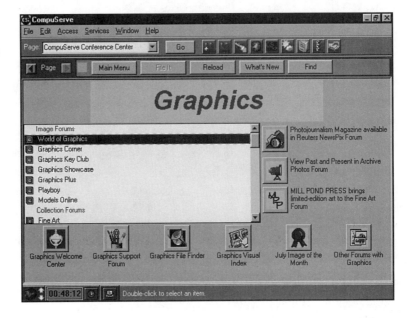

You can find graphics in many forums in addition to the Go Graphics area. The following list names some of CompuServe's more popular graphics forums and gives examples of what you can expect to find in each one. This should give you a head start toward finding the pictures you need.

 **CAUTION** **Because of the nudity in many of these graphics forums, you may** want to restrict access to them if you have younger CompuServers in your household. See Chapter 4 for details.

- Archive Photos Forum (GO ARCHIVE) specializes in historical images.

- Computer Art Forum (GO COMART) features computer-generated images.

- Fine Art Forum (GO FINEARTS) is chock full of images of famous paintings, pictures, and sculptures.

- Glamour Graphics Forum (GO GLAMOUR) contains thousands of model and fashion photographs, like the one shown in Fig. 9.2. (Note that this forum contains some graphics that are not suitable for children.)

**Fig. 9.2**
A typically glamorous
graphic from the
Glamour Graphics
Forum.

- Graphics Corner (GO CORNER) offers photographic-quality scanned images of various sorts.

- Graphics Gallery Forum (GO GALLERY) features scanned images from organizations such as the Smithsonian Institute, NASA, and the U.S. Coast Guard.

- Graphics Plus Forum (GO GRAPHPLUS) features high-resolution true color images in JPG, TIFF, and EPS formats. Images in this forum are the highest-resolution you can find on CompuServe.

*CAUTION*    **While you can view most of these images from within** CompuServe, other programs might not contain viewers that support some of these high-resolution formats. It's also possible that your computer/ monitor may not be capable of displaying these images at their true resolution.

- Graphics Showcase (GO GRFSHOW) offers a showcase of the collections of individual contributors to CompuServe's graphics forums.

- Human Form Photo Forum (GO PHOTOHUMAN) contains photographs of the human form, including swimsuit and lingerie photos. (Note: some adult-only content.)

- Photography Forum (GO PHOTOFORUM) is a repository of thousands of photographs from both professional and amateur photographers.

- Quick Pictures Forum (GO QPICS) is stocked with plenty of low-resolution artwork and clip art.

- Reuter NewsPictures Forum (GO NEWSPI) functions as the primary online source for news photographs from Reuters and other news services.

**CAUTION**  **The NewsPictures forum, like most graphics forums, includes** images that are copyrighted by their creators. In general, you're free to lift these images for your own personal use, but you're not licensed to reproduce them in a professional publication. Ask for more details in the individual forums.

# Searching forum libraries and downloading files

Let's say you know which forum has the file you want. After you enter the forum, how do you find that file? It's really quite easy.

When you enter a forum, click the Forum Libraries button, select the Search tab, and enter specific criteria that matches the file you want to find (see Fig. 9.3). By default, you can search by file name or keyword. Click the More icon to expand the searchable criteria.

When you click the Search icon, CompuServe searches the forum's libraries for any and all files that match your search criteria. Matching files appear in the File Search Result list.

**TIP**  **Many of the files you find will have .ZIP extensions. This indicates** that the file is compressed or "zipped." You'll learn more about compression and decompression later in this chapter.

# Choosy CompuServers choose GIFs

GIF is a file format used to create many of the graphics images found in CompuServe graphics libraries. Pronounced "jiff," GIF stands for Graphics Interchange Format.

GIF files are popular among CompuServers because they can be created and viewed on all major computer platforms, including DOS, Windows, and Macintosh. Also, when compared with graphics formats such as BMP and PCX, GIF files are quite efficient. They take up less disk space and can be downloaded faster than files in other formats.

Although CompuServe can display GIF files automatically, you may want to obtain a separate Windows- or DOS-based GIF viewer program to use outside CompuServe. You can find dozens of these types of programs in the Graphics Support Forum (GO GRAPHSUP). The following files are just a few of those available:

- CVIEW.ZIP (ColorView), a shareware Windows viewer

- DCVW21.ZIP (ColorView), a shareware DOS viewer

- MMK10.ZIP, a freeware Windows viewer

- OVIP1.ZIP, a shareware DOS viewer

- PWVIEW.ARC, a Macintosh viewer

- QGIF.SIT (QuickGIF), a shareware Macintosh viewer

- REVEAL.ZIP, an SVGA-capable DOS viewer

- VPIC.ZIP, a DOS viewer

- WINGIF.ZIP (WinGIF), a shareware Windows viewer

- WINVIE.ZIP (WinView), a Windows viewer

- PS.ZIP (Paint Shop Pro), a shareware Windows viewer  (This is my personal favorite; it handles GIF, JPG, PCX, and 32 other graphic formats.)

If you want more information about these viewers, go to the Graphics Support Forum and download or view the files PROGS.IBM (for DOS and Windows viewers), PROGS.MAC (for Macintosh viewers), or PROGS.TXT (for viewers for other types of computers).

Other file types are supported in specific graphics forums. For example, the Graphics Plus Forum prides itself for its support of higher-resolution images, including those in JPG and EPS formats. (The JPG format is also very popular on the Internet.) You should be able to find viewers for these file formats in the forum at GO GRAPHPLUS.

While GIF is the current standard for graphics on CompuServe, CompuServe is trying to establish a new standard—the PNG format. PNG graphics can be compressed smaller than GIF files can, but with better resolution. So far this format has been slow to catch on; however, CompuServe 3.0 is PNG-capable in case you encounter any PNG files.

**Fig. 9.3**
Note the criteria you
can choose from when
searching through the
libraries in a forum.

If you want to see a more complete description of a file, click the Description
icon. To download the file to your computer, click the Retrieve button. You
are asked to name the file you're about to download and to specify the
directory on your hard disk that you want to download it to. Specify the
name and directory and click Save, and the file is downloaded automatically
to your hard disk.

**TIP** **You can also choose to download a file at a later time. Just select**
the file, click the Retrieve Later icon, and respond to the question of where
the file should be saved. Then you're free to go about your business. When
you return and want to download the file, click the To-Do List button on
the main toolbar, and click the Process Next button. This is a great way to
make the most of your online time and to postpone downloading delays.

# Finding files with File Finders

If you didn't know which forum to search, finding a file on CompuServe
would be a bit of a pain. Fortunately, CompuServe offers several ways to
search across forums for a particular file.

Several **File Finders** are available, which can search multiple forums for
different kinds of files. Specifically, CompuServe offers the PC File Finder,

the Macintosh File Finder, the Windows File Finder, the Graphics File Finder, the Games File Finder, the Adult File Finder, and the ZDNet File Finder.

# Tracking down files with the PC File Finder

The PC File Finder (GO PCFF)—and its companion for Mac files, the Macintosh File Finder (GO MACFF)—enable you to perform cross-forum searches for files. Actually, File Finder is just a big database with file descriptions pulled from various forum libraries. So when you search "across forums" with File Finder, you're really just searching a list of files in a central database.

**CAUTION**   **Because File Finder is a compilation, it might not always be** complete or completely up to date. File Finder doesn't include files from every forum, and it's only updated approximately once a month. So it's possible that the file you want won't show up in a File Finder search. In that case, you'll need to directly access the correct forum to find the file.

From File Finder's main menu, select Access File Finder. You'll see the Select Search Criteria screen shown in Fig. 9.4. This menu provides a list of criteria you can use to control the file search.

**Fig. 9.4**
Searching for files with
PC File Finder.

```
CompuServe                                          _ 6 X
File  Edit  Access  Services  Window  Help
Page: PC File Finder            ▼     Go
◀ Page  ◉        Main Menu    File It    Reload   What's New    Find

  🖳  Select Search Criteria

  Current selection: 220841 file(s)
  📄 Keyword            [ ]
  📄 Submission Date    [ ]
  📄 Forum Name         [ ]
  📄 File Type          [ ]
  📄 File Extension     [ ]
  📄 File Name          [ ]
  📄 File Submitter     [ ]
  📄 Display Selected Titles
  📄 Begin a New Search




  ◆ ▲ 01:01:28 ▶  🖳  Double-click to select an item.
```

You can search according to the following criteria:

- *Keyword* looks in the file's description for words you supply.

- *Submission Date* lets you search for files submitted since a specified date.

- *Forum Name* searches for files in only the forum you specify. (If you choose this criteria, you can only look in one forum at a time.)

- *File Type* narrows the search to files in certain categories (ASCII, Binary, Image, Mac, and Graphics).

- *File Extension* lets you specify a file extension to search for, such as .ZIP, .TXT, .DOC, and so on.

- *File Name* enables you to search for the particular file by name. This is a great way to narrow your search if you know the name of the file for which you're looking.

- *File Submitter* lets you search by the user ID of the person who uploaded the file.

After you specify your criteria, all you have to do is double-click Display Selected Titles. CompuServe then displays a list of files that match your criteria. Highlight a selection from the list and click the Select button to see a detailed description of the file. From this dialog box, you can Mark the file for later retrieval, or you can go ahead and Retrieve (download) or View now using the Open button.

If you choose to retrieve the file now, you'll see the Save As dialog box, which prompts you to enter a name for the file and to select the directory on your hard disk where you want to download the file. Enter that information and click Save, and the download begins; CompuServe alerts you when the download is complete.

**TIP** **A better way to find software across different libraries is with the** CompuServeCD File Finder. Unlike the PC File Finder, CompuServe CD File Finder enables you to search across forum libraries offline (without racking up CompuServe access charges), and then you can go online to download files. Refer to Chapter 11, "Other Ways to Automate Your Sessions," for more information about file searching with CompuServeCD.

## Finding Windows files with the Windows File Finder

The Windows File Finder is the part of the PC File Finder that searches for Windows-related programs only. It works just like the PC File Finder; GO WINFF to access it.

## Finding graphics files with the Graphics File Finder

The quickest and easiest way to find graphics files is with CompuServe's Graphics File Finder (GO GRAPHFF). File Finder is a database of file descriptions from CompuServe's various graphics forums; you can conveniently search it with keywords. It is designed to provide quick and easy access to graphics files across the CompuServe service.

Graphics File Finder works exactly the same as PC File Finder. Just enter your search criteria and begin your search. Because CompuServe has literally hundreds of thousands of graphics images available in its libraries, the Graphics File Finder is the best way to search for pictures when you're not quite sure what you're looking for.

 **TIP** **You can also preview CompuServe images in the libraries of the** Graphics Visual Index Forum (GO GRFINDEX). These libraries include low-resolution "thumbnails" that can be displayed as many as 24 images to a page; virtually all CompuServe graphics can be previewed from this forum.

## Finding games files with Games File Finder

The Games File Finder works just like the other File Finders, but it searches CompuServe's forums for games and games-related files. GO GAMESFF to access this File Finder.

## Finding adult files with Adult File Finder

CompuServe offers a separate File Finder for adult-oriented files. Adult File Finder (GO ADULTFF) works the same as the other File Finders; it searches a select group of adult-related forums.

## Finding files on ZDNet

All of the previously mentioned File Finders work on the CompuServe service itself. However, if you want to search for files on the related ZDNet service, you need to use the ZDNet-specific File Finder. GO ZNT:FILEFIND to search for files on ZDNet.

# Finding and downloading files from the Internet

One of the key attractions of the Internet is the sheer volume of information stored out there—*somewhere*. To find this information and download it to your computer, you need to master CompuServe's FTP program. FTP provides the fastest way to retrieve files from Internet sites. (For more detailed information on using FTP to find and download files from the Internet, see Chapter 24.)

## Protect against deadly viruses

Anytime you download an executable program file from another computer, you run the risk of downloading a computer virus. Viruses are programs that attach to other programs (*not* to graphics files or documents, by the way) and then damage your computer system when you run the infected file. Viruses are real, and they're very dangerous to your computer system.

Commercial online services like CompuServe screen all the files they've made available for downloading, this isn't the case with files you download from the Internet. Because the Internet isn't really monitored, you have no guarantees about the safety of files you find anywhere on the Net.

Now, if you're downloading files from a major Net site, such as a large U.S. university or a major corporation, you're probably okay. These organizations tend to police the files on their servers. But if you're downloading from a site you've never been to or heard of before, who knows where those files have been.

The best protection is prevention. Practice "safe computing," and use an antivirus program to scan for viruses on all files you download from the Net. The Microsoft Anti-Virus or the Norton Antivirus are both good programs, and they work. When it comes to the safety of your computer system, it pays to be a little bit paranoid.

# Getting binary with USENET graphics groups

USENET has a certain area of newsgroups devoted exclusively to graphics files. These newsgroups are called **binary** groups because graphics files are stored in an encoded binary format. If you try to read a binary graphics file, it will look like some gibberish ASCII characters; you need to decode the file to actually see the graphics.

 **TIP**    **See Chapter 23 for more information on accessing USENET** newsgroups and decoding binary newsgroup files.

Most of USENET's graphics files are in the **alt.binaries.*** area. There you'll find individual newsgroups devoted to such topics as clip art, multimedia, animal pictures, astronomy photos, cartoons, pictures of celebrities, and fine art—and lots and lots of "erotic" pictures. Use CompuServe's USENET newsreader (GO USENET) to access these groups, and then you can choose the files (disguised as messages) that you want to download and decode.

 *CAUTION*    **Many of the alt.binaries.* groups are sexual in nature and contain** at least some very mature pictures. You probably want to monitor your children if they venture into this area.

There are also several newsgroups devoted to the art of creating graphics and to the support of graphics programs. Look for these groups in the **comp.graphics.*** area.

# Graphics on the Web

Quite a few Web sites specialize in graphics and graphics-oriented resources. The best place to hunt for graphics on the Web (IMHO) is at the Yahoo Image Surfer site (**http://isurf.yahoo.com/**). This site is a visual directory of tens of thousands of Web graphics. As you can see in Fig. 9.5, you can search for various types of graphics. Then, when the "hits" are returned, you can search for more pictures that look like the ones listed! It's pretty neat and very effective.

So if you need a graphics image, it would seem that you have two options: you can purchase a CD-ROM of clip art graphics (expensive and limited in selection), or you can get on CompuServe (or the Net) and browse through an almost unlimited selection of graphics files. I know which one I choose!

**Fig. 9.5**
Searching for actors
and actresses at
Yahoo's Image Surfer
Web site.

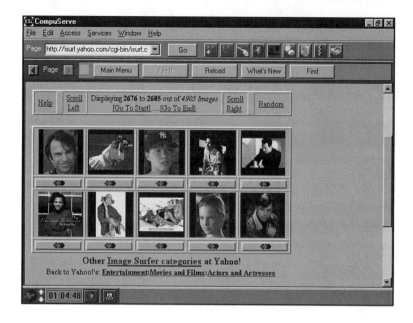

# Decompressing your files

Many of the files you find on CompuServe are stored in a special compressed
format. In some cases, multiple files are compressed into a single compressed file. This makes the files smaller and shortens the time needed for
downloading.

To use these files, however, you have to decompress them. Several different
methods can be used for decompressing; the method of decompression you
use depends on the method of compression that was used. The following
sections outline the two most popular decompression methods.

## Executable decompression

The most common method of compression creates an executable file, which
has the extension .EXE. To decompress one of these files, all you have to do
is "run" the file as a normal program.

For example, let's say you have a compressed file named FILENAME.EXE.
To decompress the file, type the following at the DOS prompt (or click the
Windows 95 Start button and select Run):

   **FILENAME**

Either way, the file automatically decompresses itself.

# PKUNZIPping your files

The second most popular means of compressing files uses a method called PKZIP. When files are compressed using PKZIP, they have the file extension .ZIP, as in FILENAME.ZIP.

To decompress a ZIP file, you need the PKUNZIP utility. You can download a copy of PKUNZIP from the Macmillan Computer Publishing Library (GO MACMILLAN). Under the file name PK204G.EXE, this file is compressed as an executable file. So all you have to do is type **PK204G** at the DOS prompt to decompress this main file. Then you're ready to tackle any file with the .ZIP extension.

**TIP**   **You can put a Windows front end on PKUNZIP by using the** WinZIP program. You'll still need PKUNZIP, but WinZIP will let you do all your ZIPping and UNZIPping without having to mess with DOS. You can find the WINZIP.EXE file in the MCP Library (GO MACMILLAN).

To decompress a ZIP file, type the following at the DOS prompt (or click the Windows 95 Start button and select Run):

   **PKUNZIP FILENAME.ZIP**

PKUNZIP does the rest, automatically unzipping all of the files in the compressed file.

Although other compression formats (such as ARC) are in use, they're not used very often. If you know how to work with executable files and ZIP files, you'll be okay.

# Part III: Getting More out of CompuServe

# 10

# Making Your Sessions Automatic with CompuServe Navigator

● In this chapter:

- **What is Navigator and how does it work?**

- **Creating a Navigator script**

- **What is an online session with Navigator like?**

- **Scheduling Navigator to run while you're away**

*Save money by using Navigator to automate many of your online tasks. . . . . . . . . . . . . . . . . . . . . . . . . . . . . . .* ➤

**M**any CompuServers use something called an "autopilot" program in addition to the main CompuServe software. These programs enable you to automate certain CompuServe operations and to perform some of these operations offline, on your own time—when the CompuServe bill isn't adding up. The most popular of these autopilot programs is CompuServe Navigator, which is available directly from CompuServe.

# What is Navigator?

When you use CompuServe, there are some things that you don't have to do online—like reading e-mail and forum messages. If you store the messages you want to read on your personal computer, you don't have to read them online while the CompuServe meter ticks away. This is where CompuServe Navigator (also called CSNav) comes in.

This chapter is based on version 1.1.1 of CompuServe Navigator for Windows. CompuServe has announced that this will be the last version of Navigator: no new versions will be developed or released. The folks at CompuServe stopped development on CSNav because only a small fraction (less than 5%) of CompuServe users actually use CSNav or any other autopilot program.

However, CSNav will still be available for downloading (GO CSNAV), and it will still be supported by CompuServe. There just won't be any updates or new versions released.

 *CAUTION* **CSNav 1.1.1 is not fully compatible with CompuServe 3.0. In** particular, the filing cabinets share different structures. If you want to use both programs and their respective filing cabinets, make sure that CompuServe 3.0 and CompuServe Navigator are installed in different directories on your hard drive.

## Should I use Navigator?

CSNav is a great program for certain types of CompuServe users. If you send and receive a lot of e-mail, or if you visit CompuServe forums for the express purpose of reading and sending messages, you'll find CSNav to be extremely valuable. Because all tasks that consist mainly of reading and writing can now be done offline with CSNav, you'll avoid CompuServe charges while you sit staring at the screen.

On the other hand, if you do a lot of database searching or file retrievals, you won't find much use for CSNav; you'll want to stick to the regular CompuServe software. That's because most of what you do is very interactive, and CSNav can only automate tasks that are noninteractive.

What if you do both kinds of tasks? Well, if you're a lot like me, you'll end up using both CSNav and the regular CompuServe software. I use CSNav for sending and receiving forum messages and e-mail, but I use the regular software for just about everything else. I've found that the two programs complement each other quite well.

Should CompuServe's lack of future development on CSNav impact your decision? Well, if you want the latest and greatest features, you'll have to look elsewhere (see Chapter 11 for information on other autopilot programs). However, CSNav is perfectly adequate for most needs, and CompuServe does continue to support it in case users run into difficulties, so it's not a big risk.

## How does Navigator work?

Navigator works in two separate passes (online sessions). For the first pass, you instruct the program to connect to CompuServe and automatically download message headers from your favorite forums. After Navigator disconnects, you browse through the headers and decide which full-text messages you really want to read.

In the second pass, Navigator reconnects to CompuServe and downloads the messages you selected. After Navigator disconnects again, you can read the full messages at your leisure, without running up your CompuServe bill.

# Getting your own copy of Navigator—and getting it to work!

CSNav for Windows is available through a CompuServe download. All you have to do is GO CSNAV. From there, you can read a little about CSNav, go to the CSNav support forum, or download the software.

Downloading CSNav is a snap. The installation program creates three icons: CompuServe Navigator, Scheduler, and Help. Scheduler is an automatic timer program discussed later in this chapter. The Help icon launches the CSNav Help files. (You can delete the Help icon, if you want; Help is always available from CSNav's menus.)

**TIP**    **Get online support for CSNav in the CSNav Windows Support Forum (GO WCSNAVSUP).**

## Setting CSNav's configuration options

Before you first use Navigator, you need to set a few configuration options. Begin by launching CSNav, pulling down the Settings menu, and selecting General. This displays the General Preferences dialog box. You probably don't need to change anything in this dialog box right now.

---

## CSNav versus other autopilot programs: Which is better?

Chapter 11, "Other Ways to Automate Your Sessions," examines several available autopilot programs. Assuming that you're looking for a Windows program, how does CSNav stack up against the competition?

First, CSNav is the "official" CompuServe program. In the real world, that may mean nothing more than that you'll get prompt responses in the support forums, or that CSNav will always be compatible with any changes CompuServe instigates. It certainly doesn't mean that unofficial programs will be incompatible.

Second, CSNav is a big program. It takes up more than 4MB on your hard disk (not counting any files shared with the regular CompuServe software); NavCIS and GoCIS (the other two popular

Windows autopilots) take up less than 2.5MB each. If disk space is an issue, one of the other programs might be the better choice.

On the plus side, CSNav installs in the same directory as your other CompuServe software, and the two products work well together. If you're familiar with CompuServe, you'll find that using CSNav is a snap. The other autopilot programs may take some getting used to.

The bottom line is that most CompuServe users prefer the similarities between CompuServe and CSNav. However, if you have special needs, or if you want a program that's under constant development with the guarantee of future support, check out NavCIS, the leading competitor.

You do, however, want to click the Advanced button to display the Advanced Preferences dialog box. Of the many options in this dialog box, I recommend that you turn on the following:

- Verbosity

- Auto Save (in both the Script and Session windows)

- Auto Check

- Current Pass

- Auto Increment Pass

- Passes: 2 (This is very important: it sets up CSNav for the two-step operation you need for true autopiloting.)

- Clear Session Window

- Mail Summary

- Mail Messages

- News Summary

- News Stories

- Forum Summary

- Forum Messages

 **TIP** Make sure you *don't* turn on Library Abstracts. That option downloads the contents of forum libraries every time you log on, which can be quite time consuming.

Click OK to save your settings, and then click OK in the General Preferences dialog box.

 **Q&A** *Why won't CSNav connect (or log in) to CompuServe?*

Somehow, your general connection settings have gotten messed up. Pull down the Settings menu and select Session to display the Setup Session Settings dialog box. Check all the boxes to see if they're correctly filled in; the settings should be set similar to those of your CompuServe 3.0 software (described in Chapter 2). Also click the Modem button to check your modem settings.

# Launching and exploring Navigator

Launching CSNav is as simple as double-clicking the CSNav icon in the CompuServe program group. When the program launches, it displays a screen that looks something like the one in Fig. 10.1.

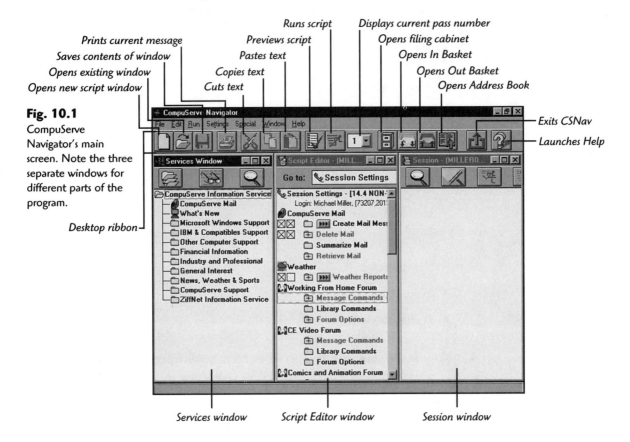

Prints current message
Saves contents of window
Opens existing window
Opens new script window

Runs script
Previews script
Pastes text
Copies text
Cuts text

Displays current pass number
Opens filing cabinet
Opens In Basket
Opens Out Basket
Opens Address Book

Exits CSNav
Launches Help

**Fig. 10.1**
CompuServe Navigator's main screen. Note the three separate windows for different parts of the program.

Desktop ribbon

Services window        Script Editor window        Session window

The CSNav screen is made up of the following important parts:

- The desktop ribbon, which contains all the icon buttons for essential operations. (I won't go into a lot of detail about this ribbon, because many of the buttons are similar to the buttons on the normal CompuServe 3.0 interface.)

- The Services window, which lists all available CompuServe services and forums.

- The Script Editor window, where you create the scripts that tell CSNav what to do online.

- The Session window, which records the results of your CSNav sessions.

Working with CSNav is as easy as dragging items from the Services window into the Script Editor window to create a script. You instruct CSNav to run your script, and the results are recorded in the Session window.

Pretty easy, eh?

# Creating a Navigator script

The default Script Editor window already has a few items in it—specifically, items for Session Settings and CompuServe Mail. CSNav assumes that you want to start each session by logging in and that you want to retrieve any waiting e-mail. (Good assumptions, all things considered.)

Your job is to add other operations you want to automate to the Script Editor window. CSNav makes this easy by including just about every possible service, forum, and operation in the Services window.

## Finding and dragging the services you want

When you first look at the Services window, you see a tree diagram. Because the tree has not been expanded, you see only the upper-level topics, signified by the file folder icons. To see more services, expand the upper-level topic folders by double-clicking specific folder icons.

 **TIP** **Think of the tree diagram in the Services window as a multilevel** outline: the main heading is the root directory, the second heading is the first level of directories, and so on. All directories branch off of the root directory, and subdirectories branch off of main directories.

When you expand the tree diagram, many more services and forums become visible. Note that individual services and forums have a different icon; anything that has a folder icon can be expanded to yet another level.

You can scroll through the entire list of services and forums. When you find one you want to include in your CSNav script, drag it from the Services window into the Script Editor window, placing it in the position that corresponds to the order in which you want it to execute. You can drag as many services as you want into the Script Editor window. Just remember that the more services you include in the script, the longer it takes the script to run.

 **TIP**    **To ensure the fastest execution of your script, place the mail icon** at the *end* of your CSNav script; when you have no mail waiting, this setup cuts down your online time by a few seconds.

## Creating a script from scratch

As you've already learned, CSNav's default script comes preconfigured with Session Settings and CompuServe Mail items in place. But what if you want to create a completely new script? Or what if you have two different scripts that you use at different times, for different purposes?

To create a new script, simply pull down the File menu and select New. This opens a new Script Editor window, which is mostly empty and definitely untitled. I say mostly empty because all scripts begin with the Session Settings item. (After all, your script has to log on to CompuServe before it can do anything else.)

Now that you have a clean slate, you can drag any items from the Services window into this new script. When you complete the script, save it by pulling down the File menu and selecting Save As. In the Save As dialog box, give the script a File Name and click OK.

You can create as many scripts as you want, and you can use different scripts at different times. For example, you might want to create a simple script (with just mail and one or two forums) for times when you're busy, and a more complex script (with multiple forums) for that one time a week when you have time to read everything.

To change scripts, close any that are open, pull down the File menu, select Open, and find the new one you want to open. There's no limit to the number of scripts you can create with CSNav, so don't be shy!

# Fine-tuning your script, forum by forum

Once you've dragged all the forums and services you want into the Script Editor window, it's time to determine just what you want CSNav to do in each service. Although there are lots of things you could do, I'll give you my recommendations for what you should do.

In my opinion, the best CSNav script is a two-pass script. On the first pass, you have CSNav perform essential operations (such as retrieving and sending e-mail, grabbing weather reports, and so on) and then you go to the selected forums to download message headers. On the second pass, you have CSNav retrieve messages you marked when you were offline between the two passes.

How do you instruct CSNav to do all of this? Begin by scrolling to the top of your script, to the CompuServe Mail item. Note that there are two boxes next to certain operations; these boxes are for the first pass (left) and the second pass (right). When a box is checked, that operation is activated for that pass. Because you'll probably want to retrieve and send e-mail messages on both passes, check both boxes: Create Mail Message and Retrieve Mail.

 **CAUTION**  If you don't see two check boxes (for two passes), you need to reconfigure CSNav for two-step operations. See the section "Configuring Navigator" earlier in this chapter for instructions.

 **TIP**  When a file folder icon is closed and has a + on it, you must "open" (expand) the folder to see any subsidiary operations. You do this by clicking the folder icon. You can also click an open folder icon, which has a – on it, to close (contract) it.

Next, move to your first forum item. Expand the Message Commands item and then expand the Summarize Messages item. Click the left check box next to Since and then click the related arrow button. When the Search for Message Summaries dialog box appears (see Fig. 10.2), select which sections in that forum you want CSNav to visit. Click OK when you're done.

 **TIP**  If you're visiting a forum for the first time, only section *numbers* will appear in the Search for Message Summaries dialog box. Once you've visited that forum, section *names* will appear.

**Fig. 10.2**
Use the Search for
Message Summaries
dialog box to select
which sections in a
forum you want to
visit.

Move down and expand the Retrieve Messages item, and then expand the
Marked Items folder. Click the right check box next to the Marked folder.

**TIP** **Any items that appear in green text have tasks that will be**
performed on the current pass. Any items with red text have tasks that will
not be performed this pass because the corresponding box has not been
checked. Any items with blue text have tasks that will not be performed
on the current pass but that will be performed on the next pass.

# Using CSNav to download files

So far, I've shown you how to use CSNav to
manage forum messages and e-mail. Although you
can also use CSNav to find and retrieve forum
files, I don't always recommend it.

It's actually a little quicker to use the normal
CompuServe software to find and download
specific files. And it's a *lot* quicker to use
CompuServeCD's file finder to perform this
operation. If you have CompuServe CD, I
recommend that you use it to find and download
your files. If you don't have CompuServeCD, use
CompuServe 3.0 and the PC File Finder (GO
PCFF).

The reason I don't recommend CSNav is that
when you use CSNav to search for files, you have
to edit your script to turn on the Search Library

operation on the first pass. And because you must
do this one forum library at a time, you can't
search multiple forums. This decreases the
likelihood that you'll find the file you're looking
for on the first pass, and it may take several passes
to find the file you're looking for. (And even
though you could also download the entire file
list from any given forum library and then search
the abstract list while offline, the long download
time needed for the abstracts makes this method
inefficient as well.)

Using CSNav to download a specific file is
effective and efficient only if you know the file's
exact name and forum location. If you're *searching* for files, I recommend that you forget CSNav
and use the other tools you have at your disposal.

Finally, make sure that you always have the most up-to-date list of forum sections. Expand the Forum Options item and click the first (left) box next to Update section names.

Repeat these steps for every service in your script.

 **TIP** **If you want to delete an item from the Script Editor window,** select the item, click the right mouse button, and choose Delete from the pop-up menu.

When you're done, you have a completed script and you're ready to run. Now let's see how you send CSNav online to do your bidding!

# Going online with Navigator

Running a CSNav script is fairly easy. All you have to do is run the first pass, do a little offline work, and then run the second pass. Read on for a little more detail.

## Making the first pass

To begin, go to the desktop ribbon and set the Pass box to 1. Click the Run button, and CSNav connects to CompuServe and runs all first-pass operations in your script. When the script is complete, CSNav automatically disconnects from CompuServe.

 **TIP** **You can run CSNav while it's minimized in the background, which** leaves you free to perform other Windows tasks.

The results of your first pass appear in the Session window (see Fig. 10.3). If you have any waiting e-mail, double-click the e-mail item to read your mail; otherwise, let's concentrate on viewing your forum message summaries.

**Fig. 10.3**
The results of CSNav's first pass: note the Message Summaries icon and the number of threads downloaded in each forum.

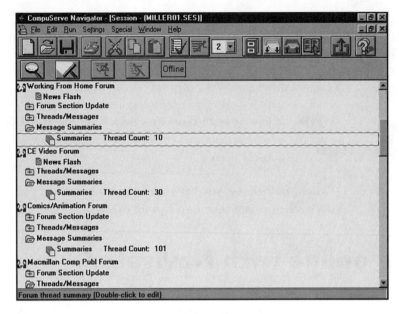

## Working between passes

Double-click the first Message Summaries item, and a Summaries window like the one shown in Fig. 10.4 appears. Double-click the message threads you want to download and read.

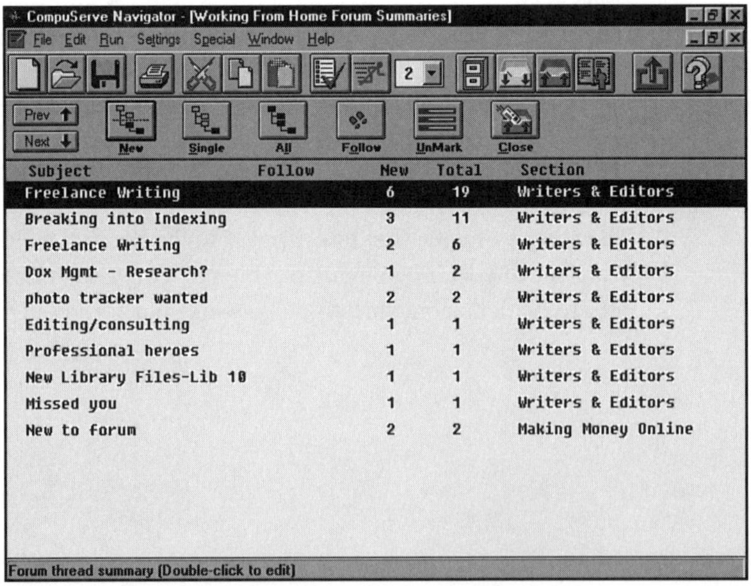

**Fig. 10.4**
Selecting the message threads you want to download.

**TIP** **By default, when you select a thread, CSNav downloads only** those messages that have been posted since your last session. However, you have other options. Once you've selected a thread, you can click the Single button to retrieve only the thread's last message; you can click the All button to retrieve both old and new messages; or you can click the Ignore button to indicate you don't want to retrieve any messages in the thread.

When you finish selecting the threads in this forum that you want to download, click the Next button to select threads in the next forum in your script. When you reach the end of your last forum, click the Close button.

## Making the second pass

Now it's time to download your selected messages. Set the Pass box in the desktop ribbon to 2 and click the Run button. CSNav reconnects to CompuServe and runs all your second-pass operations. When the script is complete, CSNav automatically disconnects from CompuServe again. The results of your second pass appear in the Session window, below your first-pass results.

## Reading messages offline

You can now read the messages CSNav just downloaded—at your leisure. When you click the first message item in the Session window, a new window appears (see Fig. 10.5). This window shows the text of the first message.

## Navigator and CompuServe Mail

One of the most common uses of CSNav is for automating the sending and receiving of CompuServe Mail. Because you don't want to waste valuable online time composing and reading mail messages, it only makes sense to do your writing and reading offline and to have CSNav automate the actual transmission of the messages.

Using CSNav to create mail messages is covered in Chapter 6, "Pushing the Virtual Envelope: Sending and Receiving CompuServe E-Mail." For now,

suffice it to say that creating an e-mail message with CSNav is very similar to creating one with CompuServe 3.0.

The keys to efficiently using CSNav for this purpose are that you must make sure you have the e-mail item in all of your CSNav scripts, and you must activate the item for both first and second passes. This way, you'll automatically get any messages sent to you, and any messages you've recently composed will be automatically sent.

**Fig. 10.5**
Reading messages offline.

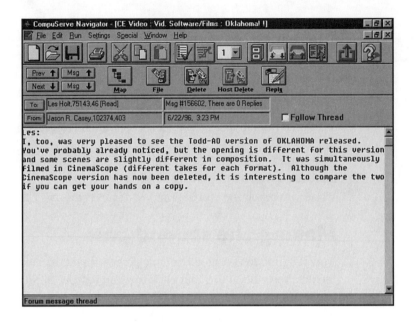

In this window, you have the following options for how to proceed:

- Click the Msg ↓ button to read the next message in this thread.

- Click the Msg ↑ button to read the previous message in this thread.

- Click the Next ↓ button to read the first message in the next thread.

- Click the Prev ↑ button to read the first message in the previous thread.

- Click the Map button to view a map of all messages in this thread.

- Click the File button to file a copy of this message in your file cabinet.

- Click the Reply button to compose a reply to this message.

# Putting Navigator on a daily schedule

Another of CSNav's handy features is its capability to run unattended sessions using the CompuServe Scheduler program. Scheduler is a program that launches CSNav at the times and on the dates you specify. Using Scheduler, you can have CSNav download message headers and e-mail whether you're around or not!

You can launch Scheduler by selecting its icon in the CompuServe program group. From the main Scheduler window, you can create launch entries that launch CSNav at specified times.

## Say when!

The most important part of Scheduler appears when you click the <u>W</u>hen button. The When dialog box (shown in Fig. 10.6) looks a little daunting, but it's pretty easy to figure out.

**Fig. 10.6**
Scheduling a time to run CSNav with CompuServe Scheduler.

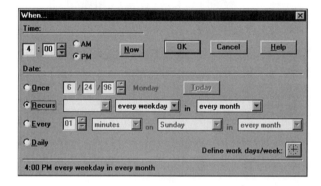

With the parameters in this dialog box, set the options described here to control when Scheduler runs CSNav:

**Time**   If you want it to run at a particular time, select the time (and click AM or PM) at which you want Scheduler to launch CSNav.

**Once**   If you want to schedule a single session, select <u>O</u>nce and enter the date on which you want Scheduler to launch CSNav.

**Recurs**   If you want to schedule a session that recurs, click <u>R</u>ecurs and specify the frequency with which you want the session to recur.

**Every**   If you want to schedule a session that runs on a regular basis, click <u>E</u>very and indicate the day or the frequency in a day or a month.

**Daily**   If you want to run a session at the same time every day, click <u>D</u>aily.

Filling in these options is actually easier than it appears to be, and you'll get the hang of it quickly.

## Who launches Scheduler?

Just creating a launch session won't do much for you unless the Scheduler program itself is running. That means Scheduler must be running all the time so that it can tell CSNav when to launch.

To ensure that Scheduler is running whenever Windows is running, place the Scheduler program in Windows' Startup group. This will ensure that Scheduler is launched automatically whenever you launch Windows.

Now you're set! Scheduler and CSNav will do their things, and you will get your e-mail whether you're around or not.

# Other Ways to Automate Your Sessions

● **In this chapter:**

● Evaluate NavCIS, GoCIS, and OzCIS

● How do autopilot programs compare the regular CompuServe software?

● Investigate CompuServeCD

● Other ways to cut your CompuServe bills

*Use an autopilot program to do your CompuServe chores—without even hooking up to CompuServe!* . . . . . . . . . . . ⊛

The best way to cut back on your CompuServe bills is to do some of your CompuServe chores without actually hooking up to CompuServe. Programs that allow you to do this are called autopilot programs because they do their things automatically, without your direct involvement.

# A little background info on autopilot programs

Any program that automates aspects of your CompuServe online sessions is called an **autopilot** program. Using an autopilot program is kind of like planning an automobile trip well ahead of time. Instead of wasting time on the road fumbling through maps and asking for directions, you do all the preparatory work at home at your leisure.

In general, autopilot programs download message headers (not the full messages) from selected forums so that you can choose which messages you want to read before you go online. The programs go back online and download only the messages you select. You then can read those messages offline, at your own pace and at no charge.

# Reviewing autopilot programs for Windows

In Chapter 10, "Making Your Sessions Automatic with CompuServe Navigator," you learned about CompuServe Navigator for Windows, the most-used autopilot program today. But CSNav isn't the only program available. Third-party autopilot programs have been available since the early days of CompuServe. Many of these programs are shareware or freeware, but some of the newer ones are sold commercially. Most are available for download from CompuServe. I'll discuss the best Windows-based autopilots later in this chapter.

Note that with version 3.0, CompuServe switched to a format called HMI for most of its forums. Older autopilot programs won't work with HMI forums. Therefore, you'll want to pick from those programs that are HMI-compatible. The following table lists autopilot programs that (as of the time of writing of this book) are HMI-compatible.

**Table 11.1 HMI-compatible autopilot programs**

| Program | GO Command |
|---|---|
| CISComm (DOS) | GO CISCOMM |
| CompuServe Navigator (Macintosh & Windows) | GO CISSOFT |
| NavCIS (Windows) | GO DVORAK |
| OzWin II (Windows) | GO OZWIN |
| TapCIS (DOS) | GO TAPCIS |

# NavCIS: The best autopilot program for Windows

Although some may disagree, I think NavCIS (GO DVORAK) is the best third-party autopilot program for Windows. NavCIS is a commercial program from Dvorak Development that sells for $99.95. (Dvorak also offers a trial "timed edition" of NavCIS for free downloading via CompuServe; if you download it and then decide to buy the full edition, you get a $30 discount.)

 **TIP** **For you computer gurus, Dvorak Development is a software** company run by John Dvorak, noted columnist and pundit for several leading computer publications.

NavCIS' main screen is shown in Fig. 11.1. NavCIS makes consistent and frequent use of the Windows environment and conventions. For example, when you want to add a new forum to your list, all you have to do is drag a forum icon to the desktop. When you want to perform a library search in a given forum, you drag a library search icon over and drop it on the appropriate forum icon.

In addition, NavCIS uses voice support, so you get aural reinforcement for all your actions. You can choose from a number of voices, including John Dvorak himself and Kermit the Frog. (Personally, I prefer Kermit to Dvorak!)

NavCIS is available in its full edition ("Pro") and in a special timed edition ("TE"). The TE provides a good way for you to try out the program; if you like it, you can download/purchase the Pro edition.

**Fig. 11.1**
NavCIS for Windows is
easily the best third-
party autopilot
program available.

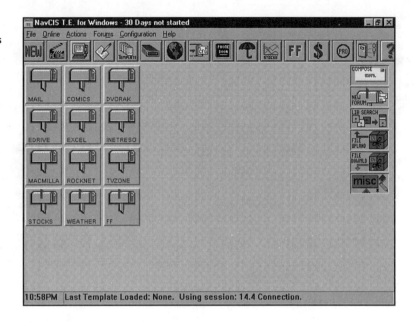

## GoCIS: Another good Windows autopilot

GoCIS (GO WUGNET) is my second favorite third-party Windows autopilot program. Originally known as WinCIS, GoCIS was developed by Logix Systems and is distributed by Patri-Soft. GoCIS costs $59 and is a shareware program.

Unfortunately, GoCIS isn't as easy to use as NavCIS is, which is why it earns a lower rank. Even though initial setup isn't complex, the learning curve is a bit steep. To its advantage, however, it is a very powerful program, and it includes a nice interactive mode (that works similar to the regular CompuServe software) in addition to the autopilot features.

Unlike most other autopilot programs, GoCIS was written in VisualBasic—which means it won't run by itself. You need to have the VisualBasic runtime program VBRUN300.EXE installed on your hard drive to run GoCIS.

## OzWin II: An old DOS friend in Windows clothing

OzWin (GO OZWIN) is a familiar name to many DOS users because it is the progeny of the most popular DOS-based autopilot program: OzCIS. Ozarks West Software is the publisher behind OzWin II (their second-generation

Windows product). If you're an OzCIS/DOS user, you just might want to check out OzWin. OzWin is a commercial program that you can order directly from the OzCIS forum (GO OZWIN) for $89.

Unlike NavCIS and GoCIS, OzWin is not very graphical or straightforward. In fact, a lot of the more powerful features of the program are buried beneath multiple menus and dialog boxes, and documentation is written in such technical terminology that it doesn't really help you find things. In its defense, OzWin is probably the most powerful autopilot program available; but to access that power, you'll sacrifice some ease-of-use.

## Should you use an autopilot program?

Is an autopilot program better than the regular CompuServe software? Well, it depends on what you're doing online.

If all you want to do is send and receive e-mail and forum messages, an autopilot program is the way to go. Autopilots automate these activities almost completely (composing and reading messages offline), which saves you a lot of money. On the other hand, if you participate in a lot of interactive communications—conferencing, database searching, or travel reservations—you need to use the regular CompuServe software.

In reality, you'll probably end up using both kinds of programs. I use an autopilot program on a daily basis to keep up on forum messages and to grab my e-mail. Whenever I want to do something more interactive, like search a database, I fire up regular CompuServe. I also use the CompuServe software to browse through unfamiliar forums to determine whether I want to add them to my automated list. CompuServe is also my choice for browsing through news and weather reports.

My recommendation? If you're a heavy CompuServe user, use a combination of the regular CompuServe software and autopilot programs. If you're an occasional user, skip the autopilots completely. By doing only the bare minimum online (at the fastest modem speeds available) and taking care of the more time-intensive activities (such as reading messages) offline, you save money on your CompuServe connect charges. Depending on the amount of time you spend on CompuServe, you could reduce your monthly CompuServe bill to as little as one-fourth of your previous charges!

# CompuServe on a silver platter with CompuServeCD

CompuServeCD is a subscription-based CD-ROM meant to supplement your normal CompuServe membership by offering lots of stuff on the CD-ROM that isn't available online. First and foremost, it's a full-fledged multimedia magazine on disk—complete with audio and video and all sorts of extras. Second, CompuServeCD includes a database for all the files available on CompuServe, which can make it much easier for you to find a file without incurring connect-time charges. Finally, each issue of CompuServeCD comes with an updated version of the CompuServe Directory, listing all of the services available on CompuServe.

## Let's get spinning: How to get a copy of CompuServeCD

First, you need to get the most recent copy of CompuServeCD. CompuServe mails you a new disc every two months or so. For demonstration purposes, I'll refer to issue 196W, which came out in mid-1996.

The best way to get your hands on a copy of CompuServeCD is through CompuServe. To do so, GO CCD to access the CompuServeCD Online menu. From here, you can get a product overview, you can join the CompuServeCD forum, and you can order your own copy of CompuServeCD. It will cost you $5.95 (U.S.) per issue, plus shipping and handling.

## Playing CompuServeCD

If you're using Windows 95, CompuServeCD is automatically launched when you insert it in your CD-ROM drive. If you're using an older version of Windows, you'll have to run the SETUP.EXE file on the CD.

 **Q&A**  *Why can't I hear any audio?*

This could be the result of several problems. (1) You could have a faulty connection on either your sound card, your speakers, or your CD-ROM drive. (2) You could have an incorrect sound drive installed on your PC. (3) The volume on your speakers might be turned down.

**Q&A** *My system locks up when I run one of CompuServeCD's movies. What should I do?*

Lockups generally happen when you have incorrect video drivers installed on your system. For starters, select a driver/configuration for standard VGA (640x480) with 256 colors. (You can also try a higher resolution combination, but make sure you're running 256 colors.) If you still have problems, try updating your video driver to a newer version. It's also possible that you have insufficient memory available to run movies properly; try closing other Windows applications before you start CompuServeCD.

## Between the grooves: What's on CompuServeCD

When you launch CompuServeCD, you're presented with a Start Up screen like the one shown in Fig. 11.2. To open the magazine, click the main screen where it says "Click this button to launch the latest edition of CompuServeCD." Note that when you open the magazine, the original Start Up screen stays open; you'll use this screen to access some of the other features of CompuServeCD.

**Fig. 11.2**
CompuServeCD's Start Up screen gives you access to the features of CompuServeCD.

After you open the magazine, a brief animated sequence runs across your screen and you're left with the Cover screen. From here, you can do the following:

- Go to featured articles and services
- Turn to the next page in the magazine
- Go to a list of Departments
- Go to the next Department
- Open the Browse window
- Go to the Outbox
- Open CompuServeCD's Help system

 **TIP** **The Outbox is a place where CompuServeCD stores anything that** needs to be done later online. So if you're batching a lot of files to download, for example, CompuServeCD stores the instructions in the Outbox.

## Cutting CompuServe access time with File Finder

In Chapter 9, "Finding and Downloading Files," you learned how to use CompuServe's online File Finder to locate specific files for downloading. With CompuServeCD, you can locate the files you want before you connect to CompuServe, which saves you on access charges.

CompuServeCD contains a complete list of all files available on CompuServe, so you can search the CD's database instead of the online database. The advantage is that you don't have to worry about running up the meter while you're connected to CompuServe.

 **TIP** **CompuServeCD includes only the files that were active as of the** date it was created. If you're looking for very new files (those created within the past 2–3 months), you will have to connect to CompuServe and use the File Finder or access the forum libraries directly.

To launch CompuServeCD's File Finder, go to the original Start Up screen, click the Find It Online button, and then click the File Finder button. When the File Finder window appears (see Fig. 11.3), enter your search criteria and click the Search button to initiate your search.

**Fig. 11.3**
Use CompuServeCD's
File Finder to find files
you want to download.

After you find the files you want on CompuServeCD, you can have the program connect to CompuServe and automatically download the selected files to your hard disk. In fact, unlike the online version of File Finder, CompuServeCD's File Finder even lets you download files from multiple forums in a single operation. (If you're using the online File Finder, you have to go to each forum manually to download files; CompuServeCD automates this task.)

Searching for files offline and downloading them in a batch can save you a lot of time and money. I think the File Finder feature alone makes the subscription to CompuServeCD worth the money.

## Searching for files on CompuServeCD

In addition to searching for files on CompuServe itself, you can also search for any files contained on CompuServeCD. With the CompuServeCD Disc Index, you can search for any file located on the CompuServeCD disc.

To do so, go to the original Start Up screen, pull down the Indexes menu, and select Run CompuServe Disc Index. When the Disc Index window appears, select the first button on the toolbar to search the Disc Index.

**TIP** **The Disc Index is cumulative, so you can search for files located on** current or previous issues of CompuServeCD.

## Searching for CompuServe services with the CompuServe Directory

The final part of CompuServeCD is an updated version of the CompuServe Directory. This guide to all current CompuServe services is a great place to hunt down obscure forums and services without wasting online time using the Find command.

To open the CompuServe Directory, go to the original Start Up screen, click the Find It Online button, and then click the Directory button.

 **TIP** You can also use the Que CompuServe Directory located at the **back of this** book to look up specific CompuServe services.

# 12

# Going Global

- ● **In this chapter:**

- ● **CompuServe's language options**

- ● **How to find international versions of CompuServe**

- ● **Make CompuServe talk in other languages**

- ● **Resources for users outside the United States**

*CompuServe is big all around the world!* . . . . . . . . . . . . **>**

C
ompuServe has more than 6 million users worldwide. While 4.5 million of those users are Americans, at least a million and a half CompuServers live outside the United States. A variety of CompuServe features and forums serve this international user base. This chapter examines how users around the world can get the most out of CompuServe.

# Configuring CompuServe for different languages

Any version of CompuServe can display information in English, German, French, or Spanish. You change the default language (which is English to begin with) by pulling down the Access menu and selecting Preferences. From the Connection tab, click the Define Advanced button to display the Define Advanced Settings dialog box (shown in Fig. 12.1). Pull down the Language sent from CompuServe list and select a language. You can also tell CompuServe which country you're connecting from. To do so, pull down the Country setting list and select your current country.

**Fig. 12.1**
Defining language and country settings.

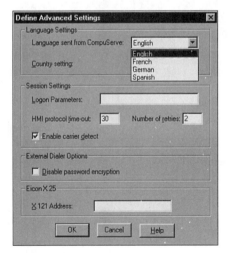

**TIP**  **This language option affects only the messages sent from** CompuServe; it does not affect the CompuServe interface or anything that arrives over the Internet.

# CompuServe in other languages is still CompuServe

In addition to the language feature described above, you also obtain country-specific versions of the CompuServe 3.0 software. At the present time, the software is available in French, German, and Spanish versions (in addition to the English version, of course). Just GO CISSOFT, and pick the country version you want.

The country-specific versions of the CompuServe software include localized menus and graphics. So if you use one of them, you won't have to deal with English being mixed in with the French, German, or Spanish.

# Making CompuServe speak other languages

CompuServe's software comes configured with voice support in English. When it "speaks" to you (saying "Welcome to CompuServe," when you log on, for example) the voice is in English. Well, actually, she has an American accent, derived from CompuServe's roots in Columbus, Ohio. However, you can change the voice you hear in CompuServe so that it speaks in other languages. Specifically, the voice can speak in German, French, or Spanish—or in English with a British accent!

All you have to do is download a special file (there's a separate one for each language), save it in your C:\CSERVE\SUPPORT directory, and then run the file. Each file is self-executing, which means that you can click the Windows 95 Start button, select Run, and enter the program's name, and the file installs itself automatically.

 **TIP** **There's also a file in the standard American English language that** contains sounds for more events than CompuServe automatically comes with.

The files you want are found in the WinCIM Technical Support Forum (GO WCIMTE) in the Install/Upgrade library. Table 12.1 lists the specific files you can download to make CompuServe speak in other languages.

**Table 12.1   CompuServe's foreign language sound files**

| Language | File | Language | File |
|----------|------|----------|------|
| American English | WCMWAV.EXE | French | WCFSND.EXE |
| British English | UKWAV.EXE | Spanish | WCSSND.EXE |
| German | GERWAV.EXE | | |

# CompuServe's global resources

Throughout this book, I talk about a number of CompuServe resources, and many more are listed in the "Que CompuServe Directory" at the end of this book. Although all of these resources are available to every CompuServe member, they're available almost exclusively in English.

If you're using CompuServe outside the U.S., you might like to locate the resources specific to your area of the world. With that in mind, Table 12.2 lists a variety of non-U.S. resources—sorted according to the country and region—that are available on CompuServe.

**Table 12.2   Global resources available on CompuServe**

| Country/Region | Resource | GO Command |
|----------------|----------|------------|
| Australia | Australian Associated Press Online | AAPONLINE |
| Australia | Australian/New Zealand Research Centre | ANZCOLIB |
| Australia | Pacific Forum | PACFORUM |
| Australia | Pacific Vendor Forum | PACVEN |
| Belgium | Belgium Forum | BELFORUM |
| Benelux | Hoppenstedt Benelux | HOPPBEN |
| Benelux | Microsoft Benelux Forum | MSBF |
| Benelux | Microsoft Benelux | MSBEN |
| Canada | Canada Forum | CANADA |
| Canada | Canadian Company Information | COCAN |

| Country/Region | Resource | GO Command |
| --- | --- | --- |
| Europe | European Community Telework Forum | ECTF |
| Europe | Other European Company Information | COEURO |
| Europe | European Forum | EURFORUM |
| Europe | European Railway Schedule | RAILWAY |
| Europe | European Co. Research Centre | EUROLIB |
| Europe | Federation of International Distributors Forum | FEDERATION |
| Europe | Microsoft Central Europe Forum | MSCE |
| Europe | Microsoft Central European Services | MSEURO |
| Europe | Telework Europa Forum | TWEUROPA |
| Europe | World Community Forum | WCOMMUNITY |
| France | Agendus Quo Vadis | QUOVADIS |
| France | ARN | ARNFR |
| France | Associated Press France en Ligne | APFRANCE |
| France | Claris France Forum | CLARFR |
| France | France Forum | FRFORUM |
| France | Informatique France Forum | INFOFR |
| France | Le Bihan & Cie | LEBIHAN |
| France | Microsoft France Forum | MSFR |
| France | Microsoft France | MSFRANCE |
| France | *PC Direct France* Forum | PCDFRA |
| France | US Robotics France | USRFRANCE |
| France | Windowshare France Forum | WSHARE |
| Germany | BertelsmannUnivsallexikon | BEPLEXIKON |
| Germany | Borland GmbH Forum | BORGER |

continues

## Table 12.2   Continued

| Country/Region | Resource | GO Command |
|---|---|---|
| Germany | CA-Clipper Germany Forum | CLIPGER |
| Germany | CA Micro Germany Forum | CAMICRO |
| Germany | CPV Datensysteme | PCIND |
| Germany | *DER SPIEGEL* Forum | SPIEGEL |
| Germany | Deutsches Computer Forum | GERNET |
| Germany | Deutsches Internet Forum | GERINTERNET |
| Germany | Deutsches NT Forum | GERNT |
| Germany | Deutsches Science Fiction Forum | SCIFID |
| Germany | Deutsches Windows 95 Forum | DEUWIN95 |
| Germany | Deutschland Info | INFOGER |
| Germany | Deutschland Online | GERONLINE |
| Germany | Deutschland Online Forum | GERLINE |
| Germany | DPA-Kurznachrichtendiendst | DPANEWS |
| Germany | Dr. Neuhaus Forum | NEUHAUS |
| Germany | German Company Information | COGERMAN |
| Germany | German Company Research Center | GERLIB |
| Germany | IBM PSP Deutschland Forum | OS2UGER |
| Germany | Lotus GmbH Forum | LOTGER |
| Germany | Magna Media Forum | MAGNA |
| Germany | PEARL Forum | PEARL |
| Germany | Prisma GmbH Forum | PRISMA |
| Germany | Toshiba GmbH Forum | TOSHGER |
| Germany | Vobis AG Forum | VOBIS |
| Germany | Corel WordPerfect GmbH Forum | WPGER |

| Country/Region | Resource | GO Command |
|---|---|---|
| Germany | Ziff *PC DIREKT* Forum | PCDIREKT |
| Germany | Ziff *PC Professionell* Forum | PCPRO |
| Germany | Ziff *Windows* Deutschland Forum | GERWIN |
| Hong Kong | Hong Kong Forum | HONGKONG |
| Ireland | Northern Ireland News | NIRELAND |
| Israel | Israel Forum | ISRAEL |
| Italy | Italian Forum | GO ITALFOR |
| Italy | Microsoft Italy Forum | MSITALY |
| Italy | Microsoft Italy | MSITA |
| Japan | Japan Forum | JAPAN |
| Latin America | Latin America Forum | FORLATIN |
| Latin America | Microsoft Spain/Latin America Forum | MSSP |
| Latin America | Microsoft Spain/Latin America | MSSPAIN |
| Mexico | Mexico Forum | MEXICO |
| Netherlands | Netherlands Forum | NLFORUM |
| Netherlands | Netherlands Professional Forum | NFPROF |
| Spain | Microsoft Spain/Latin America Forum | MSSP |
| Spain | Microsoft Spain/Latin America | MSSPAIN |
| Spain | Spanish Forum | SPFORUM |
| United Kingdom | AA Accommodation | UKACCOMM |
| United Kingdom | AA Days Out | UKDAYSOUT |
| United Kingdom | AA Golf | UKGOLF |
| United Kingdom | AA Restaurants | UKREST |
| United Kingdom | AA Roadwatch | AAROADWATCH |
| United Kingdom | British Books in Print | BBIP |

continues

**Table 12.2 Continued**

| Country/Region | Resource | GO Command |
|---|---|---|
| United Kingdom | British Trade Marks | UKTRADEMARK |
| United Kingdom | PA News Online | PAO |
| United Kingdom | *PC Direct UK* Forum | PCDUK |
| United Kingdom | *PC Magazine* UK Forum | PCUKFORUM |
| United Kingdom | *PC UK Online* | PCUKONLINE |
| United Kingdom | Reuters UK News Clips | UKREUTERS |
| United Kingdom | UK Book Reviews | UKBREVE |
| United Kingdom | UK Communications Forum | UKCOMMS |
| United Kingdom | UK Company Information | COUK |
| United Kingdom | *UK Computer Shopper* Forum | UKSHOPPER |
| United Kingdom | UK Computing Forum | UKCOMP |
| United Kingdom | UK Film Reviews | UKFILMS |
| United Kingdom | UK Forum | UKFORUM |
| United Kingdom | UK Historical Pricing | UKPRICE |
| United Kingdom | UK Issue Lookup | SEDOL |
| United Kingdom | UK Newspaper Library | UKPAPERS |
| United Kingdom | UK Professionals Forum | UKPROF |
| United Kingdom | UK Research Centre | UKLIB |
| United Kingdom | UK Shareware Forum | UKSHARE |
| United Kingdom | UK Theatre Reviews | UKTHEATRE |
| United Kingdom | UK TV Soap Previews | UKSOAPS |
| United Kingdom | UK Video Reviews | UKVIDEO |
| United Kingdom | UK Weather | UKWEATHER |
| United Kingdom | UK What's On Guide | UKWO |

# Going Traveling

● **In this chapter:**

- **Search travel-related databases**

- **Visit travel-related forums**

- **Make your own travel arrangements with eaasySABRE, Worldspace Travelshopper, and OAG**

- **Venture onto the Internet for more travel-related resources**

*Make all your travel plans without leaving the comfort of your keyboard!* . . . . . . . . . . . . . . . . . . . . . . . . . . . . . . . . **⊘**

ompuServe puts the world at your fingertips—literally. Through various online databases, forums, and reservation systems, you can plan for a trip anywhere in the world, taking care of everything from start to finish—including making all your travel and lodging reservations. It's all very convenient: you can do it without leaving the comfort of your computer keyboard, thanks to CompuServe's various travel-related resources.

# Before you go, do your research

Before you go anywhere, you can check out all the details from your personal computer. Thanks to the valuable services CompuServe offers, you can plan the perfect trip without having to pore over mounds of brochures from hotel chains and chambers of commerce.

Most of CompuServe's travel-related services can be accessed from the main Travel screen (GO TRAVEL), shown in Fig. 13.1. Stop there first to see what's available.

**Fig. 13.1**
CompuServe's Travel screen gives you access to numerous travel-related services.

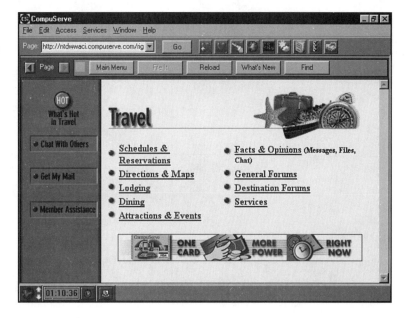

# Travel-related databases

If you need data about wherever it is you're going, the best place to look is in a CompuServe database. Table 13.1 highlights some of the more popular travel-related databases.

### Table 13.1    Popular travel-related databases

| Database | Contents | GO Command |
| --- | --- | --- |
| Adventures in Travel | Articles by professional travel writers | AIT |
| Complete Guide to America's National Parks | News and information from the National Park Service | PARKS |
| Department of State Advisories | Advisories and warnings for Americans traveling abroad | STATE |
| Golf Guide Online | From the Lanier Golf Database, a comprehensive listing of more than 12,000 golf courses across the U.S. and 1,200 more courses worldwide | GLF |
| Lanier Bed & Breakfast Database | Data on more than 9,000 North American inns | INNS |
| Outdoors News Clips | News on environmental and outdoor activities | OUTNEWS |
| Travel Britain Online | A database of U.K. events and destinations | TBONLINE |
| UK Travel | A service for travelers to Britain | UKTRAVEL |
| Zagat Restaurant Survey | Thousands of restaurant reviews | ZAGAT |

I have found ABC Worldwide Hotel Guide and Adventures in Travel to be the most useful services for my needs. But then again, I'm not much of a golfer or a camper; if I were, I'd use those databases, too.

 **TIP**    **If you need information or action on passport or Visa applications,** see the Visa Advisors and Electronic Visa guide (GO VISA).

# Travel-related forums

If raw data isn't enough, go for the face-to-face (or keyboard-to-keyboard) contact that's available via CompuServe's travel-related forums. Although many forums may prove fruitful, depending on your destination, you might need an extended list of the more popular forums among CompuServe travelers:

Air Canada Forum (GO AIRCANADA)

Belgium Forum (GO BELFORUM)

California Forum (GO CALFORUM)

Canada Forum (GO CANADA)

Carribean Travel Forum (GO CARIBFORUM)

Colorado Forum (GO COLORADO)

Deutschland Forum (TO GERLINE)

European Forum (GO EURFORUM)

Florida Forum (GO FLORIDA)

France Forum (GO FRFORUM)

Hawaii Forum (GO HAWAII)

Hong Kong Forum (GO HONGKONG)

Inns and Lodging Forum (GO LODGING)

Israel Forum (GO ISRAEL)

Italian Forum (GO ITALFOR)

Japan Forum (GO JAPAN)

Latin America Forum (GO FORLATIN)

Mexico Forum (GO MEXICO)

Mexico Travel & Culture Forum (GO MEXTRAVEL)

Native's Guide to New York Forum (GO NYNY)

Netherlands Forum (GO NLFORUM)

New York Newslink (GO NEWYORK)

Ohio Travel Forum (GO OHIO)

Outdoors Network (GO OUTDOORS)

Pacific Forum (GO PACFORUM)

Recreational Vehicle Forum (GO RVFORUM)

Spanish Forum (GO SPFORUM)

Travel Software Support Forum (GO TSSFORUM)

United States Travel Forum (GO USTRAVEL)

UK Forum (GO UKFORUM)

World Community Forum (GO WCOMMUNITY)

The granddaddy here, of course, is the Travel Forum (GO TRAVSIG). It's the place to get advice from seasoned travelers of all sorts.

The World Community Forum (GO WCOMMUNITY) is also an interesting place to visit. As you can see in Fig. 13.2, this forum is available in several languages, but all the messages are synchronized so that visitors of various nationalities can read the same messages in their native tongues!

**Fig. 13.2**
Get multicultural with the World Community Forum.

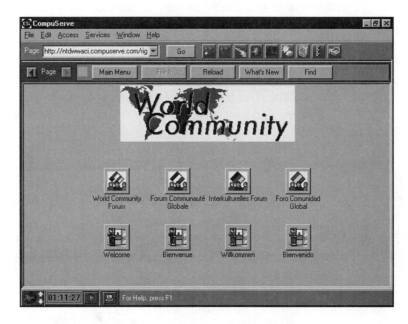

# Booking your travel with reservations

Now that you know where you want to go, you'll want to arrange the details of getting there. CompuServe offers four commercial services that you can use to make all your reservations, including those with airlines, hotels, and car rental companies. And all you have to do is tap a few keys on your keyboard (and pay the bills later!).

Of the four reservation services on CompuServe, three are run by airlines or airline consortia, and they are free of charge. The fourth, Official Airline Guides (OAG), is not run by an airline, and it charges you for its use. (Frankly, the free ones run by the airlines are easier to use and are more comprehensive than the OAG service, anyway!)

## Using eaasySABRE

eaasySABRE (GO SABRE) is the travel reservation system of American Airlines. (Note the two A's in EAAsy—for American Airlines.) Sabre lets you make airline, hotel, and car rental reservations around the world—and on all major airlines, not just American.

If you're an eaasySABRE member, you can go right into the service. (Just select <u>A</u>ccess eaasySABRE CIM from the main menu.) If you're not a member, you can either apply for membership (at no charge) or browse through the system. On your first visit, it's a good idea to set up your Travel Profile (for frequent flyer numbers, rental car information, and so on). Then on subsequent visits, all you have to do is enter your membership number and password, and you can go ahead and make your reservations.

**TIP**   **You don't have to be an eaasySABRE member to browse through** eaasySABRE. You *do* have to be a member, however, to make actual reservations. Note that there is no charge to establish an eaasySABRE membership.

To make airline reservations, choose Flights & Fares. When you see the screen shown in Fig. 13.3, you need to enter the information outlined in the following list.

- *Departure City or Code.* If you don't know the code for this city's airport, just type the city name; eaasySABRE prompts you later with a list of possible airports.

**Fig. 13.3**
Using eaasySABRE
to make airline
reservations.

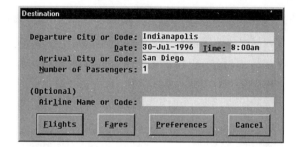

 **TIP** eaasySABRE, like all reservation systems, bases all reservations on
airport codes; it does not use the actual name of the city.

- *Date of departure.*

- *Time of departure.* Enter the earliest possible time you want to depart
  that day.

- *Arrival City or Code.* This is the airport at your destination.

- *Number of Passengers.*

- *Airline Name or Code.* This is optional; fill it out only if you have an
  airline preference.

If you want to set your flying preferences (such as the class of service), click
the Preferences button. Otherwise, click the Flights button to see a list of
available flights. To get more detail on a given flight, select the flight and
click the Detail button. You can check out the prices by clicking the Fares
button.

After you have selected your flight, highlight it and click the Select button.
You'll be presented with the Itinerary screen, for confirmation. From here,
you can elect to see more details, to delete or confirm your reservation, or to
arrange hotel reservations, car rentals, or additional flights. (Car rentals and
hotel reservations work like flight reservations. After you fill in some basic
information, eaasySABRE does the rest of the work for you.)

When you finish making all of your reservations, you're returned to the
itinerary screen. Check all the information for accuracy, and then click
Confirm.

That's it. Your trip is all set—and you didn't have to leave your keyboard!

# Using Worldspan Travelshopper

Worldspan Travelshopper is a reservation system like eaasySABRE. It is jointly owned by TWA, Northwest Airlines, and Delta. As you can with eaasySABRE, you can use Travelshopper to make reservations on any major airline and to make hotel and car rental reservations.

To access Travelshopper, GO WORLDCIM. From there, Travelshopper operates almost exactly the same as eaasySABRE does. You proceed by entering a variety of options, and you end up with an Itinerary screen (just like you did with eaasySABRE).

With Travelshopper, however, you need to make your hotel and car rental reservations separately from your flight reservations. They don't all feed into the same itinerary, like they do in eaasySABRE. For this reason, I prefer eaasySABRE to Travelshopper. Even though the results are the same, it's easier to do it all from one screen in CompuServe.)

# Using the United Connection

The newest kid on the block—in terms of airline reservations, anyway—is the United Connection (GO UNITED). Run by (surprise!) United Airlines, it's available only to members of their Mileage Plus plan. (Don't worry, you can enroll online if you want to, and enrollment is free.)

When you plan a trip, you can choose to pick flights based on prices or schedules. You can also make car rental and hotel reservations. Once you get into the system, it works pretty much the same as eaasySABRE and Travelshopper. Although it defaults to United flights (as you might guess), it does list flights from all airlines.

When should you use the United Connection? If you're a Mileage Plus member and you like to fly United, this should be your system of choice. Otherwise, I'd stick with eaasySABRE.

# Using the Official Airline Guide system

The Official Airline Guide (GO OAG) is the oldest travel service on CompuServe. As such, it's a bit archaic in its mode of operation. For example, no graphical interface is available; instead, you have to do everything in terminal mode and master some obscure commands and abbreviations.

In addition, OAG costs you money to use (it's an extended service)—unlike eaasySABRE, Travelshopper, and the United Connection, which are free. So unless you just have a hankering to use OAG, I recommend that you stick with eaasySABRE.

It's important to note, however, that one reason OAG charges a fee is that it offers more options than either of the other services. For example, you can find out which in-flight movies will be shown on your trip, and you can make cruise ship reservations, as well as airline reservations.

 **TIP** **My advice? If you don't need the additional information and** services, and if you're not a travel professional, skip OAG and use eaasySABRE instead.

# Traveling with CompuServe

There are several things you should do *before* you take a trip if you want to use CompuServe once you get to wherever you're going.

The most important thing to do is to make sure that CompuServe is properly installed on your portable computer. Your portable should also have a modem installed and properly configured. Check your setup before you head out the door; you don't want to get halfway across the country before you realize that your software, modem, or whatever isn't working properly!

Next, look up the CompuServe access number for your destination city (GO LOGON). After all, you don't want to make a long-distance call back home whenever you use CompuServe, do you?

Finally, make sure that you have the proper accessories for using your PC and modem on the road. Make sure you have things like extra batteries (fully charged, of course), battery charger, mouse, modular telephone cables, and so on.

Suffice it to say that the best way to prepare for foreign travel is to use CompuServe to talk to members from your destination country. Your fellow members will be willing and eager to help you hook up to CompuServe (and to better enjoy their country).

Here are some other tips for using CompuServe while traveling abroad:

- Find out as much about connecting to CompuServe from your destination country as you can before you leave the States. You may need to take special equipment or prepare different connection configurations (different modem commands, for example). Check the CompuServe forum for your destination country, or look for general information in the mobile computing forums (GO MOBILE).

- In Europe, if you can't connect through normal methods, try calling the local number for INFONET. INFONET is a pan-European service that serves many different types of online users. Normally, you can connect to INFONET with your modem. Then, once you're connected, direct INFONET to access CompuServe.

- If a foreign phone system issues ring signals that sound like busy signals to your modem, you can get around it by hooking up both your modem and your telephone to the same line with a Y-connector (available at any local Radio Shack store). Dial the connect number with the telephone, listen for the connect signal on the other end of the line, and then start your modem connect procedure. You also may be able to work around this by adding an X2 to your modem initialize string in CompuServe's Modem Control Strings dialog box.

## Crossing borders and phone systems

If you're traveling abroad, you'll have to deal with the peculiarities of foreign phone systems. Many of them just aren't as reliable as the systems in the U.S. And the less reliable the system is, the harder it is to get a good connection to CompuServe.

In addition, some phone systems just work differently from the ones here in the States. Wires may be hooked up differently, modem commands may work differently, or the tone/pulse system may perform differently. You name it: anything you deal with can be different when you travel abroad. You may also have to deal with operator-assisted calls, strange dialing schemes, dial tones that sound like busy signals, or... well, who knows what you'll encounter.

- If you have to go through a human operator before you can connect your modem, use the Y-connector scheme described above. That way, you can talk to the operator through one leg of the Y on the telephone, and then—when the call is put through—you can activate your modem (and CompuServe) through the other leg of the Y.

- Some foreign phone systems won't let your modem automatically disconnect. That means that when you think you're disconnected from CompuServe, you may still be connected! To be safe, check to see if you're really disconnected by picking up the receiver of your telephone and listening for the dial tone.

- In the U.K., CompuServe connections are best made using one of British Telecom's PSS Dial Plus nodes, the Mercury system, or through CompuServe's direct-dial number in London.

- Foreign phone lines are often noisy. This can make connections difficult and can even cut you off in the middle of a call. To ensure against such problems, use a modem with good error-correcting protocols, such as an MNP or V.42 modem. In addition, you probably want to connect at a lower speed, perhaps as low as 1200 or 2400 baud. (Higher-speed connections have more trouble with noisy lines.)

# Travel the Internet for more resources

CompuServe probably has all of the travel information and services you'll need, but it's still worth checking the Internet to see if there's anything of interest there.

To begin with, several newsgroups (GO USENET) are devoted to travel issues. Those include **rec.travel**, **rec.travel.air**, **rec.travel.asia**, **rec.travel.cruises**, **rec.travel.europe**, **rec.travel.marketplace**, and **rec.travel.usa-canada**. Use these to connect with other travelers who share your interests.

You'll also find many Web sites of interest when you're planning a trip. Check out the following sites:

Airlines of the Web (**http://haas.berkeley.edu/~seidel/airline.html**) has links to all major U.S. and international airlines.

Air Traveler's Handbook (**http://www.cs.cmu.edu/afs/cs.cmu.edu/ user/mkant/Public/Travel/airfare.html**) is a great site for air travelers, with basic info and links to a lot of other air travel resources on the Net.

BizTravel (**http://www.biztravel.com/guide/**) is a good site for business travelers.

City.Net (**http://www.city.net/**) provides a comprehensive guide to cities around the world, with lots and lots and *lots* of hotlinks!

GNN Travel Resource Center (**http://gnn.com/meta/travel/ index.html**) is one of the Web's premier travel-related sites.

Subway Navigator (**http://metro.jussieu.fr:10001/bin/cities/english**) is a unique site that displays routes of subway systems in cities around the world.

Travel Weekly (**http://www.traveler.net/**) offers up-to-the-minute travel news.

TravelData Guide to Bed & Breakfast Inns (**http://www.ultranet.com/ biz/inns/**) lists thousands of bed & breakfast inns across America.

Travelocity (**http://www.travelocity.com/**) is a first-class site that lets you make airline, hotel, and auto reservations.

TravelWeb (**http://www.travelweb.com/**) provides information and reservations for most major hotel chains.

USA CityLink Project (**http://www.NeoSoft.com:80/citylink/**) lists Web pages for selected U.S. cities and states.

Virtual Tourist II (**http://wings.buffalo.edu/world/vt2/**) is a map-based interface to City.Net; this one is highly recommended!

Gee whiz! With all this travel information available, why would you want to stay home?

# Using CompuServe for travel: A personal experience

I've been using CompuServe as a travel aid for years. I've even attempted to use CompuServe while on a trip to the U.K.—and succeeded! So I guess you might call me an old hand at online travel.

Here's just one example of how I've personally used CompuServe while traveling. I go to San Diego several times a year; I like to think of San Diego as my home-away-from-home. (The weather's perfect all year 'round; everyone should go there at least once.) For my last trip, I decided to rely heavily on CompuServe for my pre-travel activities.

First, I used CompuServe's Web browser to search for hotels in the La Jolla area—that's where I like to stay. Then I started hanging out in the California Forum's San Diego section, and I even asked some of the locals to tell me which hotel was best. Finally, I used the forum to find out what special events were happening in San Diego during my trip.

When I had decided on a hotel, I used eaasySABRE to take care of my car rental, as well as my hotel and plane reservations. Then, for about a week before my trip, I used CompuServe to find out what the weather was like in San Diego so I could pack appropriately.

Finally, once I got to my hotel in San Diego, I plugged in my portable computer and logged in to the local CompuServe node (having retrieved the San Diego access number before I left home). So, even though I was on vacation, I could keep track of the world at large through daily CompuServe sessions.

As you can see, I can vouch for how helpful CompuServe can be when planning a trip. If I hadn't used CompuServe, it would've been harder to find all the information I needed and to make the right decisions. Instead, I relied on CompuServe and had a good time on my vacation!

# 14

# Getting Informed

● **In this chapter:**

- **Discover CompuServe's basic news services**

- **Learn about extended, executive, and international news options**

- **Access CompuServe's weather reports and maps**

- **Where can I find sports scores and stories online?**

- **Read online newspapers and magazines**

*Make CompuServe your source for up-to-the-minute news, weather, sports, and stock quotes* . . . . . . . . . . . . . . . . . ⊖

**W**ith CompuServe, you can get just about all the news you want: current news headlines, in-depth news analyses, and specialized industry and company news. You can also catch the latest sports scores, consult "live" weather forecasts and maps, and get updated stock quotes. And, if that isn't enough, you can use CompuServe's Internet services to venture onto the Internet and find even *more* news, weather, and sports services—including online newspapers and magazines!

# All the news that's fit to print (on-screen!)

CompuServe offers a variety of news services, from basic services to fancy customized services. When you GO NEWS, you're taken directly to CompuServe's main News menu (see Fig. 14.1). From there, click your chosen service to start reading the latest news!

**Fig. 14.1**
CompuServe's main
News menu.

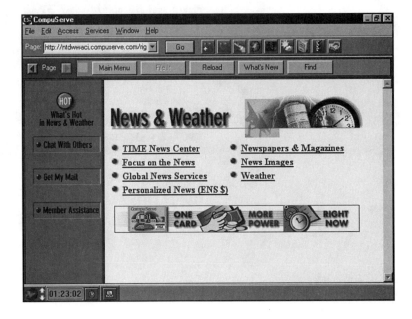

# Focus on the News

Of all the news areas available on CompuServe, the best is probably Focus on the News (GO BAD). This area incorporates a lot of different news services (including the Associated Press) and a lot of different types of news (U.S. news, world news, health news, computing news, news summaries, headlines, and weather). As you can see in Fig. 14.2, this is a good place to head for a daily dose of news.

**Fig. 14.2**
Getting the focus on the news.

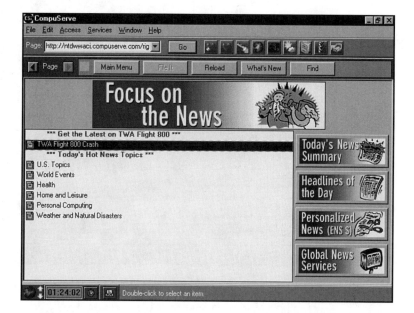

# The latest news from the cable news experts

One of the most-respected news gathering organizations belongs to Cable Network News (CNN), Ted Turner's cable-based news network. Now there's a version of CNN available on CompuServe. GO CNN to access the main screen of this multi-dimensional service.

CNN Interactive offers a wide variety of news services—some on CompuServe itself, and some on a direct link with CNN's site on the World Wide Web. You'll find breaking news stories, features, forums, and even a "letters to the editor" section. This is one heck of a service with many layers to explore; CNN Interactive is well worth checking out.

## TIME for the news

Another good general news area is the TIME News Center (GO TIME). This area, shown in Fig. 14.3, includes breaking news from the Associated Press, as well as features and pictures from the current issue of *TIME* magazine. There's even a TIME forum where you can discuss current events!

**Fig. 14.3**
You'll find a wide variety of news stories at the TIME News Center.

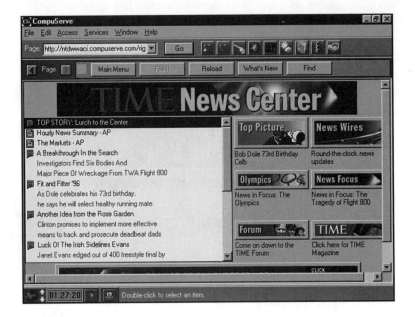

## Computer news du jour with Online Today

If you crave news about the computer industry, CompuServe offers a service called Online Today that should pique your interest. When you GO ONLINE, you're presented with Online Today's main menu. There you can read reviews of computer books (maybe this book will be reviewed soon!), peruse announcements of new hardware and software products, request information about products advertised in *CompuServe* Magazine, go "behind the screens" with news from inside CompuServe, and read the daily Monitor News.

Monitor News gives you the latest word on the computer industry. Normally, you'll find six to ten articles about such things as computer hardware and software developments or new product releases.

# The latest news for executives (and others)

CompuServe's Executive News Service (GO ENS) is a clipping service that monitors the Associated Press, the Washington Post, United Press International, Dow Jones, Deutsch Presse-Agentur, Reuters, and other news wires for current stories. ENS is updated hourly, and is perhaps the best place to look for general and business news.

You can use ENS in any of three ways:

- Search for news on specific companies by clicking the Articles button, selecting the Search tab, choosing News by Company Ticker, and then entering the company's ticker listing (see Fig. 14.4). When you click Search, you're presented with a list of recent stories about the company you've selected.

**Fig. 14.4**
Searching for company news with the Executive News Service.

 **TIP**   **GO LOOKUP to find company ticker listings.**

- Browse ENS for specific stories by clicking the Articles button, selecting the Search tab, choosing Current News, choosing a service (or services), and then clicking Search. You are then presented with a list of current stories from that service. You can preview the first few lines of a story, get the story to read online, or mark the story for later downloading.

- Clip specific stories to electronic folders. You can designate folders to hold news articles that meet such criteria as content and date range.

## News that means business

CompuServe offers more interesting news services for business people. For example, you might want to check out one or more of the following:

- ADP AdDP ADP Global Report (GO GLOREP): Up-to-the-minute news and financial information from sources around the world. (Note: This

## The low-down on clipping

Clipping news stories sounds complicated, but it's really a great way to read only the news that interests you. You can create a folder by clicking the Articles button, selecting the Create Folder tab, and clicking the New icon. When the Define Personal Folder dialog box appears, select the services you want to monitor and enter keywords (the topics you want to read about) in the Clipping terms fields. In the Expiration dates field, specify the number of days clippings should be held, and then enter the date you want your folder to expire. Give the folder a name and click OK.

When you want to view the contents of your folder, just click the Articles button, select the Read tab, and choose the folder from the list. You see a list of stories that match the criteria

you established; you can either read the stories online or mark them for later downloading.

Using ENS' personal folders is the closest thing to creating a personal newspaper devoted only to topics that interest you. I recommend folders for anyone who needs the news to be focused, easily accessible, and in one place.

To create your own personalized newspaper with stories culled from *all* of CompuServe's news services (not just ENS), consider a Windows-based software program called *Journalist*. Journalist automatically roams CompuServe's news services looking for the types of stories you pre-set and then assembles them in a desktop-published, ready-to-print newspaper. (You can order Journalist by calling Pointcast Software Corporation at 1-800-548-2203.)

is a pricey, customized service—up to $60/hour during prime access hours!)

- NewsGrid (GO NEWSGRID): A service similar to AP Online, but with more of a business focus.

- PR Newswire (GO PRNEWS): A compendium of press releases updated daily.

- The Business Wire (GO TBW): Various press releases, news articles, and other business information updated hourly.

Even with this wide assortment of services, I prefer to use the Executive News Service. It can't be beat for detailed, current business news.

## News from around the world

If you prefer your news with an international flavor, check out Table 14.1 for some non-U.S. news services available on CompuServe.

**Table 14.1  Good international news services on CompuServe**

| News service | GO word |
| --- | --- |
| AP France en Ligne | GO APFRANCE for French news |
| Australian Associated Press | GO AAPONLINE for Australian news |
| Deutsche Presse-Agentur Kurznachrichtendienst | GO DPA for German news |
| PA News Online | GO PAO for U.K. news |
| Reuter's Canadian News Clips | GO RTCANADA for Canadian news |
| Reuter's UK News Clips | GO UKREUTERS for U.K. news |
| Televisa Noticias | GO TEV for Mexican news |

Each of these services provides news in its country's official language—although I understand that Australian, British, and Canadian English are very similar to the English that we speak here in the U.S.

# How's the weather?

When you click the Weather button on CompuServe's toolbar, you get your basic local forecast, plus access to a variety of weather maps. This forecast, like every CompuServe U.S. weather report, comes directly from the National Weather Service. (If you look up weather forecasts for cities *outside* the United States, CompuServe uses the Accu-Weather service.) Fig. 14.5 shows a sample weather map on CompuServe.

**Fig. 14.5**
Viewing a satellite weather map; there's a cold front coming through!

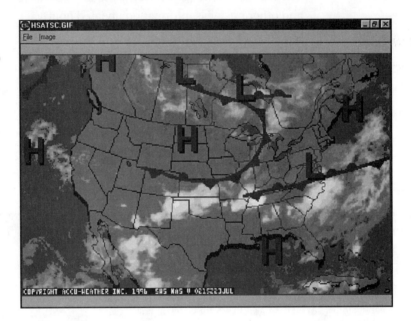

 **TIP**    To check out the weather anywhere in the world, click the Location button and enter the area you're interested in!

# Getting fanatic about sports

The best sports news on CompuServe comes from *Sports Illustrated*. When you GO SPORTS, you see a main menu that offers a plethora of sports news and features (see Fig. 14.6). Quite frankly, the *Sports Illustrated* site far surpasses any other site with sports-related information that's available on CompuServe—and it rivals any sports service on the Internet.

With *Sports Illustrated* on CompuServe, you find all sorts of sports news and information, including

- Clippings of major stories
- An online version of *Sports Illustrated* magazine
- News, scores, and statistics
- An online sports photo gallery
- Access to the *Sports Illustrated* forum
- Online fantasy sports games
- The *Sports Illustrated* online store

For my money, *Sports Illustrated* is one of the best services on CompuServe—period.

**Fig. 14.6**
All the sports news you need: Sports Illustrated on CompuServe.

# Reading online newspapers and magazines

An online magazine is, quite simply, an electronic version of a print magazine accessed through an online service like CompuServe or the Internet. But there are different types of online magazines.

Some online magazines offer the complete contents (sans ads) of their print versions; others are just forums (message sections and file libraries); others are online research databases that incorporate articles from dozens of publications. Still others forgo magazine content altogether, instead establishing services through CompuServe—services like subscription sales and a direct message line to the editorial staff. These are just some of the magazines you can find on CompuServe (with their GO words):

AI EXPERT Forum (GO AIEXPERT)

Automobile Magazine (GO AUTOLIVE)

CADENCE Forum (GO CADENCE)

CompuServe Magazine (GO COMPUMAG)

Computer Database Plus (GO COMPDB)

Computer Gaming World (GO CGWMAGAZINE)

Computer Life (GO LIFE)

Computer Shopper (GO CSHOPPER)

Consumer Reports (GO CONSUMER)

Data Based Advisor Forum (GO DBADVISOR)

DBMS Forum (GO DBMS)

DER SPIEGEL(GO SPIEGEL)

Dr. Dobb's Journal Forum (GO DDJ)

Electronic Gamer (GO EGAMER)

FORBES (GO FORBES)

FORTUNE Magazine (GO FORTUNE)

IndustryWeek Interactive (GO INDWEEK)

Internet Magazine Forum (GO INTMAG)

InternetWorld Online (GO IWORLD)

LAN Magazine Forum (GO LANMAG)

Magazine Database Plus (GO MDP)

Macleans Online (GO MACLEANS)

Money Magazine (GO MONEY)

Multimedia World (GO MMWORLD)

NetGuide (GO NETGUIDE)

NetWare Solutions (GO NWSOLUTIONS)

New York Magazine (GO NYMAG)

News Source USA (GO NEWSUSA)

PC Computing (GO PCCOMPUTING)

PC Magazine (GO PCMAGAZINE)

PC Week (GO PCWONLINE)

PC World Online (GO PCWORLD)

People Magazine Online (GO PEOPLE)

Rolling Stone (GO RSONLINE)

Selling (GO SELLING)

Sky & Telescope (GO SKYTEL)

Sports Illutrated Online (GO SIMAGAZINE)

Time (GO TIME)

Visual Basic Programmer's Journal Forum (GO VBPJFO)

Vogel (GO VOGEL)

Windows Magazine Online Forum (GO WINMAG)

Windows Sources (GO WSOURCES)

WordPerfect Magazine (GO WPMAG)

**TIP**   **Many magazines encourage the use of e-mail for submissions and** letters to the editor. If a magazine lists an e-mail address (normally somewhere near the letters column), you can use CompuServe Mail instead of snail mail (U.S. Post Office mail) to make your ideas known to the editor.

# A tour of *People Magazine Online*

To give you a taste of what an online magazine is all about, let's look at one of the more popular online magazines on CompuServe: *People Magazine Online*. When you GO PEOPLE, you're presented with an online table of contents like the one shown in this figure.

From here you can either click a button or click a feature in the scrolling list. The scrolling menu on the left part of the screen is where you find the daily news from *People*. That's right, CompuServe's online *People* actually spills the

entertainment news before it hits the magazine stand! Just double-click an article to read it on your computer screen.

And that's what an online magazine is all about—articles and pictures from the printed issue, plus forums, feedback, and the most recent news. You might be wondering if online magazines will ever replace the print rags. Probably not. After all, you can't roll up an online magazine and take it with you to the beach. But, for offering online access to current information, online magazines are great.

The table of contents for People Magazine Online.

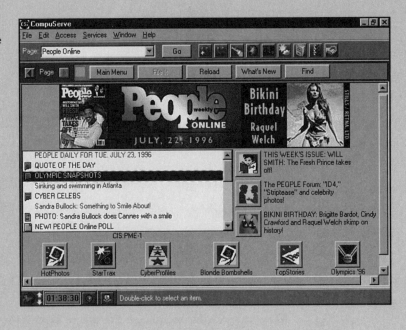

# 15

# Doing Research

● **In this chapter:**

● **What information can I find?**

● **Where to search**

● **Finding phone numbers online**

*Searching for information on CompuServe is like having access to all the information in the world—right on your computer screen!* . . . . . . . . . . . . . . . . . . . . . . . . . . . . . . . ▸

CompuServe is a great place to find things. You can find phone numbers, software programs, text files, pictures, and even new friends. But this merely scratches the surface of possibilities; you can find much more on CompuServe when you utilize the massive reference databases available to you as a CompuServe member.

# What to look up

What can you look up on CompuServe? Just about anything! Take a look at this short list of examples:

- Business, company, and financial information

- Science and medical data

- Information of interest to educators

- Newspaper, magazine, and newsletter articles

- Law and government data

- Radio and television broadcast schedules and program transcripts

- Computing information

- Sports history and current events

- Phone numbers

When you find an article, you're often given the choice of viewing brief bibliographic information (article title, author, publication date, and so on), an abstract (summary) of the important information, or the complete full-text article. The reason you have this choice of what to display is that different databases store different amounts of data.

# Where to look it up

CompuServe offers a number of different databases, but they all operate similarly and are quite comprehensive. The following sections give you a quick look at some of the most popular ones.

**TIP** **Many of CompuServe's online databases feature fairly detailed** instructions. When possible, download these instructions to your hard drive to reduce your online reading time and to keep them for future use. Also, consider selecting the least amount of information available. An abstract usually costs less than a full-text retrieval, and it doesn't take as long to download.

## IQuest

IQuest (GO IQUEST) is the most comprehensive reference database available on CompuServe. Actually, it's a collection of more than 850 separate databases, linked through the IQuest front end. Fig. 15.1 shows you IQuest's main menu.

**Fig. 15.1**
Getting started with IQuest.

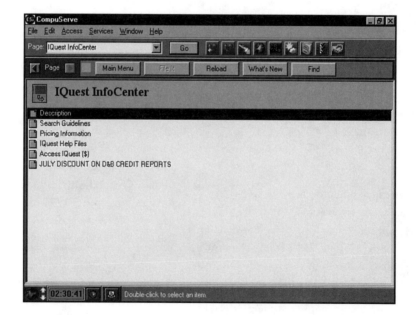

 **CAUTION** **IQuest charges can be pretty expensive: you'll pay at least a few** bucks for anything you do on IQuest. In addition, some of IQuest's databases tack on surcharges that range from $2.00 to $75.00! Take note of all applicable charges before you begin an IQuest search.

With IQuest, you can find information on just about every topic and from almost every source imaginable. You'll probably find yourself accessing IQuest frequently when you're looking for information. It is definitely the most-used reference database on CompuServe.

Note that many "separate" databases on CompuServe are actually part of the IQuest database. For example, the Management InfoCenter (GO IQMANAGEMENT) is just a subset of the larger IQuest database. So don't be surprised if you type a GO command, and it takes you to the IQuest front end!

## IQuest search tips

When you search on IQuest, understanding certain things and putting them into effect will make your search more efficient and productive.

To begin with, it doesn't matter whether you use lowercase or uppercase characters; IQuest is case-insensitive. IQuest *is* sensitive, however, to common words such as "a," "of," "the," "to," and so on. They'll slow down your search, so avoid them.

You can use such operators as AND, OR, and NOT to combine keywords in your search. For example, you can search for articles that contain both the words "Mustang AND Ford." This results in a very different search than if you use OR or NOT.

You should also use parentheses to group search items. For example, if you searched for "Ford AND (Mustang OR Pinto)," IQuest would return articles on either Ford Mustangs or Ford Pintos.

Don't forget about wild cards. IQuest uses the slash character (/) to represent one or more characters at the end of a word (kind of like the asterisk (*) in DOS file names). So to search for "Miller," "Milner," and anything else that starts with "Mil," just enter "Mil/."

Keep in mind the size of the databases involved, and remember that it's important to make your searches as narrow as possible; if you don't you'll be overwhelmed with responses. For example, to look for info on the 1994 Mustang, make sure you add "1994" to the search phrase "Mustang"; this will help make your search more efficient.

It's also a good idea to either print the data you retrieve or save it to a file. To do the former, pull down the Terminal menu and select Log to Printer. To save the data to a file, pull down the Terminal menu and select Log to File.

# Knowledge Index

Knowledge Index (GO KI) is kind of an IQuest service with training wheels. It's not quite as big as IQuest. It's also not quite as accessible; you can only access it after normal business hours (after 6:00 p.m. during the week) and on weekends. Unlike IQuest, Knowledge Index charges by the hour instead of by the search or retrieval. Rates at the time of this writing were $24 per hour.

Knowledge Index provides access to more than 50,000 journals in more than 100 databases. KI is good for general searches, as well as for more specific engineering, technical, and legal searches. Obviously, it's not as wide ranging as IQuest, nor is it as good for business or financial searches. It's a good place to start, though, and it's a lot cheaper than IQuest.

I find Knowledge Index particularly useful for searching local newspapers. I generally choose the **News & Current Affairs** option and then pick a newspaper to search. KI keeps full-text articles on file for most major U.S. newspapers, so it's a pretty comprehensive search.

# CENDATA: The Census Bureau service

The Census Bureau's (GO CENDATA) information on manufacturing, housing starts, agriculture, and more is available online through CompuServe. When you access CENDATA, you can locate tabular data reports and other data culled from the Bureau's 1990 census.

CENDATA provides access to a wide range of data—more than just the boring census stuff. CENDATA is a great source for all sorts of demographic information. (Market researchers love this database!)

# Computer Library

Computer Library (GO COMPLIB) is a family of databases maintained by Ziff-Davis. These databases, which focus on computer-related topics, include the following:

- **Computer Database Plus**, which contains articles from a variety of computer industry publications

- **Computer Buyer's Guide**, which contains specifications for a wide variety of computer hardware and software products

# Grolier's Academic American Encyclopedia

Grolier's (GO GROLIERS) is an online version of its print encyclopedia. In all, you can find more than 33,000 articles (and 10 million words) and all the topics you expect to find in a print encyclopedia. Grolier's is a good resource for students.

# Hutchinson Encylopedia

The Hutchinson Encyclopedia (GO HUTCHINSON) is an online version of the noted British print encyclopedia. It's about the same size as Grolier's (34,000 articles), but it's a little more academic in style (it's updated regularly by professors at Oxford University). Fig. 15.2 shows a screen from the Hutchinson Encyclopedia.

**Fig. 15.2**
The Hutchinson Encyclopedia *is easy on the eye and easy to use.*

# Information Please Almanac

The Information Please Almanac (GO GENALMANAC) is a collection of articles about a variety of general-interest topics. You can browse the Almanac by general categories (ranging from Astronomy to World Statistics), or you can search for specific topics.

**TIP** You can also find business almanacs (**GO BIZALMANAC**) and sports almanacs (GO SPORTALMANAC) available online.

## American Heritage Dictionary

This online dictionary (GO DICTIONARY) contains definitions and spellings for more than 200,000 words, places, and people. Many definitions also include synonyms, antonyms, and usage notes.

The online American Heritage Dictionary is another good resource for students—or anyone searching for just the right word.

**TIP** To find lists of libraries and other reference information on the Internet, go to Yahoo's lists of Libraries (**http://www.yahoo.com/Reference/Libraries/**) and Reference sites (**http://www.yahoo.com/Reference/**).

# Use CompuServe to look up phone numbers

CompuServe provides a service called Phone*File (GO PHONEFILE), in which you can look up names, addresses, and phone numbers just as you would in your local white pages. The big difference is that you can look up numbers electronically for all 80 million households in the U.S. (Think of the weight of all the phone books it would take to offer the same search capability!)

You can use Phone*File in the following ways:

- To search for a phone number if you know the person's name and address

- To search for a phone number if you know the person's last name and geographical area

- To search for a person's address if you know the person's phone number

When looking for a phone number, search by name and complete address. This keeps your search narrow and helps you find the right number faster. The slowest way to search is by state only, under the Surname and Geographical Area option; the result of such a search is a list of everyone in the entire state with that last name.

While Phone*File is a great way to find personal phone numbers, it doesn't include listings for businesses. To find the phone number of a business, you have to use Phone*File's sibling, Biz*File (GO BIZFILE).

Biz*File works like Phone*File. You can perform the following searches:

- A search for a company's phone number if you know its name and geographical area

- A search for a company's address if you know its phone number

- A search for a list of companies within a certain industry (similar to a Yellow Pages heading)

If you want to search for a toll-free number, get on the World Wide Web and go to AT&T's 800 Directory (**http://att.net/dir800/**). This site lets you search a comprehensive list of 800 numbers, either by category or name. It's a great resource if the company you need to call has a toll-free number.

# 16

# Managing Your Personal Finances

● **In this chapter:**

- ● **Get stock quotes online**

- ● **Track historical data**

- ● **Make investments online**

- ● **Locate financial information on the Internet**

*Track your financial investments online, in real time!. . . .*

W hether you're a casual or a serious investor, you'll want to know how your investments are currently performing and how you can increase the performance of your portfolio. CompuServe offers a combination of services that provide you with up-to-the-minute quotes and in-depth investment advice. All you have to do is invest the time and know where to look.

# Get the latest quotes from CompuServe

You can get quotes in many ways from CompuServe. It all depends on what kind of information you want and what you're willing to pay.

 **TIP** To look up stock ticker symbols, GO LOOKUP. To look up commodity symbols, GO CSYMBOL.

## Find CompuServe's basic quotes

When you click CompuServe's Quote button, you get access to the basic stock quote service. With this service, you can get current quotes on stock prices, including volume, high/ask, low/bid, last, change, and time of last trade or quote. These quotes are delayed by at least 15 minutes during the trading day.

When you click the Quotes button, the Stock Quotes dialog box appears (see Fig. 16.1). This dialog box lists all your favorite stocks and lets you obtain quotes and performance charts for any and all listed stocks.

First, of course, you need to add some stocks to your list. CompuServe stores your stock issues in **folders** that you create.

To create a new folder, click the Edit Folders button. In the Maintain Folders dialog box, click the Add button, enter the name of your folder, and click OK.

To add stocks to your folders, select the folder in the main folder list and then click the New button. Type the stock symbol in the Issue symbol box and click OK, and the stock is added to the folder.

You can get an "instant quote" by typing a stock symbol in the box at the bottom of the Stock Quotes dialog box and clicking the Get Quote button.

**Fig. 16.1**
CompuServe's Stock
Quotes dialog box.

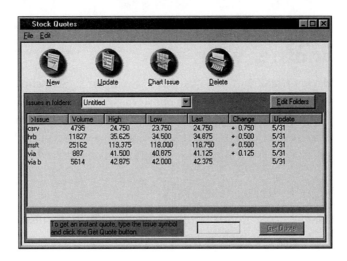

# Track your portfolio

Portfolio Valuation (GO PORT) tracks the value of your portfolio. After you enter the issues in your portfolio, the number of shares held, and the purchase price, Portfolio Valuation produces a report detailing the current value of your portfolio.

 **TIP** **Several commercial software programs are also available that** automatically retrieve stock information from CompuServe and create customized reports for your personal portfolio. One to check out is the $39.95 StockTracker from Virgil Corporation (call 1–800–662–8256 or GO STOCKTRADER).

# Get a snapshot of the current market

CompuServe's Current Market Snapshot (GO SNAPSHOT) provides a one-page report of statistics and key indicators that give you a "snapshot" of the current market. A Snapshot report is a pretty good overview of the entire stock market.

There are more detailed reports available on CompuServe, however, such as Market Highlights. Snapshot is more valuable to the casual investor or to someone who's just interested in today's overall stock market performance.

# Highlight market performance in another way

Market Highlights (GO MARKET) is similar to Snapshot, but it gives more detailed reports of the day's market activity. If you're a serious investor, you'll probably prefer Market Highlights to Snapshot. The frequency of reports and the level of detail available from Market Highlights make it a better overview for those who are really interested in the market.

# Rate your bonds

CompuServe's Bonds Listing service (GO BONDS) displays all active bonds for a company. Included in the report are quality ratings from both S&P and Moody's.

# Get complete market info, all in one place

Perhaps the most detailed daily market reports are available from News-A-Tron Market Reports (GO NAT). Here you have access to numerous reports, prices, and analyses on selected commodities and market indexes. Just look at the reports available:

- Daily Petro Analysis

- Petro Crack and Rack Spreads

- Cash Metal Prices and Analysis

- Currency Analysis and Cash Forex Prices

- Credit Market Analysis and Technical Indications

- Indications of Domestic and International Rates

- Grains Report and Cash Prices

- Livestock and Meat Report

- Foreign Exchange Quotes

- Dow Industrial News and Analysis

- S&P Index News and Analysis

- KC Value Line News and Analysis

- Stock Index News and Quotes

- Economic Calendar of Events

- Trendvest Stock Market Summary

- Trendvest Stock Market Indicators

- Trendvest Highest Stock and Fund Ratings

- Trendvest Lowest Stock and Fund Ratings

- Tax Free Money Funds

- General Purpose Money Funds

- Government Only Money Funds

News-A-Tron is definitely *the* service for serious investors. It's hard to imagine that a person would need any information not available through this service!

# Get investment advice from VESTOR

VESTOR (GO VESTOR) is a combination of services designed to assist your investment decisions and your portfolio management. VESTOR reports analyze more than 7,000 stocks, offering buy/sell recommendations and predicting future stock performance.

# Track an issue, singularly

For a more detailed report of a stock issue's history, use CompuServe's Issue Pricing History service (GO PRICES). This service gives you a day-by-day, week-by-week, or month-by-month history of an issue's pricing, up to a 12-year period.

# Track dividends pays dividends

CompuServe's Dividends, Splits, Interest service (GO DIVIDENDS) provides information for a given issue over a given period.

# Track price and volume

Pricing Statistics (GO PRISTATS) provides a snapshot of an issue's price and volume performance over a given period. Pricing Statistics also shows the percent change of the stock's performance over that period.

# Perform an in-depth analysis

Perhaps the most detailed analysis for individual stocks and bonds is available from CompuServe's Detailed Issue Examination service (GO EXAMINE). Nearly everything you want to know about a stock's performance is included in this service's reports.

# Track your funds, mutually

*Money* magazine's FundWatch Online (GO FUNDWATCH) lets you analyze more than 1,900 mutual funds. The *Money* magazine service offers the FundWatch database, which you can use to screen funds. With this database you use various criteria to find the best funds for your investment needs. FundWatch provides very detailed tracking of these funds.

# Even *more* information and analysis

If you want background information on any company you're considering investing in, you can turn to a variety of CompuServe's services. These services include both up-to-the-minute news services and massive historical databases.

Among the available services are:

- Basic Company Snapshot (GO BASCOMPAN)
- Business Database Plus (GO BUSDB)
- Company Analyzer (GO ANALYZER)
- Company Screening (GO COSCREEN)
- Disclosure SEC (GO DISCLOSURE)
- Executive News Service (GO ENS)
- Hoover's Company Database (GO HOOVER)

- Institutional Brokers Estimate Service Earning Estimate Reports (GO IBES)

- InvesText (GO INVTEXT)

- IQuest InfoCenter (GO IQUEST)

- S&P Online (GO S&P)

For more information on these and similar services, see Chapter 15, "Doing Research."

**TIP**    **To talk to other investors online, check out the Investor's Forum** (GO INVFORUM) and the National Association of Investors Corporation Forum (GO NAIC).

# Make your investments online

So far, we've looked at the data that's available online. But what if you want to act on this data and make your own investments online, via CompuServe?

Through CompuServe, you can access two commercial services that enable you to trade stocks and other issues online in real time.

- E*TRADE (GO ETRADE) is an online brokerage service provided by Trade*Plus, Inc. E*TRADE offers discount commissions, Black Scholes option analysis, around-the-clock availability, and investment management services.

- QuickWay (GO QWK) is an online brokerage service provided by Quick & Reilly. QuickWay offers customers discount commissions, current online quotes, around-the-clock availability, and portfolio evaluation services.

You can also find a number of online brokers on the Internet, including:

- Ceres Securities (http://www.ceres.com)

- Charles Schwab & Company, Inc. (http://www.schwab.com)

- Ebroker (http://www.ebroker.com)

- E*TRADE (http://www.etrade.com); the Web version of the E*TRADE service offered on CompuServe

- Lombard Securities (http://www.lombard.com)

Any of these services is fine if your transactions are simple—and if you know what you're doing. If you have more complex investments, or if you need face-to-face advice, you may want to use a more traditional brokerage firm.

# Financial information and services on the Internet

One of the best places to look for financial information and services is on the World Wide Web. Here are a few finance-oriented Web sites you might want to check out.

- American Stock Exchange (http://www.amex.com/) offers news and information on all listed companies.

- Canada Net Pages (http://www.visions.com/) is the most comprehensive resource for Canadian business and financial data.

- CNNfn (http://cnnfn.com/) is the online version of the new cable financial news network.

- Financial Information Link Library (http://www.mbnet.ca:80/~russell/) provides a list of links to financial sites around the world.

- FinanCenter Inc. (http://www.financenter.com/resources/) is an online personal finance resource center that helps you evaluate borrowing and investment options. FinanCenter includes glossaries, statistics, concise how-to reports, and professional load counselors' advice. This one is recommended.

- Hoover's Online (http://www.hoovers.com/) is a great source for company-specific information.

- Kiplinger Online (http://www.kiplinger.com/) offers the online version of the popular periodical.

- Mortgage Strategies (http://www.ais.net:80/netmall/mortgage/mortgage.html) maintains an online report that explains how to save on your mortgage interest.

- NETworth (http://networth.galt.com/), from GALT Technologies, Inc., has in-depth information on more than 5,000 mutual funds.

- PAWWS Financial Network (http://pawws.secapl.com/) provides a variety of online quotes, charts, and financial information.

- PC Quote (http://ds9.spacecom.com/Participants/pcquote/) offers real-time securities quotations and news.

- Quote.Com (http://www.quote.com/) provides financial market data, such as current quotes on stocks, commodity futures, mutual funds, and bonds. Quote.Com also supplies business news, market analysis, and commentary.

- *The Wall Street Journal* on the Web (http://www.wsj.com) has a lot of WSJ offerings, including the continually updated Money & Investing Update.

The volume of relatively free ("relatively" because some of these services come at a fee) financial information available on both CompuServe and the Internet is amazing. New sites are added daily, so visit them all and pick the ones that best fit your personal needs.

# 17

# Playing Games

● **In this chapter:**

● **Play games against the CompuServe computer**

● **Play games in real time against other CompuServers**

● **Visit CompuServe forums for gamers**

● **Play games on the Internet**

*CompuServe puts you online to experience all the latest games!* . . . . . . . . . . . . . . . . . . . . . . . . . . . . .

**S**o far, CompuServe has been a lot of work and very little play. It's time to change all that. This chapter covers some of the games you can play on CompuServe. Whether you're a casual or a serious gamer, CompuServe has lots of fun spots just for you!

# Playing games on CompuServe

There are lots of games you can play on CompuServe. Some let you play against the CompuServe computer; others let you play against other gamers. To get a complete listing of games and game-related areas on CompuServe, GO GAMES. This takes you to New Game City (see Fig. 17.1), the primo place for all game activity on CompuServe—including an Internet On-Ramp that gives you access to games on the Web.

**Fig. 17.1**
CompuServe's New Game City: if you hit only one game area on CompuServe, this is the one to hit!

## Parlor and trivia games

The easiest kind of game to play is one that lets you play against CompuServe—against CompuServe's computers, that is. The easiest type of CompuServe player-versus-computer game is the trivia game. (GO TTGAMES for a complete list of trivia games.)

Trivia games test your knowledge of useless information (my favorite type!). Among the trivia games on CompuServe are:

- Grolier's Whiz Quiz (GO WHIZ)

- Science Trivia Quiz (GO SCITRIVIA)

- ShowBizQuiz (GO SBQ)

- Stage II—Two Stage Trivia (GO STAGEII)

- The Multiple Choice (GO TMC)

- You Guessed It! (GO YGI)

Chief among these trivia games is ShowBizQuiz (GO SBQ), one of the oldest and most popular trivia games on CompuServe. Actually, ShowBizQuiz features more than 75 different trivia games, on topics as diverse as James Bond, Star Trek, Frank Sinatra, the Twilight Zone, the Three Stooges, Fred Astaire, Heavy Metal Music, Leave It to Beaver, the Flintstones, the Jetsons, English Pop Music, the Oscars, and TV Game Shows.

## Adventure games

Adventure games are electronic role-playing games. You assume the role of a character in a specific setting, and then you travel around the game's virtual world, interacting with other characters and in various situations. Some of the adventure games available on CompuServe are:

- BlackDragon (GO BLACKDRAGON)

- British Legends (GO LEGENDS)

- CastleQuest (GO CQUEST)

- Classic Adventure (GO CLADVENT)

- Enhanced Adventure (GO ENADVENT)

- Island of Kesmai (GO ISLAND)

 **TIP** **You can type** QUIT **at almost any prompt to exit from the game** you're playing.

Some of these adventure and simulation games are technically multiplayer games. Although you're still playing your own game against the computer, other gamers are also interacting in your simulation as they play their own games.

Even though most adventure games are text-based, they are some of the most sophisticated games available. Instructions are often quite complex and difficult to decipher.

 **TIP** **All online games have their own online instructions, which I** recommend you read before you get stuck and can't figure out what to do!

## Simulation games

Simulation games (often called "wargames") are played in a simulated environment. These games involve strategy and tactics as you plot your moves against both the computer and other players. CompuServe offers the following simulation games:

- MegaWars I: The Galactic Conflict (GO MEGA1)
- MegaWars III: The New Empire (GO MEGA3)
- SNIPER! (GO SNIPER)
- Air Traffic Controller (GO ATCONTROL)

Like adventure games, simulation games can be quite complex. It's imperative that you read the instructions before you get involved—and you're probably better off to download the instructions and read them offline at your own speed. (It also doesn't hurt to print a hard copy of these instructions to keep near your keyboard while you're playing!)

 **TIP** **CompuServe also includes some games that don't fit into any** established categories. Check out Biorhythms (GO BIORHYTHM), Astrology Calculator (GO ASTROLOGY), and Hangman (GO HANGMAN) for CompuServe's versions of these games.

# Playing games with other CompuServers

The next crop of games lets you play directly against other gamers through modem-to-modem (MTM) play. When you play MTM games, the CompuServe computer acts as a go-between so you can challenge another CompuServer located anywhere in the world!

There are various places to meet other MTM players to discuss MTM and multiplayer game play, including:

- Modem Games/Games Challenge Forum (GO MODEMGAMES)
- Modem-to-Modem Gaming Lobby (GO MTMLOBBY)
- Modem-to-Modem Game Support (GO MTMGAMES)
- Multiplayer Games Forum (GO MPGAMES)

Among the many more complex MTM games available on CompuServe are Battleship, Conquest, F-16 Combat Pilot, Falcon 3, Flight Simulator, Populous, Tank, Vette!, and many more.

The best way to initiate an MTM game is to enter the Modem-to-Modem Challenge Board (GO MTMCHALLENGE). The Challenge Board is a worldwide database of CompuServe MTM game players. It is the place to search for other CompuServers who might want to engage in MTM play.

 **TIP** **You can search the Challenge Board for MTM players by name,** phone number, or specific game titles.

You use the Challenge Board to identify potential MTM opponents. When you choose an opponent, you then invoke the CHALLENGE command. This automatically sends an e-mail message to your opponent, requesting a match. If your opponent accepts the challenge, your game will be played in the MTM Gaming Lobby.

From here, use CompuServe to establish the connection. Then withdraw from CompuServe and run the game with its own communications protocol. When you finish, drop the game's connection and reenter CompuServe. The whole process is pretty easy if you just follow the prompts CompuServe displays on your screen.

# CompuServe games forums

CompuServe has a lot of other places for gamers to hang out. Chief among these places are the various gaming forums. GO GAMECON to get a list of current game forums and news, or check out some of the sites in this list of the most popular resources:

- Action Games Forum (GO ACTION) focuses on shoot-'em-ups and other action games, including DOOM and Descent.

- Bridge Forum (GO BRIDGE) is for Bridge aficionados.

- Chess Forum (GO CHESSFORUM) is for serious chess players at all levels.

- Electronic Gamer Archives (GO EGAMER) contains archives of walk throughs and reviews from the popular gaming magazines.

- Epic MegaGames (GO EPIC) is the forum for Epic, the leading developer of shareware computer games. (You can also buy Epic games or download an Epic Game-of-the-Month.)

- Flight Simulation Forum (GO FSFORUM) is the electronic hangar where players of various flight simulation games huddle between fantasy flights.

- Game Developer's Forum (GO GAMDEV) is for programmers developing new computer games.

- Game Publisher Beta Forum (GO GAMBETA) provides a place for game publishers to test their upcoming games.

- Gamers Forum (GO GAMERS) is the main hangout for serious gamers. Here you will find people who really know their way around various PC and video games.

- Mac Entertainment Forum (GO MACFUN) offers Mac-compatible games.

- Microsoft Home Products Forum (GO MSHOME) is where Microsoft supports its Home of products, including games like Flight Simulator.

- Microsoft Windows Fun Forum (GO WINFUN) offers a place to find support and solutions for major Windows-compatible games.

- Nintendo Promotions (GO NINTENDO) is the official source for the latest news and promotions from Nintendo.

- PC Fun Forum (GO PCFUN) provides support for DOS-compatible computer games.

- *PC World* Entertainment Forum (GO GAMING) covers state-of-the-art multimedia games.

- Play-by-Mail/Board/Card Games Forum (GO PBMGAMES) offers a place to find other PBM gamers, board gamers, and card gamers.

- Role-Playing Games Forum (GO RPGAMES) is the hangout for RPGers. Sections are available for Advanced Dungeons and Dragons (AD&D), fantasy, heroes, science fiction, and other types of role-playing games.

- Sega Forum (GO SEGA) is the official forum for Sega video games.

- Sierra On-Line Forum (GO SIERRA) is the official forum for Sierra On-Line games.

- Sports Simulations Forum (GO SPRTSIMS) is where you can find gamers who like sports simulation games (such as baseball, football, basketball, golf, and hockey).

- The Electronic Gamer Archives (GO TEG) is a repository for reviews and step-by-step "walk throughs" of the most popular computer games.

- Video Game Publishers Forum (GO VIDAPUB) is the official forum for numerous smaller video game developers.

- Video Games Forum (GO VIDGAM) is the place where all the Sega and Nintendo junkies crash.

- Windows Games Forum (GO WINGAMES) offers another forum for games on the Windows platform.

In addition, many PC game manufacturers are represented in either Game Publishers A Forum (GO GAMAPUB), Game Publishers B Forum (GO GAMBPUB), Game Publishers C Forum (GO GAMCPUB), or Game Publishers D Forum (GO GAMDPUB).

# Downloading games from CompuServe

Many games are available on CompuServe in the form of program files. You can actually download these to your PC and play them offline! Because most of these files are in individual forum libraries, you'd normally have to hop from forum to forum to find the game you want. However, CompuServe has created a way to search all the game-related forums for specific game files. The tool you use to do this is called the Games File Finder (GO GAMESFF); it makes finding game files as easy as clicking your mouse. (See Chapter 9 for more information on File Finder and downloading files.)

GO GAMESFF and then select Access File Finder. CompuServe displays the Select Search Criteria screen shown in Fig. 17.2. Unless you know the precise file name you want to search for, it's best to search by keyword. Select Keyword, and you're prompted to give up to four words that describe the game. Enter the keywords and click OK to begin the search. File Finder searches and returns a list of files that match your criteria. Choose the file(s) you want—and let the downloading begin!

**Fig. 17.2**

Searching for game files with Games File Finder.

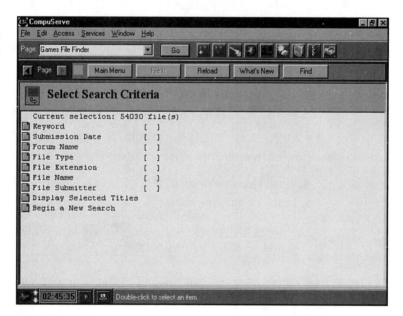

Another place to look for games to download is CompuServe's Hot Games Download Area (GO HOTGAMES). This area contains some of the most exciting and entertaining new game files and demos from the hottest professional game companies.

 **CAUTION** **Note that when you download some of these games, you are** charged the game's full retail price. (It is added to your CompuServe account.)

# Games on the Internet

If you can't get enough games and gaming info on CompuServe, you can always venture out on the Internet for even more game resources.

## Newsgroups for gamers

Let's start by looking at game-related newsgroups (GO USENET). The following newsgroup areas contain many games-related groups:

- **alt.games.\***   This area contains newsgroups for just about every major game, including Descent, DOOM, Mortal Kombat, and Tie Fighter.

- **comp.sys.ibm.pc.games.\***   This area includes groups for major PC-compatible games such as Flight Simulator.

- **comp.sys.mac.games**   This newsgroup is for all Mac-compatible games.

- **rec.games.\***   This is the main gaming area on USENET; it offers dozens of newsgroups for such traditional games as Bridge and Chess, as well as state-of-the-art Internet MUDs, exciting trading-card games, and all the major video games.

## Games on the Web

Newsgroups offer great interaction with other gamers, but you can find more cool stuff at key game-related Web sites, like these:

- BradyGAMES' Gamer Connection (http://www.mcp.com/brady/connect/): A great place to exchange gaming tips and meet other online gamers. (Sponsored by BradyGAMES.)

- EA Online (http://www.ea.com/): The Web home of Electronic Arts.

- Games Domain (http://www.gamesdomain.com/): Links to hundreds of Net-based game sites, walk throughs, home pages, electronic magazines, and MUDs.

- MUDs (http://draco.centerline.com:8080/~franl/mud.html): Lots of info about MUDs and MOOs.

- Nintendo Power (http://www.nintendo.com): Nintendo's supersite on the Web.

- NUKE (http://www.nuke.com): Perhaps the best site on the Net for games of all shapes and sizes. Recommended.

- Outland Online Games (http://www.outland.com/): A place to play graphical, real-time games with other Internetters.

- Yahoo's List of Game Sites (http://www.yahoo.com/Entertainment/Games/): A really big list of game-related resources on the Internet.

- Zarf's List of Interactive Games on the Web (http://www.leftfoot.com/games.html): A very comprehensive list of all sorts of Web-based games—from online chess to trivia quizzes, to MUDs and MUSHes.

# MUDs, MOOs, and MUSHes on the Net

In addition to newsgroups and Web sites, the Internet gives you the capability to play games in real time. You play the game live against other Internet users. These games are called **MUDs.**

A MUD (Multiple User Dimension) is more or less like a big text-based adventure-type game that's accessible via the Internet. You log into a MUD and take control of a computerized character. You can walk around, chat with other characters, explore dangerous monster-infested areas, solve puzzles, and even create your own rooms complete with descriptions, characters, and objects. In short, a MUD is a virtual world that you explore online.

There are thousands of MUDs on the Internet—way too many to list here. Each has its own atmosphere and community that should be judged individually. Some MUDs are purely games that reflect some sort of warfare between gamers and virtual enemies. Other MUDs are more

sophisticated role-playing environments. And still others attempt to reproduce aspects of the physical world in the virtual medium of the Internet.

There are also variations on MUDs. They go by names like MOOs (MUD Object Oriented), TinyMUDs (a more social MUD), MUCKs, MUSHes, and ad infinitum. They're all basically MUDs organized in slightly different ways.

You connect to a MUD using Telnet (GO TELNET). Chapter 24 explains how to use Telnet with CompuServe, but there isn't enough space in this book to go into all the details you need to fully participate in MUDding. If you're really interested in MUDding on the Net, I recommend that you check out two books from BradyGAMES: *Online Games* and *MUDs: Exploring Virtual Worlds on the Internet.* If you're interested in creating your own MUD, look for Sams' *Secrets of the MUD Wizards.*

# 18

# Going Shopping

● In this chapter:

- Shop the CompuServe Electronic Mall

- Can I order catalogs via CompuServe?

- Can I order CompuServe software from the CompuServe Store?

- Shop on the Internet

- Place and respond to classified ads

*All you need is your keyboard, your mouse, and your credit card to shop online with CompuServe . . . . . . . . . . . . . .* ➤

I f you're an avid shopper, you probably already know about CompuServe's Electronic Mall. However, you may not be familiar with all of CompuServe's shopping services. That's why I wrote this chapter—to tell you about all the ways you can shop from the comfort of your own home via CompuServe.

# Hitting the Mall

The CompuServe Electronic Mall is a virtual shopping center that houses dozens of stores. None of these stores have real storefronts; they exist only on your computer screen. But just as you can in real stores, you can browse around CompuServe's stores and order a variety of merchandise. Unlike traditional malls however, CompuServe's Electronic Mall is open 24 hours a day 365 days a year. Other advantages are that you don't have to get all dressed up to shop the Electronic Mall, and you save time, gasoline, and money shopping directly from your personal computer.

Of course, to shop from home via the CompuServe Mall, you have to use a credit card (just as you would to order from a traditional catalog merchant). In fact, using the Electronic Mall is a lot like shopping by catalog—but you use your modem instead of your phone, and you don't have to throw away the catalog (or live with the catalogs stacking up) when you're done!

To access the Mall, GO MALL. Fig. 18.1 shows the CompuServe Mall's opening screen. Once you're in, you can search by merchant or by type of goods.

 **TIP** **Because new merchants are added to the Mall monthly, you need** access to the latest Mall news and events. GO EMN to find out the latest news about new merchants, special sales, and promotions from the Electronic Mall News.

## Shopping by merchant

If you know the name of the online store you want, the fastest way to shop is by merchant. Select Quicksearch By Merchant from the main Mall menu and select Shop by Merchant in the next screen. In the dialog box that appears next, enter the store's name. If you don't know the full name, you can type a partial entry, and CompuServe will supply a list of candidates. In that list, double-click the merchant you want.

**Fig. 18.1**

Get out your shopping cart—you're entering the CompuServe Mall!

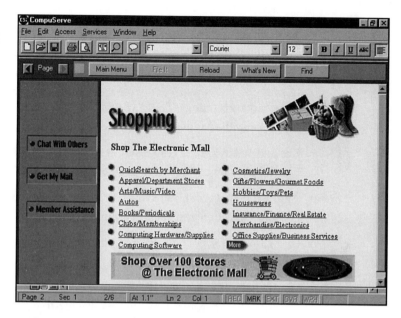

When you enter the store, you're usually presented with a menu that includes such choices as browsing the store, searching for merchandise, ordering a catalog, talking to customer service, or placing an order. I say that you're *usually* presented with a menu because the merchants all run their own shops. Some merchants only offer catalogs; some don't have online customer service; some offer additional services. In addition, some stores are completely text-based, whereas others let you see the merchandise before you buy. They're all different (just like the stores in a real mall). The thing to remember is that when you enter a store, you should look for and follow the on-screen directions.

## Shopping by department

Even if you don't have a specific merchant in mind, it's still easy to use the Electronic Mall. Just pick the department you want, and then select from the group of merchants in the directory. You're taken to a specific store where you can follow the on-screen directions to complete your shopping.

# CompuServe's other shopping services

In addition to the Electronic Mall, CompuServe offers a variety of other shopping-related services. Let's take a look at some of the major ones.

- Directory of Catalogs (GO DTC): You can order a variety of catalogs from CompuServe merchants.

- Shopper's Advantage (GO SAC): A discount shopping club that offers discounts of up to 50% off suggested retail prices.

- AutoNet New Car Showroom (GO NEWCAR): A great place to view and compare features and specifications on more than a thousand vehicles.

- SOFTEX (GO SOFTEX): A great place to purchase software online by downloading it from CompuServe.

- CompuServe Store (GO ORDER): The place to buy all sorts of CompuServe merchandise—from software to coffee mugs.

- Consumer Reports (GO CONSUMER): Chock full of product reviews and comparisons, this is definitely the place to stop before you shop.

# Shopping on the Internet

There are many places to shop on the Internet because companies think they'll make a fortune setting up "virtual shopping malls" on the Net. Take a look at these Web sites to get an idea of what's available:

- AutoSite (**http://www.autosite.com/**): A great place to compare new car features and prices.

- Branch Mall (**http://branch.com:1080/**): A mass of Internet retailers with catalog entries ranging from art to vacations.

- CDNow! (**http://www.cdnow.com/**): My favorite place to order music CDs and tapes.

- Commercial Services on the Net (**http://www.directory.net/**): Open Markets' searchable directory of commercial services, products, and information on the Net.

- EUROMALL (**http://www.internet-eireann.ie/Euromall/**): An online mall for European merchants.

- Hall of Malls (**http://nsns.com/MouseTracks/HallofMalls.html**): A list of dozens of online malls.

- Internet Mall (**http://www.internet-mall.com/**). Dozens of online retailers in one place.

- Internet Shopping Network (**https://www.internet.net/**): Another good Net place to shop.

- marketplaceMCI (**http://www2.pcy.mci.net/marketplace/ index.html**): A good collection of online merchants, hosted by MCI.

- Ticketmaster Online (**http://www.ticketmaster.com/**): Order tickets for concerts online.

- Yahoo's List of Products and Services (**http://www.yahoo.com/ Business/Products_and_Services/**): A comprehensive list of merchants accessible on the Net.

So, with all these retailers literally at your fingertips, why leave your house to shop? Just make sure your mouse is working and that there's room on your credit card, and you'll be able to shop online until your fingers are sore!

# Use CompuServe to place classified ads

If you think of the interconnected community on CompuServe as a small town, you'll understand why it offers newspaper-style classified ads. CompuServe has classified ads in hundreds of different categories—just like traditional classifieds. To see these ads, all you have to do is GO CLASSIFIEDS and select Browse/Submit Classified Ads. Then you're presented with thousands of classified advertisements, as well as the opportunity to place your own classified ads.

To browse through the ads, just scroll through the category list and highlight the category you're interested in. Click the Browse button, select a subcategory (if necessary), and browse through the list of ads displayed.

When you find an ad you want to read, highlight it and click the Read button. If you want to respond to the ad, click the Reply button; otherwise, click Cancel to return to the ad list.

Placing an ad is also simple. Just follow these steps:

**1** From the Classified Ads window, click the Submit button.

**2** When the Select Category list appears, choose a category for your ad and click OK.

**3** When the Submit Ad dialog box appears (see Fig. 18.2), enter your name, your location (a two-letter state abbreviation), the subject, and the duration the ad should run. Then enter your text, and click the Post button to send the ad.

**Fig. 18.2**
You can place a classified ad on CompuServe.

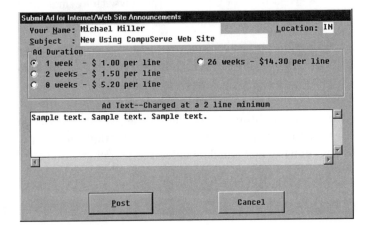

## Searching for a job via CompuServe

You can also rely on CompuServe to aid your job search. CompuServe gives you access to E-SPAN JobSearch, an online employment resource for job seekers and employers across America. Every week E-SPAN lists more than 1,000 positions.

Job seekers can browse E-SPAN listings via the classified ads (GO CLASSIFIEDS and select the Job Search category) or directly from E-SPAN (GO ESPAN). When you're in E-SPAN, you select a job category and the area of the United States that you're targeting. Then you're presented with

a list of potential jobs in your category and region.

When you select a listing and click Read, the full ad appears in a separate window. If you want to answer the ad, click the Reply button; otherwise, click the Cancel button.

If you're an employer, you can place ads for prospective employees through E-SPAN. Contact E-SPAN via CompuServe Mail (76702,1771) or at their toll-free number (1-800-682-2901).

# 19

# Sharing Your Opinions

● **In this chapter:**

- **Vent your spleen in CompuServe forums**

- **Discuss politics and other controversial issues**

- **Explore controversial content on the Internet**

- **Communicate with the White House and the rest of the Federal government**

*When you want to share your opinions with people that count, CompuServe is the place to go!* . . . . . . . . . . . . . . . . . ▶

I f you think of CompuServe as a typical American town, you would expect to be able to walk right up to the town's courthouse and talk with your elected officials. Well, believe it or not, you can do that with CompuServe; you can even talk directly to the White House! But if that's too intimidating for you, feel free to vent in the lively debates that take place in some of CompuServe's issues-oriented forums.

# Argue the issues in CompuServe forums

While most CompuServe forums inspire much debate (often over trivial issues), the bulk of the issue-oriented discourse takes place in a handful of hot forums. Check out the forums listed here if you want a look at the hottest of the hot.

> Issues Forum (GO ISSUESFORUM)
> (includes a special Rush Limbaugh section)
>
> Global Crisis Forum (GO CRISIS)
>
> Political Debate Forum (GO POLITICS)
>
> Republican Forum (GO REPUBLICAN)
>
> Democratic Forum (GO DEMOCRAT)
>
> Religion Forum (GO RELIGION)
>
> Electronic Frontier Foundation Forum (GO EFFSIG)
> (focuses on electronic freedom of speech issues)
>
> Entertainment Drive Forum (GO EFORUM)
>
> CNN Forum (GO CNNFORUM)

# Issues on the Net

CompuServe discussions look downright genteel compared to the free-for-alls you find in that wild and woolly West we call the Internet. Some of the best (i.e. the loudest and most vicious) discussions take place in USENET newsgroups. Crank up your CompuServe newsreader (GO USENET) and take a look at these groups:

- **alt.fan.rush-limbaugh, alt.flame.rush-limbaugh,** and **alt.rush-limbaugh**: Three groups that generate some of the heaviest message traffic on all of USENET.

- **alt.philosophy.debate**: A good place to discuss philosophical issues.

- **alt.politics.***: A collection of newsgroups covering Bill Clinton, Newt Gingrich, and all the degrees in-between.

- **alt.religion.***: Dozens of newsgroups discussing all of the major religions—and some of the minor ones.

- **soc.religion.***: More newsgroups discussing religious issues.

- **talk.***: Hundreds of newsgroups discussing philosophy, politics, religion, abortion, the environment, and other controversial issues (a good place to start if you want to stir things up a bit).

# Mr. CompuServer goes to Washington

Do you have an opinion you'd like to share with your representatives in Washington? Well, all you have to do is turn on your PC (and that doesn't stand for politically correct, buster!). By connecting to CompuServe, you can forge an electronic link with those government bozos you're always complaining about.

## Speaking your mind on the White House forum

When you GO WHITEHOUSE, you're taken to the White House forum. This forum is broken down into sections based on such topics as Defense, Health Care, Economy, Environment, Commerce, and Social Security.

**TIP** **You should feel free to speak your mind in the White House forum.** Even though the White House monitors the discussions to keep track of the pulse of the American public, it's unlikely you will have to worry about the FBI preparing a file on everyone who leaves a message in the forum!

# Searching for important documents in the library

No, you won't find the Watergate papers in the White House forum's libraries, but you will find other official documents. In fact, the libraries on this forum are loaded with official documents. (All files in the library come directly from the White House; no other uploading is permitted.)

What sorts of files are they? Just about every official announcement that comes from the President or Vice President ends up in these libraries. You'll find radio addresses, official statements, briefings, speeches, and letters. All of these files are available for your reading pleasure—either online or at a later date when you decide to download.

# Sending mail to the White House

We all know that the President doesn't spend his entire day reading all the messages in CompuServe's White House forum. So addressing a message to him on the forum might just be a waste of time. (Although members of the White House staff do supposedly review and respond to forum messages when appropriate.)

There is, however, a way to send e-mail directly to the President or Vice President of the United States. GO PRESMAIL, and you will be presented with the opportunity to send a letter directly to the White House.

 **TIP** You can also send a standard e-mail to the President at the address president@whitehouse.gov.

All e-mail sent via CompuServe to the White House must follow a standard format. So when you initiate your message, you'll be presented with the White House Mail window shown in Fig. 19.1. Select the recipient of your mail (the Prez or the VP) and your reason for writing. Then enter your real name and address and click the Create button.

Next you need to identify your topic and the guise under which you're writing (whether you're writing as a Business Person, a Student, or a Working Person, for example). You will need to enter the subject of your letter and the organization you're associated with (if necessary).

**Fig. 19.1**
Sending e-mail to the
President.

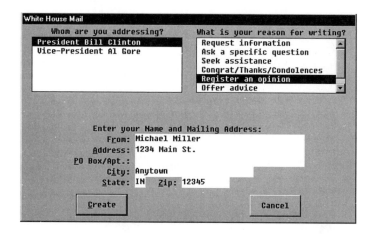

Finally, you enter the text of your message, which can be no more than 40 lines long. When you're done, click $\underline{S}$end Now, and it's off to the White House with your opinions and advice.

## Sending U.S. Mail letters to Washington

When e-mail isn't enough, you can also use CompuServe to send U.S. Mail letters to the President, Vice President, and members of the Senate and House of Representatives. This service costs $1.00 per message.

To send what CompuServe calls a CONGRESSGram, GO GRAMS and select which branch of government you're writing (White House, Senate, or House of Representatives). You'll be asked for the recipient's name and title (Senator or Representative), and then you can start typing your message. (You can write up to 88 lines with 69 characters each.) When you're done, CompuServe automatically prints out the letter and arranges for the U.S. Postal Service to deliver it.

# Accessing the government via the Internet

There are lots of ways to access the government via the Internet. Begin by tracking the following newsgroups (GO USENET):

- **alt.politics.\***: Where dozens of groups let everyone voice their opinons about current political events.

- **clari.news.gov.\***: Contains a large amount of official government news in various groups.

- **soc.politics**: A single group that focuses on political issues.

After you're done there, it's time to head to the World Wide Web. Many government and political organizations—including the White House—have Web sites. Look at this representative list (no pun intended):

- AllPolitics (**http://allpolitics.com/**): A great political information site that's jointly run by CNN and TIME (see Fig. 19.2).

**Fig. 19.2**
The AllPolitics Web site is full of political information.

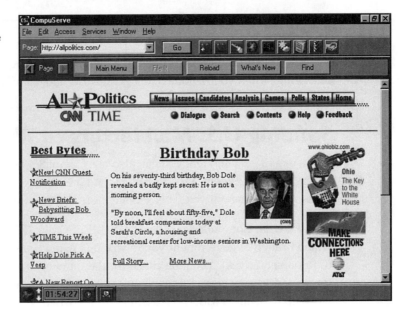

- America Vote's National Town Hall (**http://www.americavote.com/ vote**): A means by which you can send Washington your opinions on issues of the day. The site also provides information on Congressional bills and other related issues.

- American Voter '96 (**http://voter96.cqalert.com/**): A good site for discussion on the 1996 election.

- CapWeb (**http://policy.net/capweb/**): An "unauthorized"—but comprehensive—guide to the U.S. Congress, with lots of contact information.

- CBS Campaign '96 (**http://www.cbsnews.com/campaign96/**): CBS News' official Web site covering the fall elections.

- Contacting Congress (**http://ast1.spa.umn.edu/juan/congress.html**): An independent site at the University of Minnesota that lists contact information for each Congressperson.

- Electronic Democracy Forum (**http://edf.www.media.mit.edu/**): Where you can read and discuss Newt Gingrich's Contract with America.

- IRS Online (**http://www.irs.ustreas.gov/prod/**): A good source for tax information and forms you can download.

- Library of Congress: Federal Government Page (**http://lcweb.loc.gov/global/legislative/congress.html**): Has lots of links to other government and political pages.

- Political Activism Resources (**http://kimsoft.com/kimpol.htm**): A page full of political information and links, from Korea (of all places).

- Thomas: Legislative Information on the Internet (**http://thomas.loc.gov/**): In the spirit of Thomas Jefferson, this server provides the full text of current House and Senate legislation.

- U.S. House of Representatives (**http://www.house.gov/**): Where you'll find your congressperson online.

- U.S. Senate (**http://www.senate.gov:70/**): A Gopher server for the Senate.

- WebActive (**http://www.webactive.com/**): A great site for Web-based political activism.

- White House (**http://www.whitehouse.gov/**): The official Web site of the President. (This page includes a tour of the White House and sound bites from Socks the cat.)

- Yahoo's List of Government Resources (**http://www.yahoo.com/Government/**): The master list of government-related Net resources.

- Yahoo's List of Politics (**http://www.yahoo.com/Politics/**): A good place to start if you desire controversy.

- Yahoo's List of Society and Culture (**http://www.yahoo.com/Society_and_Culture/**): Another good place to look for controversial topics.

I think it's kind of neat how CompuServe, the Internet, and e-mail make it easy to communicate with the leaders of our government. The information superhighway truly is helping to bring democracy back to the people!

# 20

# Talk to Us at Que

● **In this chapter:**

● Learn about Macmillan Computer Publishing (MCP)

● Visit the MCP Forum on CompuServe

● Discover MCP and Que on the World Wide Web

● Contact the author on the Web and through e-mail

*Visit Que on CompuServe and on the Internet!. . . . . . . .* ➤

**T**his chapter is about Que's presence on CompuServe (in the Macmillan Computer Publishing Forum) and on the Internet (via the Macmillan Information SuperLibrary Web site). You can find me and other Que staff members and authors in both of these places. (If you think this is blatant self-promotion, you're right!)

# But first... a little bit about Macmillan Computer Publishing

You might be saying: Wait a minute, what's this Macmillan Computer Publishing outfit? I thought this book was published by Que?

You see, it goes like this. Que is a business unit in a larger organization called Macmillan Computer Publishing (abbreviated MCP). MCP is made up of the following twelve business units, each of which runs as a separate publishing company.

- Que, the largest publisher in the computer book industry

- Adobe Press, the official book publisher for Adobe Corporation

- Borland Press, the official book publisher for Borland Corporation

- BradyGAMES, which focuses on books about computer games and video games

- Hayden Books, which focuses on books for creative professionals and Macintosh users

- Lycos Press, the official book publisher for the Lycos Web site

- New Riders, which focuses on books about CAD and networking

- Que Education & Training, publisher of computer textbooks for the education and corporate training markets

- Sams, which focuses on programming and new technology publishing

- Sams.net, which focuses on Internet-related books

- Waite Group Press, an esteemed publisher of technology and programming books

- Ziff-Davis Press, the official book publisher for Ziff-Davis magazines

All of these imprints are represented in MCP's CompuServe forum.

 **TIP** **Oh, in case you're interested, MCP is a unit of Macmillan** Publishing, which is a unit of Simon & Schuster, which is a unit of Paramount, which is a unit of Viacom. (Don't worry, I won't be testing you on that!)

# Que on CompuServe

MCP's CompuServe forum (GO MACMILLAN) is designed to give you access to all the folks who produce our books, including authors, editors, developers, and management staff. Just as the ads in the back of our books claim, you can do all of these things in the MCP Forum:

- Leave messages and ask questions about Que books and software

- Download helpful tips and software

- Contact the authors of your favorite Que books

- Present your own book ideas

- Keep up to date on all the latest books available from each of MCP's imprints

Many of the Que editorial and managerial staff members visit the forum on a regular basis. Personally, I try to check in every few days so I can answer any questions that might come up.

## A variety of message sections

As you can see in Fig. 20.1, the MCP Forum currently has a variety of message sections, broken up by computer-related topic. If you're not sure where to post a message, try the General section; it provides a good place to start.

What kinds of messages can you expect to see in the MCP Forum? Well, we get a lot of questions about our books, the software in our book/disk products, and the software we write about. In addition, we get questions from potential authors who are considering writing new books.

**Fig. 20.1**
The message sections on MCP's CompuServe Forum.

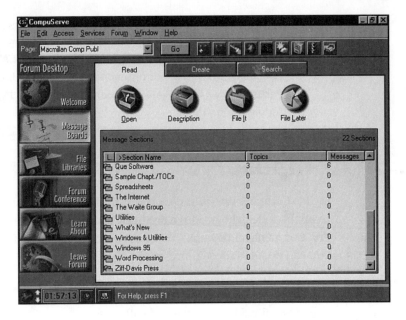

## Conferencing with authors

The MCP Forum also holds author conferences several times a month. During those conferences you can "talk" online—in real time—with Que authors concerning their latest books. Upcoming conferences are always listed in the opening notice that you see immediately when you enter the forum.

After an author conference, the **SysOp** (Systems Operator, the person who administers the daily workings of the forum) generally uploads the entire text of the conference to a forum library file. And just in case you missed out on the conference with your favorite author, you can review the highlights of any conference you miss.

## Cool stuff in our libraries

Just as the message sections contain some very scintillating conversation, the MCP Forum libraries contain a lot of neat files. For example, you might find any of the following things in our library sections:

- Electronic book listings and new book announcements
- Macros and other application helper programs

- Shareware graphics and DTP programs and utilities

- Files and sample code from programming and database books

- Shareware and freeware utilities

- Internet programs and utilities

- Games and game add-ins, including many for EPIC and DOOM

- Demos of multimedia programs

- Press releases for new books

In short, there's a lot of good stuff in the MCP libraries. GO MACMILLAN and check it out!

# Que on the Internet

Que and MCP are part of the Macmillan Information SuperLibrary Web site, located at **http://www.mcp.com/**. Some call it a "supersite" because it has sections for each of MCP's businesses, as well as for books from other Macmillan publishing groups (such as Frommer's travel books and Weight Watcher's cookbooks). As you can see in Fig. 20.2, the SuperLibrary gives you access to a number of neat areas.

**Fig. 20.2**
The Macmillan
Information
SuperLibrary
Web site.

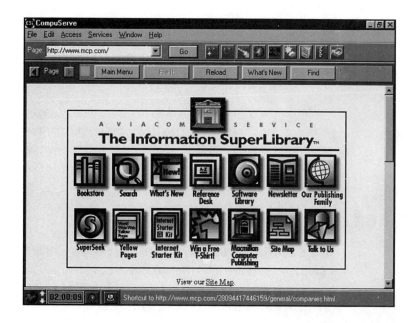

From the SuperLibrary, you can…

- Use New Riders' Official World Wide Web Yellow Pages (**http://www.mcp.com/nrp/wwwyp/**) to search the Web for specific types of sites.

- Use the new SuperSeek engine (**http://www.superseek.com/**) to explore multiple directories and search engines.

- Read the latest copy of the SuperLibrary newsletter (where I write a monthly column called Miller's View).

- Use the Reference Desk (**http://www.mcp.com/refdesk/index.html**) to obtain information about upcoming book releases.

- Find out What's New (**http://www.mcp.com/general/new.html**) with Que and Macmillan.

- Search the Software Library (**http://www.mcp.com/softlib/software.html**) for programs and utilities to download.

- Look for a bookstore near you (**http://www.mcp.com/cgi-bin/do-searches.cgi**), hotlink to technical bookstores on the Net (**http://www.mcp.com/general/techbook.html**), or contact our international distributors (**http://www.mcp.com/bookstore/distrib.html**).

- Search the Bookstore (**http://www.mcp.com/cgi-bin/do-bookstore.cgi**) for information on MCP books—and even place an order online if you want.

- Browse through the personal Web pages of some Que and MCP authors (**http://www.mcp.com/authors**).

In addition to the main SuperLibrary page, you can go directly to Que's section in the SuperLibrary (**http://www.mcp.com/que**). There you can find information specific to Que books, including announcements for upcoming releases.

# Your author online

My presence is felt in several places on the Macmillan Web site. First, I write a monthly column for the SuperLibrary newsletter; you can read it online or download it and read it later. In addition, I have a personal Web page (**http://www.mcp.com/people/miller**); I hope it's not too self-indulgent.

Most importantly, I've created a special Web page for this book. The *Using CompuServe, Third Edition* Web page (see Fig. 20.3) is located at **http://www.mcp.com/people/miller/cis3top.htm**. This page contains information that's not in this book, including updates and corrections. I recommend that you check it out.

**Fig. 20.3**
The Web page for
*Using CompuServe,
Third Edition.*

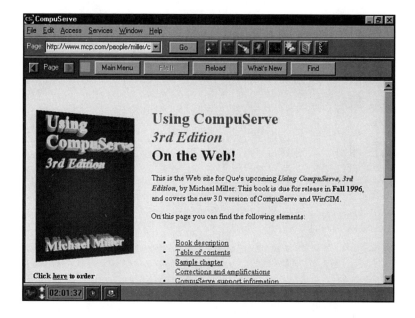

Finally, feel free to contact me via e-mail. I appreciate your comments about this book (or about anything else, for that matter). Your feedback on the previous edition helped to make this one better.

You can contact me at either of these addresses:

CompuServe: 73207,2013

Internet: **mmiller@mcp.com**

I look forward to hearing from you!

# Part IV: Surfing the Internet from CompuServe

# All About the Internet and CompuServe's Internet Services

● **In this chapter:**

- **What is the Internet?**

- **What can you do on the Internet?**

- **Exploring the Internet with CompuServe**

- **Answers to common Internet-related questions**

- **Is CompuServe the best way to connect to the Internet?**

*The Internet opens up online worlds beyond even what CompuServe itself has to offer. . . . . . . . . . . . . . . . . . . .* ⊙

**Y**ou've heard about the Internet. It's in all the newspapers, and you even hear mention of it on television from time to time. You don't know exactly what the Internet is, but it sounds neat—like something you'd probably want to get involved with. The problem is, you don't even know where to start. How do you find out more about the Internet? And more importantly, how do you get connected to it?

The answers to your questions are here in this chapter. Read on—I'll tell you all about the Net and how you can use CompuServe to connect to it.

# What the Internet is and what it *isn't*

First things first: what *is* the Internet?

Let's start with what the Internet *isn't*. It isn't a thing. You can't touch it or pick up a box of it. It isn't even a *collection* of things. The Internet is nothing tangible at all.

The Net is really just a way to connect various computers. The Internet is made up of hundreds of thousands of computers, each connected to the others via the "wiring" of the Internet. All the things you can do on the Internet are found on the computers that are connected to the Net.

Think of the Internet as if it were a utility like the electric company. When you hook electricity up to your house, what happens? Does your house start to glow? Does it spin? Does it sprout a second story? No. When you hook electricity up to your house, *nothing happens at all.*

Nothing happens, that is, until you plug something into a wall socket. You can plug lots of things into your sockets: televisions sets, radios, vacuum cleaners, blenders, and any other electric appliance you can think of. Only *after* you've plugged in the appliance can you can start doing things. When you plug in your blender, you can make milk shakes or daiquiris or margaritas. The electricity itself doesn't make your milk shake, but because you're hooked up to the electric company, you have the capability to make milk shakes if you want.

The Internet is like the electric company. When you hook your computer up to the Internet, *nothing happens*. Your computer doesn't start to glow or spin or grow an extra disk drive. No, nothing at all happens until you plug in an

Internet "appliance." You can plug in an e-mail appliance to send messages, or an FTP appliance to download files, or a World Wide Web appliance to browse hypertext documents. All this is possible because you're connected to the Net, but the Net itself can't do it for you.

# How the Internet works

The Internet is really pretty simple. You start with a computer—*your* computer. It's on your desk, all by itself, so it's truly a *personal* computer.

Next, you hook your computer up to a *network* of other computers. If you're at work, you may hook into the company's local area network (LAN). If you're at home, you'll use your PC's modem to dial into and connect with CompuServe—a network comprised of you and about three million other CompuServe users.

But wait! You're not connected to the Internet yet—you're just connected to CompuServe, which is a kind of wide area network or WAN (a network of computers not localized in a single location). It is not yet connected to anything else. You see, the final and most important step is to get CompuServe to tap into the big backbone that is the Internet. This lets you (the user who is connected to the CompuServe network via your modem and local phone lines) piggyback onto the Internet.

Once you're connected to the Internet, you can connect to any one of the hundreds of thousands of other networks that are connected to the Net. Each one of these networks boasts thousands of users (very few networks have CompuServe's three million-strong subscription), so the inter-connection of these networks gives you access to more than *50 million* computer users all around the world.

That's right, once you're connected to the Net, you can communicate with 50 million of your closest friends! You can send them e-mail, share cool files, or even read online documents "published" on something called the World Wide Web. In short, you can do just about anything imaginable—providing the computer networks allow it.

Yet the Internet isn't a commercial service like CompuServe. The Internet is only the connection between individual, *private* computers. There's no one really running the Internet; there's no help desk, no technical support, and no documentation. What you find on the Net is uncensored, untested, and un-warranteed. Sometimes the connection doesn't even work all that well! So if you're comfortable with the sanitized, monitored world of CompuServe, think twice before you venture into the wild, wild, West of the Internet. You just never know what you'll find there!

# Things you can do on the Internet

The Internet lets you do anything that the computers connected to the Net are capable of. Certainly most of the big computers on the Net (called Internet **host sites**) let you do a lot. Many of these host sites contain thou-sands of files you can download. Host sites also let you connect to online special interest groups (called **newsgroups**) and display hypertext World Wide Web documents. All you have to do is use CompuServe to get out on the Internet, and then connect to these sites. Then you'll be on your way to becoming a certified Net cruiser.

## Browse hypertext documents with the World Wide Web

The neatest part of the Internet is kind of a subset of the Net called the **World Wide Web** (GO WEBCENTRAL). The Web consists of hundreds of thousands of online "documents" called **Web pages**. Each Web page sort of looks like a page from a book, complete with different types of text and graphics. The big difference is that the text on a Web page can be **hyperlinked** to other documents. That means that when you're reading one Web page, you're just a mouse click away from related (and linked) informa-tion on a totally different Web page.

You can browse Web pages with something called a **Web browser**. CompuServe 3.0 has its own built-in Web browser, so you can experience Web pages in the familiar format of standard CompuServe services. You can also use third-party Web browsers such as Netscape Navigator or Microsoft's Internet Explorer with CompuServe 3.0. See Chapter 24, "Wandering the World Wide Web," for more information.

**TIP** **CompuServe also lets you create your own Web pages. See** Chapter 25, "Creating Your Own Web Pages," for more details.

## Communicate with others via e-mail and newsgroups

Another thing you might like to do on the Net is to communicate with other Internetters. In fact, the most common use of the Net is talking to other Net users!

There are two main ways to communicate with other users on the Net. The first is one you're probably already familiar with: electronic mail (GO MAIL). You can use the Internet to send e-mail to any of the 50 million other users on the Net, as well as to users of other online services, such as America Online or Prodigy. (See Chapter 6, "Pushing the Virtual Envelope: Sending and Receiving CompuServe E-Mail," for more information on sending e-mail across the Internet.)

The second way to communicate with other Internauts is through something called a **USENET newsgroup** (GO USENET). A newsgroup is kind of like a CompuServe forum, in that it's a virtual "place" for you to exchange messages with others who share your interests. (See Chapter 22, "Forums on the Internet: USENET Newsgroups," for more information on Internet newsgroups.)

## Find and download files with FTP and Gopher

Another popular use of the Net is to find and download computer files. This sounds a little boring, but if you consider that any information you might be looking for is going to be stored in a file somewhere on the Net, you realize that it's important to learn how to access files. There are various ways to find files on the Net; use whichever method is applicable to your situation.

Two of the most popular methods of downloading files from the Net are FTP and Gopher. FTP (GO FTP), which stands for file transfer protocol, is the fastest way to download files—*if* you know exactly where they are. If you don't know where to look for your files, you should use the method called

Gopher, which is accessible via the World Wide Web. (See Chapter 23, "Finding and Downloading Files on the Internet," for more information on FTP and Gopher.)

## Operate somebody else's computer with Telnet

**Telnet** (GO TELNET) lets you access another computer and operate it as if your PC were a terminal connected to that computer (kind of like the way users had to connect to mainframe computers before personal computers became popular). Most Telnet host computers are UNIX-based, or they are larger mainframes and minicomputers. They won't have the fancy graphical user interfaces you're used to with Windows and the Mac.

With Telnet, you can connect to another computer to find and download specific files, search databases for specific information, access services available only at the host computer, and communicate with users who have accounts with the host computer. You can also choose to play text-based games (like MUDs and MOOs) with other gamers. (See Chapter 23, "Finding and Downloading Files on the Internet," for more information on Telnet.)

# Connecting to the Internet with CompuServe

You'll be pleased to know that you have fairly complete access to the Internet as part of your CompuServe membership. From within CompuServe 3.0, you can access all the services you just read about, including the World Wide Web, e-mail, USENET newsgroups, FTP, Gopher, and Telnet. To access CompuServe's Internet services, GO INTERNET. From there you have access to all of CompuServe's Internet services; nothing else is required, and there is no additional cost.

The great thing about using CompuServe to access the Net is that you don't need to do anything new or extra. You don't have to establish a new account, or install new software, or learn to use a new program. All you have to do is GO INTERNET, and you have full access to CompuServe's Internet connection.

# Learn more about the Internet—on CompuServe!

CompuServe has a complete area devoted to the Internet. When you GO INTERNET, you gain access to a wide variety of Internet-related services and forums, including the following:

- **What's Hot on the Internet**  Kind of a What's New section for Internet-related topics.

- **World Wide Web**  GO gives you access to WebCentral (a great place to find Web software and sites), and Home Page Wizard enables you to create your own home pages on the Web (see Chapter 25 for more details).

- **Discussion Groups**  Access to USENET newsgroups.

- **Internet Specials & Offers**

- **File Downloads**  Access to FTP for file downloading.

- **Remote Login**  Gives you access to Telnet.

- **Internet Phone by VocalTec**  Lets you use your Internet connection to actually talk to other users—kind of like a low-tech telephone.

- **Internet forums**  Places where you can communicate with other CompuServe users about Internet-related issues.

- **Internet Q&A**  A great place to find answers to common Internet-related questions.

- **Home Page Wizard**  The software that lets you create your own Web pages.

- **Publish Home Pages**  A place where you can upload the pages you create with Home Page Wizard and search the pages created by other CompuServe members.

- **CompuServe Parental Controls Center**  Enables you to limit your household's access to certain types of content on the Net.

If you're an Internet newbie, I recommend that you check out some of CompuServe's various Internet forums:

- Internet Commerce Forum (GO INETCO) is all about using the Internet for business purposes.

- Internet Developer's Forum (GO INETDE) is for developers of Web pages and Web sites.

- Internet Magazine Forum (GO INTMAG) is run by *Internet* Magazine.

- Internet New Users Forum (GO INETNEW) is a great place for new Internet users.

- Internet Publishing Forum (GO INETPUB) is for those interested in publishing content on the Internet.

- Internet Resources Forum (GO INETRES) is full of tools and software for more experienced Internet users.

- Internet WebMasters Forum (GO INETWEB) is the place where Internet WebMasters and administrators hang out.

continues

continued

- InternetWorld Magazine Forum (GO IWORLD) is run by *InternetWorld Magazine*.

- NetLauncher Support Forum (GO NLSUPPORT) supports the CompuServe's NetLauncher Internet software (used by the SpryNet service).

In addition to these forums, CompuServe also offers the Java Support Forum (GO JAVAUSER), the Internet Welcome Center (GO INETWC), and the Netscape User's Forum (GO NSUSER), all of which interest many Internet users.

The Internet New Users Forum (GO INETNEW) is especially helpful if you're just getting started. Also, the Internet Welcome Center (GO INETWC) is a good place to learn more about CompuServe's Internet-related services.

If you're at all interested in the Internet, I recommend you spend some time in these forums. You'll find lots of beginners just like you, as well as those who've been there and can give you some guidance.

# Answers to the most common questions about the Internet

Over the past two years I've talked to a lot of Internet users—both beginners and more experienced users. Many of these users had similar questions, so I thought I'd share those questions (and the answers) with you.

## If I'm hooked up to CompuServe, am I also hooked up to the Internet?

If you have a CompuServe membership, you have automatic access to CompuServe's Internet connection (GO INTERNET). When you access one of CompuServe's Internet services (such as FTP or the World Wide Web), you are connecting—via CompuServe—to the Net. But none of the other CompuServe services you use are part of the Internet—and no one from the Internet can access them without a valid CompuServe membership.

### Can I use CompuServe to send e-mail to a friend of mine who has an Internet account?

Yes you can. To send e-mail, you need to know the recipient's Internet e-mail address, which will be in the format *username@domain.name*. When you enter the address, preface it with "INTERNET:" (as in **INTERNET:***username@domain.name*), and you're ready to send Internet e-mail. (See Chapter 6 for more information on sending and receiving e-mail.)

### What if I don't know my friend's Internet e-mail address?

You're out of luck. There's no general directory of Internet e-mail addresses, so you'll have to call up your friend and ask for his address.

### Why did I get so many nasty messages from other users after I posted a newsgroup article?

Nasty responses to a newsgroup posting are called **flames**. You get flamed when you do something that other users regard as being in poor form. For example, if you're the two-hundredth guy to ask the question "what's this newsgroup all about?," you won't make any friends—and you will probably be flamed. It's always good to "lurk" in a newsgroup for a while before you start posting messages; it will help you find out what's acceptable behavior and what isn't.

### Why can't I access a certain site?

The most common reason you can't reach a particular Internet site is that it's too busy. You see, an Internet site is just a computer, more or less like your PC. When too many people use it at once, it slows down, and it won't let anyone else sign on until one of the current users signs off. Some popular sites are nearly impossible to access during busy times of the day. Of course, it's also possible for a site to close down, move, or just terminate its access to the Internet.

### Why is the Internet so slow sometimes?

The Internet is just a bunch of computers connected by a bunch of wires. When too many people use it (or use a particular computer site) at the same time, it gets overloaded and slows down. Try accessing a different site or logging on later when things might not be so busy. In addition, some of the most popular sites have **mirror sites** that "mirror" their contents in an attempt to alleviate some of the traffic load.

### How can I keep certain family members from accessing objectionable content on the Net?

Go to the Parental Controls Center (GO CONTROLS). Click on the Internet Controls button and follow the instructions given in Chapter 4, "Making CompuServe Safe for Children."

### Can I use Netscape or another third-party Web browser with CompuServe?

By default, CompuServe uses its built-in Web browser. However, you can alter the settings so that CompuServe uses a third-party browser such as Netscape Navigator or Microsoft's Internet Explorer. Pull down the Access menu and select Preferences. When the Preferences dialog box appears, select the General tab, check Use external Internet Browser, and Select a new Internet Browser. When you finish, click OK.

### Is it safe to give my credit card number in transactions over the Internet?

Some people say yes, some say no. I do it myself. Giving out your credit card number to an Internet merchant is no less dangerous than handing your credit card to a waiter in a restaurant.

Note, however, that the Internet is an unsecured environment. A talented hacker can grab messages willy-nilly, and one of these could include your credit card number. While this is unlikely, if you want to be ultra-cautious, you can wait until secure credit transactions are in place (sometime in 1997) before you send sensitive information over the Internet.

### Can anyone on the Internet gain access to the files on my personal computer?

No. Your personal computer is protected from the Net via "firewalls" put in place at CompuServe. You can get out, but no one else can get in.

### Can I create my own personal Web page?

Yes you can. See Chapter 25 for more information.

### What's the best way to learn more about the Internet?

Okay, I'll admit this question is a set up. The best way to learn more about the Internet is by reading books from Que! I recommend two books in particular:

- *Using the Internet.* This is a great general book for casual Internet users, and it tells you everything you need to know to get you started with the Net—whether it's through CompuServe or an Internet Service Provider.

- *Special Edition Using the Internet.* This book is the best (and certainly the biggest) book you'll find about the Net. In 1,200+ pages, it contains exhaustive information on just about every Internet topic you can think of. It even comes with a CD-ROM that contains hundreds of Internet software programs!

For more information on these and other Que books, ask your local bookseller or use CompuServe's built-in Web browser to visit Que's World Wide Web site at http://www.mcp.com/que.

## CompuServe: The *best* way to connect to the Net?

I need to come clean with you. CompuServe offers a really easy way to connect to the Net. It's a great way to get started with the Net and lots of CompuServe users are as happy as clams connecting this way. But it's actually not the best Internet connection you can make.

You see, using CompuServe to connect to the Net gives you only *limited* access to the Internet. You have to use CompuServe's tools for newsgroups and e-mail, so you can only do those things that CompuServe lets you do.

If you want a *better* Internet connection—one that lets you use any tools you want—you need to supplement CompuServe with a set of dedicated Internet software tools. When you connect to

CompuServe 3.0, you use what is called a PPP connection; it lets you open multiple, simultaneous sessions on the Internet. That means that you can run other PPP programs while you're using CompuServe.

The other tools connect to other sites on the Net. These tools can be designated Internet e-mail programs (like Eudora), designated FTP programs (like WS-FTP), designated USENET newsreaders (like Free Agent or NewsXPress), or designated Web browsers (like Netscape Navigator or Microsoft's Internet Explorer). You can find many of these programs in the libraries of the Internet

continues

continued

Resources Forum (GO INETRES) or in the software area on Macmillan's Information SuperLibrary Web site (http://www.mcp.com/).

Of course, you don't have to use CompuServe as your Internet connection. You can also connect to the Net using an independent Internet Service Provider (ISP). A good ISP will give you complete Internet access—and let you use whatever software you want in order to do whatever you want to do. In addition, many ISPs charge less per hour to connect to the Net than you pay to CompuServe for similar services. Therefore, it pays to shop around for the best deal if you're a heavy Internet user.

Where can you find an ISP? Well, CompuServe itself offers dedicated Internet connections through what it calls SpryNet. SpryNet is a full-service Internet Service Provider that's separate from, but owned by, CompuServe itself. Call 206-957-8000 for more information on using SpryNet for your Internet connection.

If you want to search for the best ISP for your needs, check out the Ultimate Guide to ISPs from the folks at c|net (http://www.cnet.com/Content/Reviews/Compare/ISP/).

# 22

# Forums on the Internet: USENET Newsgroups

● In this chapter:

● **What is USENET?**

● **How is a USENET newsgroup like a CompuServe forum?**

● **What kinds of newsgroups are there?**

● **Accessing USENET newsgroups from CompuServe**

*If you like CompuServe forums, you'll love USENET newsgroups!* . . . . . . . . . . . . . . . . . . . . . . . . . . . . . . ▶

**O**kay. You know a little bit about the Internet, and maybe you've even exchanged e-mail with someone on the Net. However, you're not an Internet expert yet. You want to learn more.

The best way to get more is with USENET newsgroups. A **newsgroup** is a little like a CompuServe forum without file library and conference capabilities. You exchange messages with other users and follow discussion threads on major topics.

Remember, though, that USENET is not part of CompuServe. Even though you can access USENET newsgroups via CompuServe, these groups exist on a separate network and follow different guidelines than you're used to with CompuServe. You'll need to know subtle differences in terminology and etiquette in order to master these newsgroups and avoid being flamed as an Internet "newbie" by users in that awful non-CompuServe world of the Net. (Yeah, the Net community can be a little testy at times. Get used to it!)

# What *is* USENET?

USENET is a quasi-network (actually a set of rules and protocols) that operates within the confines of the Internet. Its purpose is to distribute messages to and from users with similar interests by using special forums called newsgroups.

Like a CompuServe forum, a USENET newsgroup is an electronic gathering place for people with similar interests. In a newsgroup, users post messages (called articles) about a variety of topics; other users read these articles and sometimes reply. The result is a kind of ongoing free-form discussion in which literally hundreds of users may participate.

Because USENET is separate from CompuServe, you can't access it in the same way you access CompuServe forums. You need to use the special newsreader that CompuServe provides. CompuServe also provides the link to USENET, which you access when you GO USENET.

# If you like forums, you'll *love* newsgroups!

In many ways, a newsgroup is like an old-fashioned town meeting: anyone can attend and anyone can speak his or her mind. At times, things can get a bit disorganized, and it's not uncommon for several people to talk about different things at the same time. But, all in all, a lot of interesting opinions are expressed and everyone can read them.

Does this description sound familiar? Yes, the loosely organized chaos of a USENET newsgroup is very similar to what you experience in the message sections of most CompuServe forums. You trade messages and opinions with others of similar interests, and messages related to a single topic are grouped in threads.

 **TIP**   **See Chapter 7, "The Heart of CompuServe: Fun with Forums," for** more information on forums, forum terminology, and forum "etiquette."

There are some differences between forums and newsgroups, however. Table 22.1 gives you an overview of some basic differences.

## Table 22.1   Comparison of forums and newsgroups

| Feature | CompuServe Forums | USENET Newsgroups |
| --- | --- | --- |
| Number available | 750+ | 15,000+ |
| Contain multiple sections | Yes | No |
| Contain file libraries | Yes | No |
| Moderated (by a SysOp) | Yes | Some (but not many) |
| Messages are grouped into threads | Yes | Yes |
| Old messages scroll off | Yes | Yes |
| Messages are called: | Messages | Articles |

The main difference between forums and newsgroups, however, is the culture. Whereas CompuServe forums tend to be relatively friendly places where newcomers are welcome, USENET newsgroups can be a bit insular and downright hostile to "newbies." In fact, it's quite common for old Netters to flame newbies mercilessly; if you're new to a newsgroup and overstep your bounds, you're likely to see some of this behavior.

**TIP** **A flame is a very nasty message sent to a user who has annoyed** the flame's author. It's not uncommon to see flame wars between two or more newsgroup members in a feud.

I'm not quite sure why this cultural difference between forums and newsgroups exists. It may be that for all the years before the Internet's rapid growth the Net was very much a closed society. Nonetheless, the cultural difference does exist. So be cautious when you join a new newsgroup; sit back and survey the lay of the land before you try to adapt to the culture.

# The different kinds of newsgroups

Just like CompuServe forums, USENET newsgroups are organized in a fairly rigid fashion. When you look at the name of a newsgroup, you see something that looks like this:

**first.second.third**

The first part of the name is called the hierarchy; think of it as the major topic area, or the first level of an outline. The second part of the name is a subtopic of the major topic, like the second level of an outline. The third part of the name denotes a subtopic of the subtopic like the third level of an outline. For example, a newsgroup in the recreational section that discusses the art of the cinema is called the rec.arts.cinema group.

## Newsgroup etiquette

One thing you need to know about USENET newsgroup users is that they generally don't like naive beginners (whom they call "newbies"). Most newsgroups are kind of "old boys clubs," and it's tough to break in and become one of the gang.

When it comes to newsgroups, it pays to look before you leap. That means you should "lurk" a bit: just read the articles and get a feel for the newsgroup's atmosphere before you make your first posting.

When you do post your first article, try not to ask repetitive questions or flame other subscribers. Be patient, be polite, and be concise.

Also remember that (as in CompuServe forums) blatant advertising is not acceptable. Even moderate self-promotion is often frowned upon.

**TIP** **Not all newsgroup names have three parts. As a bare minimum,** two parts are required (the hierarchy and the subtopic). On the other end of the spectrum, some very narrowly focused interest groups establish four or even five levels to accurately describe their topics.

There are dozens of different hierarchies in USENET. Table 22.2 lists the major USENET hierarchies easily accessible through the CompuServe connection.

**Table 22.2 USENET hierarchies available on CompuServe**

| USENET Hierarchy | Topics |
| --- | --- |
| alt | Alternative topics; generally related to areas that inspire a lot of different opinions |
| bionet | Biological topics |
| comp | Computer-related topics |
| k12 | Education-related topics |
| misc | Miscellaneous topics |
| news | Topics related to netnews system administration |
| rec | Recreational topics |
| sci | Scientific topics |
| soc | Topics related to social issues |
| talk | Conversational and controversial topics |

# What isn't listed on CompuServe

Actually, other hierarchies are available that aren't listed on CompuServe's main newsgroup list. Most of these are niche-oriented and have a limited number of subscribers. There are also newsgroups within the main hierarchies that CompuServe doesn't list. For example, CompuServe doesn't list any of the alt.sex newsgroups.

Even though CompuServe's USENET newsreader doesn't list certain groups, you can gain access to them. You can access any USENET group by entering its name manually, which you'll see how to do later in this chapter. So if you don't see a particular newsgroup listed, type it in. Chances are good that it's there!

**TIP** **You should definitely check out one particular newsgroup:** compuserve.general. This group deals with CompuServe in general and CompuServe's Internet services in particular.

To participate in a newsgroup, you first need to subscribe to that group, which you can do (for free) directly from CompuServe's USENET newsreader. After you're a member, you can retrieve and post articles from and to the group as frequently as you wish. You can also "unsubscribe" when you get tired of a particular group.

**Q&A** *I can't find the newsgroup I want to subscribe to.*

This may be one of the newsgroups that CompuServe doesn't list. But you can still access it. Try clicking the Subscribe by Name button (in the Subscribe to Newsgroups window) and then entering the newsgroup name manually.

# The Internet connection: accessing USENET newsgroups from CompuServe

You can GO USENET to access the general USENET area on CompuServe. From there, you can read information about newsgroups and newsgroup etiquette, and you can access the USENET newsreaders. To launch the newsreader, select USENET Newsreader (CIM). The main USENET Newsgroups menu appears (see Fig. 22.1).

**Fig. 22.1**
The main USENET
Newsgroups menu.

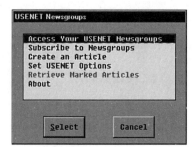

**CAUTION** **USENET exists on a network outside of CompuServe, which means** access to newsgroups may be a little slower than what you're used to with normal CompuServe services.

In the main USENET Newsgroups menu, choose one of the following options:

**Access Your USENET Newsgroups:** You can do this only after you subscribe to them.

**Subscribe to Newsgroups:** You have to do this before you can access the groups.

**Create an Article:** Create an article for a specific newsgroup to which you have subscribed. (You can subscribe at any time.)

**Set USENET Options:** This is the very first thing you need to do.

**Retrieve Marked Articles:** Have CompuServe download all articles you've marked.

**About:** You can access basic Help information.

**CAUTION** **CompuServe claims no responsibility for the content of USENET** newsgroups because they originate outside of CompuServe. You may want to avoid some newsgroups if you find them to be offensive, or you may want to supervise your children's access to them. In other words, USENET isn't as squeaky clean as CompuServe is. Be careful!

# Setting your options and creating your signature

The first thing you need to do is set your newsgroup options. Do this by selecting Set USENET Options from the main USENET Newsgroups menu. When the Options dialog box appears (see Fig. 22.2), enter your name, your organization (optional), and the number of default articles you want to see when a new newsgroup is listed. (I recommend 100 as a good round number.)

**Fig. 22.2**
First you need to set your newsgroup options.

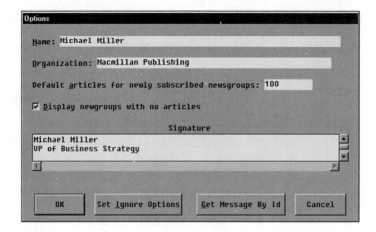

If you want, you can finalize things by creating a signature that will be added to the end of all your newsgroup postings. Your signature should be distinctive yet to the point; you don't want it to be more than four lines long. When you're done, click OK.

**TIP** **As you can see, there are two buttons at the bottom of the** Options dialog box: Set Ignore Options and Get Message By ID. Set Ignore Options lets you instruct the newsreader to ignore certain messages in a newsgroup. Get Message By ID lets you retrieve messages by ID number instead of by thread name. Both of these options are obscure and should be reserved for use by more advanced users.

## Subscribing to newsgroups

Now you need to subscribe to some newsgroups. Subscribing to a newsgroup consists of simply instructing your newsreader to retrieve articles for that group. If you don't subscribe to a group, you can't access its articles.

Begin by selecting the Subscribe to Newsgroups option from the USENET Newsgroups main menu. You see the Subscribe to Newsgroups dialog box, shown in Fig. 22.3.

The easiest way to look for newsgroups is to select a hierarchy in the Browse for Newsgroups list and then click the Select button. This displays the Found list, which you can browse through until you find a group you want. Select the group or groups you want from the Found list and click the Subscribe button.

**Fig. 22.3**
Subscribing to USENET
newsgroups.

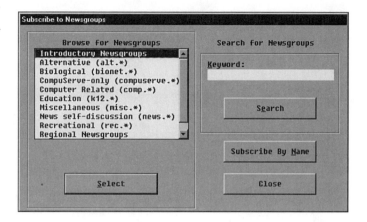

>
>
> **TIP**   **You can also subscribe to a newsgroup by its precise name (click**
> Subscribe By Name) or by hunting for newsgroups with a keyword search. To
> do this, type a keyword and then click the Search button.

# Reading articles

After you subscribe to some groups, you can access those groups to read new
articles. Click the Close button to close the Subscribe to Newsgroups dialog
box and return to the main USENET Newsgroups menu. When you select
Access Your USENET Newsgroups, the Access Newsgroups list appears.
Highlight the specific group you want to access and click the Browse button
to display a list of threads in that group. Fig. 22.4 shows a list of threads in
the alt.video.laserdisc group.

**Fig. 22.4**
Reading newsgroup
threads.

When you find a thread that sounds interesting, select it and click the Get button to retrieve and read the first article in that thread. The article appears in a new window like the one shown in Fig. 22.5.

**Fig. 22.5**

Reading a newsgroup article.

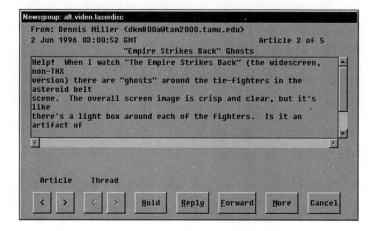

When you're reading an article, you can do the following:

- Read the next article by clicking the > button under Article.

- Read the previous article by clicking the < button under Article.

- Read the first article in the next thread by clicking the > button under Thread.

- Read the first article in the previous thread by clicking the < button under Thread.

- Mark this article to read on future access by clicking the Hold button.

- Reply to this article by clicking the Reply button.

- Forward this article to another user by clicking the Forward button.

- Perform additional operations by clicking the More button.

- Close this window by clicking the Cancel button.

In most cases, you either want to read another article or reply to this one. When you click the Reply button, the Reply to USENET Message window shown in Fig. 22.6 appears. Type your reply in the Message Contents area, make sure that Post to Newsgroup(s) is selected (not Send via E-mail), and then click Send. When you see the confirmation dialog box, click OK to send the message.

**Fig. 22.6**
Replying to a
newsgroup message.

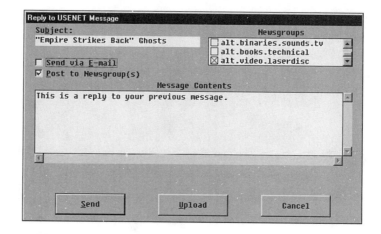

 **TIP**   You can also send messages via e-mail. Just select "Send via
E-mail" in both the Reply and Create USENET Message windows.

## Composing new articles

To post a message in a newsgroup you must first be a member of that group.
However, you don't have to be in a newsgroup to post an article. From the
main USENET menu, you can select Create an Article, and you'll see the
window shown in Fig. 22.7. Simply fill in the Subject box, enter the text of
your article, select the newsgroup(s) to which you want to post, make sure
that Post to Newsgroup(s) is selected, and click the Send button.

 **CAUTION**   You have to be a little more careful with this operation because
you won't get a confirmation dialog box. As soon as you click Send, the
message is on its way!

If you want to compose your newsgroup article as a text file while you're
offline (not connected to USENET), you can create it using a word processor
and save it as a text file with a .TXT extension. Then, in either the Reply or
the Create USENET Message window, click the Upload button. You're asked
for the name of the text file you want to upload. Enter the name of the file
and click OK. The contents of the text file are placed inside the Message
window, just as if you had typed the message there.

**Fig. 22.7**

Creating a new
newsgroup article.

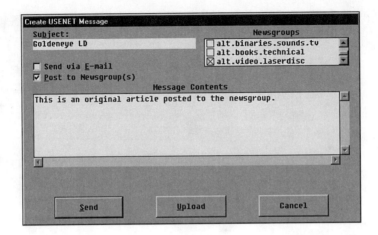

You can quote another article in a reply if you want. To do so, click Cancel to close the message window and return to the Browse window. Select the article to which you want to reply, make sure the Quoted option button is selected, and click the Retrieve button. The newsreader downloads that article to your hard disk as a text file. Then go back and reread that article, and click the Reply button. When the Reply window appears, click the Upload button, select the file you just downloaded, and click OK to load it into the Reply window. The text of the original article appears in the Reply window with angle brackets (>) setting off the quoted text.

## Q&A I'm tired of a newsgroup. How do I get rid of it?

To "get rid of" a newsgroup, you have to "unsubscribe." Go to the Access Newsgroups window and select the newsgroup you want to get rid of. Click the Remove button and confirm the removal, and the newsgroup is removed from your subscription list.

## I want to reread an article I read during my last session, but it doesn't appear in the Browse list. Where did it go?

Like messages in CompuServe forums, old articles are allowed to scroll off of USENET newsgroups. However, that's probably not the problem in this case. You see, unless you "hold" an article for future reading (by clicking the Hold button while you're reading the article), CompuServe marks the article as read. The next time you access the newsreader, CompuServe won't load articles you've already "read." Unfortunately, if this is the case, you're flat out of luck. Remember to use that Hold button next time around!

# 23

# Finding and Downloading Files on the Internet

● **In this chapter:**

- **What is FTP?**

- **Using CompuServe's FTP service**

- **Where are the best FTP sites?**

- **How does Gopher differ from FTP?**

- **Using Telnet to access remote computers**

*There are more files on the Internet than on CompuServe; use FTP and Gopher to find and download them!.* . . . . . . . . ➤

F TP isn't STP. (That's a gasoline additive.) FTP isn't FTD. (That's a flower delivery service.) FTP isn't even the FTC. (That's the Federal Trade Commission, and you don't want to mess with those government agencies!)

FTP is File Transfer Protocol, and File Transfer Protocol is just one of the many ways to download files from the Internet. This chapter will show you how to use FTP (as well as Gopher and Telnet) to find and download files.

# FTP: Your key to a treasure trove of Internet files

An FTP site is nothing more than a computer—similar in many ways to your personal computer—that's segmented into various directories and subdirectories. When you access the host computer, you have to navigate through the directories and subdirectories to find the file you want. After you find the file, you use FTP software to download the file to your personal computer.

Most FTP sites contain a large number of publicly accessible files. With FTP, it's a snap to go online and grab copies of these files for your own use.

# Using CompuServe's FTP service

It's easy to download a file with CompuServe's FTP service: just access the service (GO FTP), select a remote site from which to download, change to the right directory on the host computer, and select a file to download to your computer. It really isn't all that different from downloading a file from one of CompuServe's forum libraries.

CompuServe offers three different ways to use FTP:

- Choose from CompuServe's recommended sites
- Choose from a more comprehensive list of sites
- Enter the name of a specific site

Let's look at each of these three ways to use FTP.

**CAUTION** Internet FTP sites can be pretty popular and might have so much traffic that you can't access them during peak periods. If you have trouble accessing a site, try again a little bit later when it might be less busy.

# Choose from CompuServe's recommended sites

GO FTP, and you see CompuServe's main FTP screen, shown in Fig. 23.1. From there, click the Selected Popular Sites icon.

**Fig. 23.1**
CompuServe's main FTP screen.

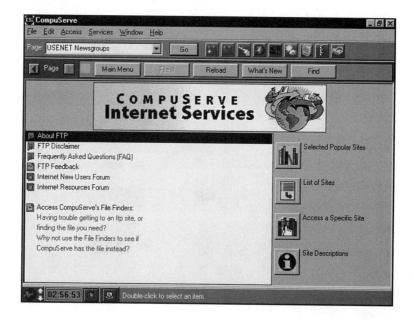

The next screen that appears displays a dozen buttons (see Fig. 23.2). Each of these buttons represents an FTP site. To access a site, all you have to do is click its button.

 **TIP** CompuServe changes the sites on this screen from time to time. If you see different buttons on your screen, it's because CompuServe decided to add more popular sites to this selection.

**Fig. 23.2**
Selected FTP sites.

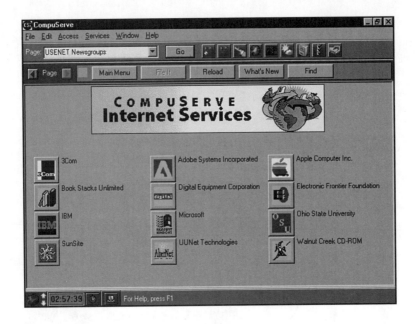

To try out FTP, select Microsoft's FTP site. You'll see the Access a Specific Site screen, shown in Fig. 23.3.

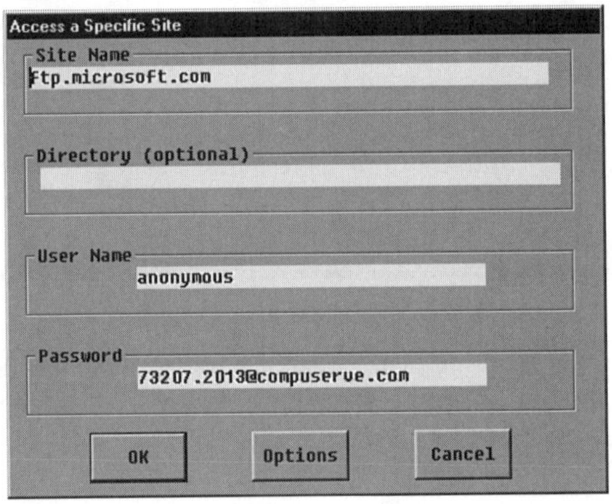

**Fig. 23.3**
Accessing an FTP site.

As you can see in the figure, this screen already contains all of the information for the site you selected (it's automatically filled in). Table 23.1 outlines the parts of this screen.

## Table 23.1  The parts of the Access a Specific Site screen

| Field | Description |
|---|---|
| Host Name | The name of the FTP site you access |
| Site Name | The FTP address for the site |
| Directory | The directory at the FTP site that holds the file for which you're looking. (Filling in this field is optional.) |
| User Name | Always filled in with "anonymous." On most sites you're not required to use your own name. (In fact, you probably can't access many sites with your own name; you must use "anonymous" instead.) |
| Password | Not a password per se, it's actually your CompuServe user ID in the form of an e-mail address (compuserve.id@compuserve.com) |

Because CompuServe fills in this information for you, all you have to do is click OK. CompuServe connects to the site and displays a message from the site. Click OK to close this screen and move to the FTP site.

**CAUTION**

**Read the site's opening message carefully! If the site is overloaded** with traffic, you'll see a message telling you that the site has reached its maximum number of connections. If this happens, try again later.

The next screen you see (Fig. 23.4) shows where you are on the host server. Don't be scared by this. Files on the host server are organized into directories just as files on your hard disk are. The left window lists all subdirectories in the current directory, and the right window lists all files in the current directory.

**TIP**

**When you access an FTP site, look for the "pub" directory. On** many sites, the publicly accessible files are stored in the pub directory.

All you have to do is double-click the directories in the left-hand window until you reach the subdirectory you want. You can move back a level by clicking the Back button; you can move all the way back to the root directory by clicking the Top button. Your current subdirectory is shown at the top of the window.

**Fig. 23.4**
The directories and files on an FTP site.

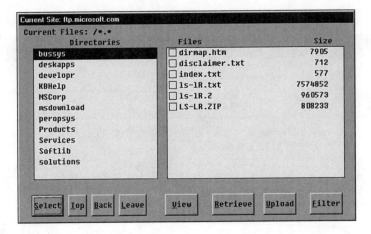

Once you're in the right subdirectory, select the file you want in the right-hand file list . You can then click either Yiew (if it's a text file that you want to read online) or Retrieve (if you want to download it to your PC).

**CAUTION** **Make sure you actually click the check box next to the file you want**; unless a check shows in the box, the file is not selected, and you can't download it or view it.

If you click Retrieve, you'll see the normal Windows Save As dialog box. Just select the directory to which you want to download, and then click Save. CompuServe automatically downloads the file to your hard disk and notifies you when the process is complete.

**TIP** **Many of the files you'll find on the Internet—as well as the files on** CompuServe's forums—are stored in a compressed format. See Chapter 9 for details on how to decompress compressed files.

# Choose from a comprehensive list of sites

That short list of preselected sites is nice, but what if you want to choose from a larger number of sites? All you have to do is go back to the main FTP screen (refer to Fig. 23.1) and click the List of Sites icon. CompuServe then displays a much longer list of FTP sites. Double-click one of the sites in the list, and the Access a Specific Site screen appears. Follow the instructions in the last section, and you're on your way!

# Go directly to a particular site

This option is for those who consider themselves to be FTP pros. This is because you have to know the address of the FTP site you want in order to use this option.

To go to a site for which you know the address, begin at the main FTP menu and click the Access a Specific Site icon. The Access a Specific Site screen appears, but this time it's blank except for the User Name line, which reads anonymous, and the Password line, which contains your Internet/CompuServe address.

 **TIP** **To find FTP and Gopher sites, use CompuServe's Web browser** to use the Archie search engine at Rutgers University (http://www-ns.rutgers.edu/htbin/archie).

Because CompuServe doesn't know where you're going, you're on your own with this screen. You need to fill in the Site Name field. You can (and should) leave the Directory field blank. When you have filled in everything, click OK to access the remote FTP server. From this point, it's the same as I described earlier: you search through the FTP site's subdirectories for the files you want.

# Exit FTP

When you finish downloading files, click the Leave button. You don't have to worry about "logging off" from the host computer; CompuServe does it automatically.

 **Q&A** *It takes a long time for CompuServe to connect to a remote site. Is there any way to speed this up?*

Remember that when you use FTP, you're accessing another computer that isn't part of the CompuServe network. It will probably take longer to log on to that computer than it does to perform normal operations in the CompuServe computer complex. There's really no way to speed this up; just be patient.

**Q&A**

### *It took so long to connect to a remote site that CompuServe "timed out" and disconnected. What can I do about this?*

If it takes too long to connect to the other site, CompuServe gets bored and "times out"—either logging off the FTP server, or disconnecting completely. The only thing you can do at that point is to reconnect with CompuServe and try it all over again.

### *I'm having trouble connecting to a site. I keep getting a* Site unresponsive *error message. What's happening?*

A site on the Internet is nothing more than a computer connected by some cable to the rest of the Internet. If too many users are trying to access that computer at any given time, it overloads and won't let any new users on until a current user logs off. When you get this error message, you can Retry the attempt, or you can Cancel and try again at a later time. I recommend you try Retry once. Then, if you still get the message, click Cancel and wait a few minutes before trying the whole thing again.

### *When I try to connect to a site, I get the error message* Connection Failed: Unable to connect to site, FTP_UNKNOWN_HOST. *What am I doing wrong?*

You're trying to access a site that doesn't exist. It's most likely that you've typed the site name incorrectly. Check your entry and then try accessing the site again. If you still get an error message, something has changed about the site itself: either the name is different, or the site has been disconnected from the Net.

### *When I try to download a file, I get the message* Download Failed. *What gives?*

This error message appears when something goes wrong with your download. Either you have too much line noise on your modem connection, the file itself is bad, or maybe the file is in the wrong format for your system. Try downloading again and see if that fixes your problem.

# Miller's recommended FTP sites

Of the thousands of FTP sites on the Internet, the following list names some of my favorites. You might want to check some of these out. Note, however, that they're all pretty popular; you might have some difficulty logging on to them during peak periods.

| Site | Description |
| --- | --- |
| ds.internic.net | InterNIC has collections of all important Internet documents and information. |
| ftp.cdrom.com | The Walnut Creek site has lots of files, which it distributes via CD-ROM. |
| ftp.cs.bham.ac.uk | University of Birmingham in the U.K. is the home of USENET newsgroup archives. |
| ftp.doc.ic.ac.uk | Imperial College in London offers lots of academic files, as well as games and utilities. |
| ftp.law.cornell.edu | Cornell University Law School is the home of many legal documents. |
| ftp.mcp.com | This is the FTP site of Macmillan Computer Publishing, parent of Que (this book's publisher). |
| ftp.microsoft.com | Microsoft's official FTP server offers a lot of official Microsoft utilities and information. |
| ftp.netscape.com | The FTP site of Netscape Communications is the place to find the latest version of the Netscape Navigator Web browser. |
| ftp.uu.net | UUNet is one of the largest Internet service providers, and the central distribution site for netnews traffic. |
| ftp.winsite.com | Winsite is a terrific site for Windows-related programs and utilities. It was formerly housed at the Center for Innovative Computer Applications at Indiana University. |
| oak.oakland.edu | This is a major mirror site that holds copies of software available at other Net sites. |
| rtfm.mit.edu | This site holds the archives of all the FAQ (frequently asked questions) lists. |
| sunsite.unc.edu | The University of North Carolina is a main site for academic information. |
| wiretap.spies.com | This site contains a rather eclectic collection of interesting documents. |
| wuarchive.wustl.edu | Washington University at St. Louis is one of the biggest FTP sites on the Net; it contains lots of archive files. |

# Digging for files with Gopher

Another tool for finding files on the Internet is a little easier to use than FTP. This tool, called Gopher, is becoming less popular as time goes by; many sites are abandoning their Gopher access in favor of access through the World Wide Web.

For those sites that still use Gopher, however, you don't have to know the directory and file name to find a particular file. All you have to do is connect to a specific site and then use Gopher to search all the files on that site in a very organized fashion.

While you can obtain separate Gopher software, it's just as easy to use CompuServe's built-in Web server to do your Gophering. To initiate a Gopher session, click the Browse the Internet button on CompuServe's toolbar, and then enter the Gopher address where you'd normally enter the Web URL. Note one important difference, though. Instead of entering the normal http: before the address, you enter **gopher:**. A typical Gopher address looks like this:

gopher://gopher.*address.domain*

Fig. 23.5 shows the Gopher menu at the University of Illinois at Urbana-Champaign (gopher.uiuc.edu).

**Fig. 23.5**
Gophering through
UIUC's site.

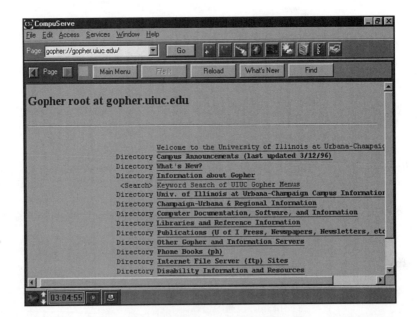

Each hyperlink on a Gopher menu represents a directory; click on any link to see the contents of that directory. When you find the file you want, click it. If it's a text file, it will be displayed on your screen; files of other types can be downloaded directly to your computer.

Gopher is easier to use than FTP; if a particular site has a Gopher service, use it.

# Connecting to host computers with Telnet

**Telnet** is kind of the lowest common denominator of the Internet. It's essentially a command-line interface to the Net that lets you communicate with computers that don't have graphical user interfaces, FTP, Gopher, or Web access.

Some activities require a command-line interface. For example, if you want to play a multi-user adventure game, such as a MUD or MOO, you have to enter a series of commands. Most MUDs and MOOs operate via Telnet.

To access CompuServe's Telnet service, GO TELNET. When the main Telnet menu appears, you can select from a List of Sites or you can Access a Specific Site. If you access a specific site, make sure you know its address and any passwords you need to access the host system.

As you can see in the figure, some Telnet sites offer a menu-driven interface. Others require manual input of command lines. In either case, it's pretty low-tech. Unfortunately, Telnet is still the only way to access some sites.

Accessing the NASA Spacelink Electronic Library via Telnet.

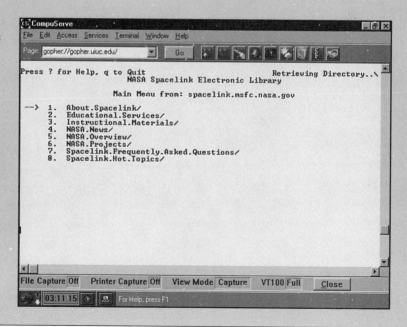

# Finding files on the Web

Of course, the absolute easiest way to find and download files is via the World Wide Web. The next chapter, "Wandering the World Wide Web," tells you all you need to know about the Web, so I won't go into details here. Suffice it to say that if a particular site offers the choice of FTP, Gopher, or Web access to its software libraries, you should choose the Web option.

# Wandering the World Wide Web

● **In this chapter:**

- **What is the World Wide Web?**

- **Use CompuServe's built-in Web browser to view Web pages**

- **What is a Web page?**

- **What can I find on the World Wide Web?**

- **Searching the Web**

- **Some good Web sites to visit**

*Due to its ability to hyperlink graphics, sound, and video from all over the world, the Web is the coolest place to be in cyberspace* . . . . . . . . . . . . . . . . . . . . . . . . . . . **>**

I f we think of CompuServe once again as an electronic version of a small town, we'll realize that like real small towns, it isn't alone in the world. Just as the main road in most small towns connects to a big interstate highway (which in turn connects to many other towns across the country), CompuServe is connected to the rest of the online world via the electronic highway called the Internet. And the biggest, brightest, and most exciting cities along the route of this online superhighway are part of what is called the **World Wide Web**.

# The World Wide Web—part of the Internet, but different

The World Wide Web, like USENET, is just a part of the thing we call the Internet. In particular, the Web is the part of the Net where hundreds of thousands of computer sites display sophisticated documents called **Web pages**. These pages—which actually resemble pages from a book or magazine—contain **hyperlinks** to other documents that let you jump to related information with the click of a mouse button.

Hyperlinking sounds like something technical, but it's really quite simple. It's the ability to click on a highlighted word or graphic and cross-reference a related document somewhere else on the Web. It's like electronically browsing an encyclopedia. For example, when I read an article in an encyclopedia, I usually stumble across a reference to a related article, which references another article. Before I know it, I have every volume of the encyclopedia open in front of me. It's the same way with hyperlinks on the Web: you can click to jump from document to related document, and pretty soon you'll have no idea where you started.

What's on the Web? Lots and lots and lots of things. You'll find Web sites run by corporations trying to sell you something, universities trying to educate you, and individual users just out to have fun. You can find Web pages devoted to TV shows, art galleries, magazines, scientific facts, and beer. (There are *several* "beer pages" on the Web.) Like the rest of the Net, the variety is seemingly endless.

# Browsing the Web from CompuServe

You view Web pages with a **Web browser**. A browser is a software program that lets you display Web pages on your computer. When your browser goes to a Web page, it downloads the contents of that page to your computer's hard disk. Depending on the size and complexity of the page, it can take from several seconds to several minutes to fully display the page.

Web browsers have only been around for a couple of years. The break-through browser was Mosaic, which was developed at the National Center for Supercomputing Applications (NCSA) at the University of Illinois. Today dozens of browsers are available, the two most popular being Netscape Navigator and Microsoft's Internet Explorer. These two browsers work pretty much the same way, and all browsers display Web pages well.

## CompuServe's built-in Web browser

CompuServe 3.0 has a built-in Web browser that is based on Microsoft's Internet Explorer browser, so anything Explorer can do, so can CompuServe.

When you click the Internet button on CompuServe's toolbar, the CompuServe display window automatically shifts to browser mode (see Fig. 24.1). The browser is also automatically activated whenever you enter a Web address (**URL**) in the GO box, or whenever you click a link to a Web resource anywhere in CompuServe. In short, you really don't have to do anything to use CompuServe's built-in Web browser because it does everything automatically for you!

### 66 *Plain English, please!*

URL is short for Uniform Resource Locator. A URL is the address that Web browsers use to locate a specific Web page. 99

**Fig. 24.1**
CompuServe's built-in
Web browser.

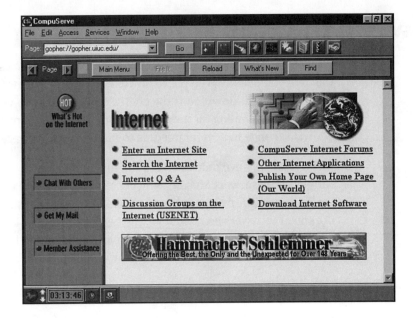

## Getting webbed!

When you click the Internet button on the toolbar, the first page you see is
CompuServe's **home page** shown in Fig. 24.1. From there, you can hyperlink
to any site listed on that page, or you can jump directly to a specific page.

 *Plain English, please!*

A **home page** is the opening screen of a Web site.

Jumping to a hyperlinked page is easy. Position your cursor over the blue
underlined text (your cursor will change to a hand with a pointing finger) and
click the left mouse button. To jump to a specific page for which there is not
a link, enter the page's URL in the Page text box at the top of the screen and
press Enter. Alternately, you can enter a URL in CompuServe's GO box.

 **TIP**   **Almost all URLs for Web pages start with http:// and contain a site**
address. The http (which stands for hypertext transfer protocol) tells the
browser that you're going to be reading a Web page as opposed to some
other type of document. As you learned in Chapter 23 "Finding and
Downloading Files on the Internet," you can also use the browser to access
Gopher (gopher://) documents.

It takes some time to actually go to a new page and have it display on your PC. The page appears in parts: text first and then graphics. Also, on many pages the graphics will be displayed in low resolution first and will then be "filled in" with higher resolution. If you think a page is taking too long to load, you can click the Stop button to halt the display where it is. If you want to restart the display, click the Reload button.

# Changing Web browsers

While CompuServe uses its built-in browser for many Web-related activities, you can choose to use another browser for other activities. For example, with the alternate browser option, you could use Netscape's browser (shown in this figure) instead of the built-in CompuServe browser.

The Netscape Navigator browser.

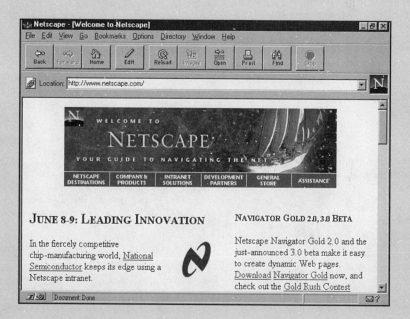

To change browsers, pull down the Access menu, select Preferences, and choose the General tab. Then select a new Internet browser and click OK.

Why would you want to use a different Web browser? Well, as fast as these browsers are being updated, a newer browser might have features that you need to use to access specific Web pages.

If you do choose to use a different browser, you'll find that it operates similarly to the CompuServe browser. All browsers do pretty much the same thing. However, some Web pages that use newer technologies might not display on older browsers.

You can move between previously displayed pages with the Back and Forward buttons. You can even mark the current page as a Favorite Place by clicking on the Add to Favorite Places button on CompuServe's toolbar.

# Reading a Web page

Information on the Web is displayed in pages. A Web page can contain some or all of these elements:

**Text:** The text can be in all sorts of fonts and sizes.

**Hyperlinks:** Live connections to related pages elsewhere on the Web.

**Graphics**: Large and small pictures, including live animations.

**Audio clips:** That's right—*sound* on the Web!

**Video clips:** Moving pictures, that is.

**Applets:** Built-in "mini programs" that run automatically when you access the page.

This figure shows a sample page from the Web. Each piece of underlined text is a separate hyperlink. When you position your cursor over one of these hyperlinks and click the mouse button, your screen changes to display the linked document.

Return to CompuServe's Main Menu (the Home Desktop).

The address (URL) of the current document

Stop the display of the current page or reload the page if it's already loaded.

Move back to the previous page viewed.

Move to the next page in line.

This is a hyperlink.

This is a graphic.

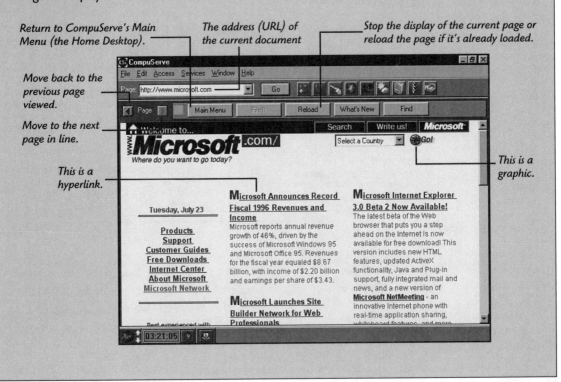

# Using the right mouse button

When you're using CompuServe's built-in browser, the right mouse button (not the traditional left button.) does some interesting things. Depending on where you position the cursor, clicking the right mouse button displays a context-sensitive pop-up menu. Options on these pop-up menus are often not available anywhere else in CompuServe—only by right-clicking the mouse can you do these things.

What can you do? Well, if you click the right mouse button while over an empty space on a Web page, you'll see the following options:

- **Save Wallpaper As**, which lets you save the background of the current page as a Windows wallpaper file on your hard disk.

- **Set As Wallpaper**, which automatically makes the background of the Web page the wallpaper for your Windows desktop.

- **Copy Background**, which copies the background of the Web page in the Windows clipboard; you can then paste the background into another Windows application.

- **Select All**, which selects all the text on the current Web page; you can then copy and paste the text into another Windows application.

- **View Source**, which displays the HTML source code for the current Web page (see Chapter 25 for more information on HTML).

- **Properties**, which displays the title, URL, size, and other properties of the current Web page.

Of course, if you position the cursor over other objects, you'll see different pop-up menus. For example, if you click the right mouse button while over a hypertext link, you have the option of jumping to the linked document (Open), or of viewing the Properties of the link. And if you click the right mouse button while over a graphic, you can save the picture to your hard disk, set the picture to be your Windows wallpaper, copy the picture to the Windows Clipboard, or view the properties of the graphic.

The lesson is, wherever you roam, click the right mouse button. You never know *what* will pop up!

## Downloading files from the Web

When you find a Web site with software libraries or archives (like the one in Fig. 24.2), it's easy to use CompuServe's browser to download files. Downloadable files should have their own hyperlinks; just click the hyperlink to initiate the download.

Before the file downloads, however, you'll see a Confirm File Open dialog box. *Don't* click the Open button (unless it's a text or graphics file you want to view on-screen); click the Save As button to save the selected file to your hard disk.

**Fig. 24.2**
One good place to download a file is Que's Software Library (http://www.mcp.com/ que/software/ index.html)

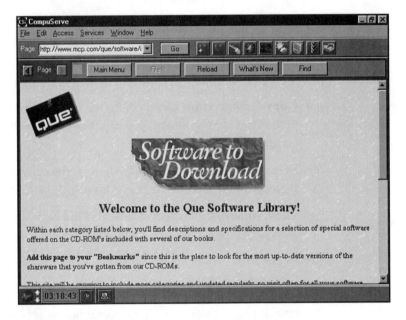

**TIP**  You can save any graphic on any Web page to your hard disk by positioning the cursor over the graphic, clicking the *right* mouse button, and selecting Save Picture As.

# Taking a quick tour of the Web

Okay, you now know a little bit about the Web and about CompuServe's Web browser, and you're itching to start browsing the Web. While the best way to learn about the Web is to begin clicking around yourself, I'll give you a quick tour of some representative sights to get you started.

**TIP**   **Web pages are in constant development. It's likely that any page** described in this book will have changed somewhat by the time you get there.

Let's start by going directly to a Web site by typing in the page's URL. Click the GO button and enter the following URL:

**http://www.paramount.com/**

The example URL takes you to the home page for Paramount, shown in Fig. 24.3.

**CAUTION**   **It's important that you type all URLs *exactly* as written especially** with regard to upper- and lowercase letters. URLs are notoriously case-sensitive.

**Fig. 24.3**
Paramount on the Web: click the graphics to enter specific site areas.

**TIP**   **Some pages display images that are hyperlinked to a number of** other pages. You know you're looking at one of these **image maps** when you pass your cursor over an image and the cursor changes into a pointing hand. Click the image to follow the hyperlink.

Now let's try using a search engine. Go to the following URL:

http://www.lycos.com

Lycos is one of the Web sites known as the "top five," so-called because they are the five search spots on Netscape's home page. (The other four are Excite, Infoseek, McKinley Magellan, and Yahoo!) As you can see in Fig. 24.4, you can go directly to various topic areas, or use the search box to search the Web for a specific topic. Let's try searching.

Enter **que** in the search box and click the Go Get It button. After a few moments, Lycos returns the results of the search (there will be several *thousand* documents). Okay, our search was too broad: it returned every word that had the letters "q-u-e" in sequence (like the words "question" and "clique"). To narrow the search, back up to the search page again and enter **que publishing** as the search term.

## CompuServe loads 'em faster!

As a Web page is loading, CompuServe displays the progress (that is, the percent of the page already loaded) in the bar at the bottom of the screen. While it sometimes seems to take forever to load a Web page (particularly ones with large graphics), CompuServe actually uses several different technologies to speed up the process.

First, CompuServe uses a "progressive display" of Web pages. That is, it loads the text first and graphics second, so you can read the page while the graphics are being loaded. It also displays the graphics in "progressive rendering," where low-resolution images are displayed first, followed by the more complex high-resolution images.

Second, CompuServe "caches" your most recent Web pages. That is, CompuServe actually stores the last few pages you visited on your hard disk.

So when you return to those pages, CompuServe reloads them from your hard disk (a much faster process than downloading from the Internet itself).

Finally, CompuServe keeps copies of the most popular Web pages on its own Web server. This way you can get access to these pages directly from CompuServe without having to go on the Web to get them. This speeds things up for you and helps to minimize Web traffic. CompuServe is a very conscientious Web citizen!

Note that because CompuServe caches the most popular Web pages on its own Web server, you may not be viewing the most up-to-date version of a page. If you think the page needs updating, click the Reload button; this loads the latest version of the page directly from the Web site.

**Fig. 24.4**
Searching the Web from Lycos.

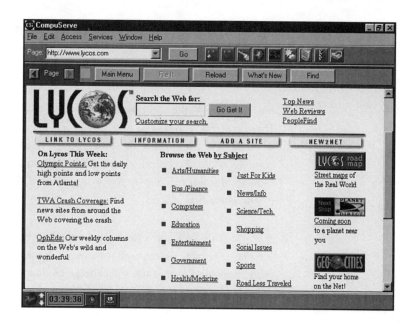

When you click the Go Get It button this time, the results are more manageable. You'll find several relevant references to Que (the publisher of this book), including the Que home page itself. The moral of this story? Try to define your search as narrowly as possible to return the most efficient results.

That should get you started on your Web cruising. To help you along, however, I've assembled a list of great "starter pages," which you can find at the end of this chapter. In addition, the "Que CompuServe Directory" at the end of this book includes lists of great Web sites intertwined with a list of CompuServe forums and services.

**Q&A** *Sometimes when I click on an audio or movie file, nothing happens. What am I doing wrong?*

CompuServe's Web browser is preconfigured to view many different types of graphics, sound, and movie files. However, as new file types become available, it's possible that the CompuServe browser won't be able to run some newer files. You'll have to wait for an updated version of the browser to view the new file types.

### Why is the Web browser slower at some times and on some sites?

Two things can slow down CompuServe's Web browser:

**1** Big, complex Web pages take longer to load than smaller, simpler pages. Therefore, if a Web page is very long or if it has a lot of graphic images, it will seem like your browser is slowing down. To speed up the display of complex pages, turn off the Load Images option at the top of the browser; this lets you display Web pages without the graphics that slow the downloading process.

**2** A World Wide Web site is just a computer. Too many people accessing the same site at the same time will overwork the site. Subsequently, all users connected at that site will experience slow downs. If this gets too annoying, try accessing that site at a different time of day.

### Why can't I access a certain Web page?

There are three main reasons why the Web browser won't connect to a Web page:

**1** You may have entered the wrong URL. URLs are notoriously particular and often quite complex. Make sure you entered the right combination of slashes and periods, and capitalized everything properly—URLs are case-sensitive. Also, don't assume that the all hyperlinks in all Web pages are correct; some hyperlinks are either old or just plain wrong.

**2** It's quite likely that the site containing that particular Web page is too busy. You see, a Web page is stored on a computer similar to your own PC. When that computer gets too much traffic, it slows down until it gets so busy it won't let anybody sign on unless one of the current users signs off. Some popular Web pages are just about impossible to access during busy times of the day.

**3** It's possible that the particular page has moved or closed down. The Web is constantly changing, which means pages frequently change or go away.

**Q&A  *Why aren't all the graphics on a page visible?***

As technology advances, some Web pages may use a newer version of HTML (the language used to create Web pages) that is not compatible with CompuServe's Web browser. Also, some types of graphics cannot be read by CompuServe's Web browser. In both cases, there's really nothing wrong with either the Web page or the Web browser; they're just not understanding each other's language. Sometimes, though, the graphics just don't load right; try clicking the Reload button to review the entire page from scratch.

# Tips for finding things on the Web

In addition to the tips listed in this chapter (and elsewhere in this book), let me give you some advice that will make it easier for you to find things on the Web.

**Use CompuServe's Home page.** This is a good resource for new developments on the Web and on the CompuServe service itself.

**Look for sites with their own lists of sites.** Many sites contain huge lists of other cool sites. Among these are:

- the GNN Best of the Net page (http://www.dec.com/gnn/wic/best.toc.html)

- The WWW Virtual Library (http://www.w3.org/hypertext/DataSources/bySubject/Overview.html)

- New Riders Official WWW Yellow Pages (http://www.mcp.com/nrp/wwwyp/)

- A complete list of FTP sites is maintained at the University of Illinois (http://hoohoo.ncsa.uiuc.edu:80/ftp-interface.html)

**Look for sites that contain good search engines.** There are lots of these sites. Among the best are:

Alta Vista (http://www.altavista.digital.com/)

Excite (http://www.excite.com/)

HotBot (http://www.hotbot.com/)

Infoseek (http://guide.infoseek.com/NS)

Lycos (http://www.lycos.com)

McKinley Magellan (http://www.mckinley.com/)

Yahoo (http://www.yahoo.com)

In addition to those search engines, these two sites let you search through other search engines:

c|net's search.com (http://www.search.com)

Macmillan's SuperSeek (http://www.superseek.com)

If you want to search through FTP and Gopher sites, you can use a search engine called Archie. One of the best Archie services is at Rutgers University (http://www-ns.rutgers.edu/htbin/archie).

**Think of the logical URL first.** If you're looking for a Web site for IBM, try http://www.ibm.com (www because it's a Web site, ibm because it's IBM, and com because it's a *commercial* site).

**Buy a book.** Lots of books list lots of sites. I can recommend a few from Que and its sister companies: *Que's MegaWeb Directory* (Que), *The Official New Riders' World Wide Web Yellow Pages* (New Riders), and *Lycos Most Popular Web Sites* (Lycos Press). You'll find thousands of listings in each book, all sorted by subject.

 **TIP** **I have several pages on the Web. Visit my personal Web page at http://www.mcp.com/people/miller/** or my CompuServe Web page at **http://ourworld.compuserve.com:80/homepages/miller01/**. I also have a special Web page for this *Using CompuServe* book: **http://www.mcp.com/people/miller/cis3top.htm**.

# Miller's list of the best Web starter pages

Table 24.1 lists Web pages that are great places to start cruising the Web. These pages all have one or more of the following attributes:

- Links to lots of other Web sites

- A great search engine to help you search the Web for the resources you want

- "Supersite" status—they have tons of information and lots of subsidiary sites within the main site

## Table 24.1 Miller's short list of Web starter pages

| Web Site and URL | Description |
|---|---|
| **Alta Vista**<br>http:// www.altavista.digital.com/ | Perhaps the best search engine on the Web; operated by Digital. |
| **Around the World in 80 Clicks**<br>http://www.coolsite.com/arworld.html | A "clickable map" of the world—click anywhere to see sites in that area. |
| **c\|net**<br>http://www.cnet.com/ | The most popular computer-related site on the Web (see Fig. 24.5). |
| **College and University Home Pages**<br>http://www.mit.edu:8001/people/cdemello/univ.html | Some of the best Web sites are at universities; use this list to cruise the academic Web. |
| **CompuServe**<br>http://www.compuserve.com/ | CompuServe's home on the Web. |
| **CUSI (Configurable Unified Search Index)**<br>http://www.eecs.nwu.edu/susi/cusi.html | A site that lets you search the Web in multiple ways. |
| **Electronic Newstand**<br>http://www.enews.com/ | Online magazines and newspapers. |
| **Excite**<br>http://www.excite.com/ | One of the "big five" search engines on the Web. |
| **HotBot**<br>http://www.hotbot.com/ | One of the newest search engines from HotWired. |
| **iGuide**<br>http://www.iguide.com/index.sml | Purported to be the "TV Guide" of the Web; a good starting point. |
| **InfoSeek**<br>http://guide.infoseek.com/NS | Another one of the "big five" search engines on the Web. |
| **Kalaidospace**<br>http://kspace.com/ | A supersite for art-related resources. |
| **Lycos**<br>http://www.lycos.com/ | One of the first search engines for the Web, and one of the "big five." |
| **Macmillan Information SuperLibrary**<br>http://www.mcp.com/ | Home of Que and other computer book publishers. |
| **McKinley Magellan**<br>http://www.mckinley.com/ | Yet another "big five" search engine. |

continues

## Table 24.1 Continued

| Web Site and URL | Description |
| --- | --- |
| **Metaverse**<br>http://www.metaverse.com/index.html | A supersite for music and counterculture resources. |
| **Microsoft**<br>http://www.microsoft.com/ | If you're using Windows, you should visit this site. |
| **Mr. Showbiz**<br>http://web3.starwave.com/showbiz/ | A supersite for entertainment-related resources. |
| **New Riders Official WWW Yellow Pages**<br>http://www.mcp.com/nrp/wwwyp/ | Part of the Macmillan Information SuperLibrary, one of the best lists of Web sites available. |
| **Newbie's Guides to the Net**<br>http://ug.cs.dal.ca:3400/franklin.html | Some great guides and lists of hot spots for new Net users. |
| **Newspapers on the Net**<br>http://www.infi.net/naa/ | A listing of online newspapers, from the Newspaper Association of America. |
| **Onramp Access**<br>http://onr.com/ | A great place for new users to start. |
| **Scout Report**<br>http://rs.internic.net/scout_report-index.html | A weekly list of newly announced Internet resources, assembled by InterNIC and the InfoScout. |
| **search.com**<br>http://www.search.com | A collection of almost all of the search engines on the Web, from c\|net. |
| **shareware.com**<br>http://www.shareware.com | The biggest collection of shareware and freeware on the Web, from c\|net. |
| **Starting Point**<br>http://www.stpt.com/ | Just what it says—a great starting point for Web exploration, with lists of sites arranged by categories. |
| **SuperSeek**<br>http://www.superseek.com | A search engine that searches other search engines, from Macmillan (see Fig. 24.6). |
| **Time Warner Pathfinder**<br>http://www.pathfinder.com/ | A terrific site, containing all sorts of Time Warner magazines (*TIME, Life, Entertainment Weekly, People, Money, Sports Illustrated, Vibe, Fortune,* etc.), Time Warner books, Warner Bros. movies, HBO, and lots of other stuff. One of the best sites on the Web. Highly recommended. |
| **TradeWinds Galaxy**<br>http://www.einet.net/ | A great supersite, with superb search tools. |

| Web Site and URL | Description |
| --- | --- |
| **URouLette**<br>http://kuhttp.cc.ukans.edu/cwis/organizations/<br>kucia/uroulette/uroulette.html | Click this site to get sent to a random site somewhere on the Web. |
| **Useless WWW Pages**<br>http://www.primus.com/staff/paulp/useless.html | The worst of the Web. |
| **WebCrawler**<br>http://webcrawler.com | A nice search engine operated by a competitor of CompuServe's, America Online. Recommended. |
| **Yahoo!**<br>http://www.yahoo.com/ | The most popular of the "big five" search engines. |
| **Yahoo! Image Surfer**<br>http://isurf.yahoo.com/ | Yahoo's index of graphics on the Web. |
| **Yahooligans!**<br>http://www.yahooligans.com/ | Yahoo! for kids. Lots of kid-friendly sites. |

**Fig. 24.5**
c|net central on the Web.

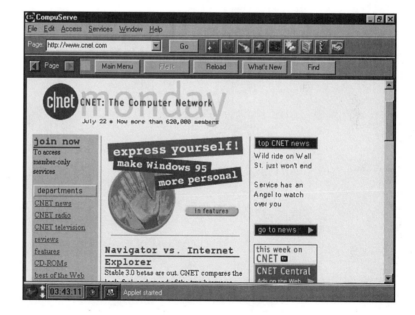

**Fig. 24.6**
Macmillan's SuperSeek
search engine.

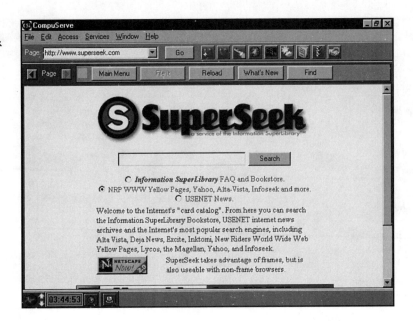

# 25

# Creating Your Own Web Pages

## In this chapter:

- **What is HTML?**

- **Downloading and installing Home Page Wizard**

- **Creating your first home page**

- **Publishing your home page with Publishing Wizard**

- **Creating more sophisticated home pages**

- **Where to find more information on HTML**

*If browsing the Web isn't enough, learn how to publish your own Web pages* . . . . . . . . . . . . . . . . . . . . . . . . . . . ⊳

**W**hen you view a Web page with CompuServe's built-in Web browser, you see the finished product, complete with graphics and hyperlinks. It looks pretty slick, if it's done right.

But what went into creating that Web page? What makes it look so good? What is the foundation behind the looks? And, more importantly, how do you create your own Web pages? Read on, and you'll find out!

# What a Web page is made of

A Web page is kind of like a word processing document with some special additions. These additions are **codes** that tell your Web browser how to display different types of text and graphics. The codes are embedded in the document, so you can't see them; they're only visible to your Web browser.

The codes used to create Web pages are part of what is called **HTML** (Hypertext Markup Language). This is the special "programming" language read by all Web browsers. Documents created with HTML can have all the fancy Web features: different font sizes, hyperlinks to other Web pages, even graphics, sound, video, and embedded applets.

If you were to see the codes revealed on a Web page, they'd look like words and letters enclosed within angle brackets, surrounding your visible text. Fig. 25.1 shows some of the code behind a sample Web page; anything inside angle brackets represents HTML code.

**Fig. 25.1**
A sample of HTML code; all the codes are within <angle brackets>.

```
<HTML>
<HEAD>
<TITLE>Using CompuServe — Home Page Wizard</TITLE>
</HEAD>
<BODY BACKGROUND="csback.gif">
<CENTER><IMG ALIGN=bottom SRC="cserve.gif" ALT="Using
CompuServe"><P>
<H1><B>CompuServe's Home Page Wizard</B><BR>
<I>New Information—<U>Not</U> in the Printed Book</I></H1>
</CENTER>
<P>
```

It's actually simpler than it looks. For example, the code <H1> is used to turn specified type into a level-one headline; the code </H1> turns off the headline type. And the code <I> is used to italicize text; </I> turns off the italics.

To create a Web page, then, you'd usually have to learn what codes result in what effects. In short, you'd need to learn how to code in HTML—sounds terribly complicated, doesn't it?

# What is Home Page Wizard?

Fortunately, CompuServe has a program that simplifies the creation of Web pages with no HTML coding required! All you have to do is enter some basic information and this program will automatically translate your document into HTML code. It then places your personal page out on the Web (via CompuServe's Web site).

The name of this program is Home Page Wizard, or HPW for short. HPW is a Windows program that lets you do the following:

- Create one or more Web pages

- Link multiple Web pages together into a single project

- Design complex Web pages that can include body text, hypertext links, header text, graphic images, and horizontal lines

- Insert background colors or images

- Size graphic images and change their proportions

- Create e-mail links

- Preview your pages before you put them on the Web

 **TIP** **Publishing Wizard is a companion program to Home Page Wizard** (which is bundled with Home Page Wizard when you download it from CompuServe). It also enables you to place your newly created home pages on the World Wide Web. Web pages created with HPW are placed on CompuServe's Web site (http://ourworld.compuserve.com).

Before you get too excited about Home Page Wizard, note that the program has some limitations. Its primary shortcoming is that it simply doesn't do complex Web pages very well. Some would say that in Home Page Wizard's quest for simplification, it oversimplifies. If you want to create complex effects (or even some modest ones), you'll have to turn elsewhere. (For example, if you want to have colored table backgrounds, or add Java applets, or insert "reply to" forms, HPW falls short.)

The next sections in this chapter cover HPW and Publishing Wizard. Later on, I'll show you how to make more sophisticated pages with separate HTML editor programs.

# Downloading and installing Home Page Wizard

Home Page Wizard is available for free from CompuServe. GO HPWIZ and click the Download the Home Page Wizard button. Then follow these steps to download and install Home Page Wizard:

**1** Select Download Home Page Wizard - HPWIZ.EXE (1.0MB), and then click the Retrieve button.

**2** When the Save As dialog box appears, elect to save the file as **C:\CSERVE\DOWNLOAD\HPWIZ.EXE**. Click Save to proceed.

**3** After the download, run the program HPWIZ.EXE. (In Windows 95, click the Start button and select Run; in Windows 3.1, choose File, Run.)

**4** As this program runs it will automatically decompress the files and execute the Setup program. You will then be asked several questions; answer them to the best of your ability or accept the default answers (by clicking OK).

**5** After the Setup program is done, you have the option to read the README.TXT file. Do so, and you will see a special text file with last-minute instructions for using Home Page Wizard.

**6** When you are asked whether to start the Home Page Wizard, select yes to start the program. (Alternatively, you can select no if you want to finish Setup for now and start Home Page Wizard at a later date.)

**TIP** **You can also GO HPWIZ to access support information as well as** access a service that converts your photos into graphics files you can use on your home pages!

After you've installed and initially launched Home Page Wizard, you should pull down the Options menu and address these three options:

- *Fonts*. This lets you select which fonts you see when you edit your pages.

- *Select*. Web Browser. This option lets you select which browser is used to preview your home pages.

- *Allow*. Extended HTML Features. When checked, this lets you use advanced features such as color backgrounds and background images on your Web pages. (I recommend that you check this option.)

# Creating your first home page—automatically

Home Page Wizard uses a series of "wizards" to lead you through the creation of your first Web page. When you launch HPW for the first time, these wizards are launched automatically. In addition, these wizards appear whenever you pull down the File menu and select New Project. Follow these steps to create your first home page:

**1** The first wizard asks you for some basic starter information. Assign a Title for this page, as well as a name for this Project. Click the Next button to proceed.

**2** The next wizard asks you for Personal Information. Fill in the blanks for your First Name, Middle Initial (MI), Last Name, City, State, Country, Occupation, Hobbies (you can list multiple hobbies in a list, separated by commas), and your e-mail address (either your CompuServe Internet address—in the form 12345.1234@compuserve.com—or a separate Internet address, if you have one). If you want to use this information on your Web page, check the Use Personal Information in Home Page box. Click the Next button to proceed.

**CAUTION** **Remember that any personal information you enter goes out on** the Web for millions of people to read. Don't put anything on your Web page that you *don't* want to share with the world.

**3** Next, you can select a template for your home page, as shown in Fig. 25.2. If you don't select a template, you have to arrange all the elements manually. If you do select a template, HPW does the arranging for you. You can choose from three basic templates, each of which is shown in thumbnail: Career, Fun, and Nature. Click the Finish button when you're done.

**Fig. 25.2**
Selecting a template
for your home page.

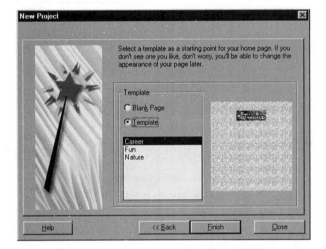

The resulting page appears on the main HPW screen. As you can see in Fig. 25.3, all HPW did was take your basic personal information and shovel it into the template. It's kind of boring, but it *is* a home page!

**TIP** **If you have created multiple pages in this project, they are listed** in the pane on the left. The current page *is* always shown in the pane on the right.

Fortunately, HPW lets you spice up your page with additional elements. The buttons along the top of the Home Page Wizard screen all work in basically the same way: you click the button and drag it to where you want to add the corresponding element. Table 25.1 lists the elements you have to choose from and gives a description of each element's function.

**Fig. 25.3**
Your first home page.

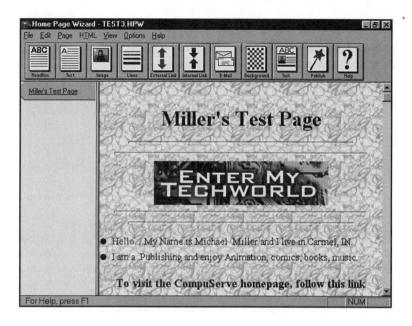

## Table 25.1   HPW's design tools

| Icon | Function | How It Works |
|------|----------|--------------|
| ABC Headline | Adds a headline | You'll be prompted for the headline text, as well as the style for the headline. (Note that you can select multiple levels of headline, with Headline 1 being the largest; you can also elect to center the headline on the page.) |
| A Text | Adds a block of text | You'll be prompted for the text itself, as well as the style for the text (centered, pre-formatted, or bulleted). |
| Image | Adds a graphic image | You'll be prompted to give the name of the image file (click the Browse button to locate files on your computer), Alternate Text for the image (to be displayed in case the image itself can't be displayed), the Size of the image, and the image Style (centered or not). |
| Lines | Adds a horizontal line | You'll be prompted for the length (as a percentage of total page width), height, and alignment (left, center, or right) of the line. |
| External Link | Adds an external hyperlink | You'll be prompted for text to be linked, the URL to be linked to, and the style of the link (centered on page or bulleted). |

continues

## Table 25.1 Continued

| Icon | Function | How It Works |
|------|----------|--------------|
| ![Internal Link icon] | Adds an *internal* hyperlink (to another page in your project) | You'll be prompted to give the linking text, the name of the page to be linked to, and the style of the link (centered on page or bulleted). If you haven't yet created the page to be linked to, click on the Add New Page button. |
| ![E-Mail icon] | Adds an e-mail link | You'll be prompted for the text of the link, the e-mail address to be linked to, and the style of the link (centered on page or bulleted). |
| ![Background icon] | Changes the background of your page | Click on the Background button. You'll be prompted as to whether you want the Default background, a custom Color background (click the Select button to see the available colors), or an Image to be used as background. (Image files to be used as backgrounds must be stored in the same directory as Home Page Wizard.) |

You can also delete elements from your page. Just click on the element you want to delete, and then click your right mouse button. When the pop-up menu appears, select Delete.

When you're finished (or even in the middle of the project), you can test your page with a browser. Just click on the Test button; you can select and launch a browser to display your home page.

 **TIP** **You must first select a Web browser by clicking on the Options** menu and selecting Select Web Browser, then entering the filename of your browser.

Once you're done with your home page, you can add additional pages to your project. That is, you can create a multiple-page Web site. To do so, click the Page menu and select Add Page to create additional pages.

All-in-all, these pages are still a little rudimentary. If you want to do something a little fancier, read ahead to the "Creating more sophisticated Web pages" section of this chapter.

# Publishing your first home page on the Web

After you create your Web pages, you need to post them to the Web. You do this with HPW's sister program, Publishing Wizard, which was installed the same time you installed HPW. To publish the Web pages in your current project, follow these steps:

**1** With your current project open in HPW, click the Publish button. You'll be presented with a series of "wizards" to help you put your pages on the Web.

**2** When the Welcoming wizard appears, click the Next button.

**3** When the Selection wizard appears, select Upload Files and click the Next button. (If you want to delete files already published, select the Delete All Files option.)

**4** When the Personal Information wizard appears, complete all relevant information and click the Next button.

**5** When the Directory Information wizard appears, complete all relevant information and click the Next button (see Fig. 25.4).

**Fig. 25.4**
Telling Publishing Wizard your personal interests.

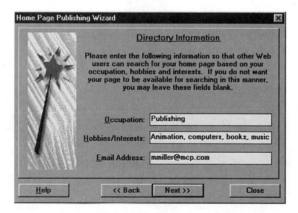

**6** When the Account Information wizard appears, enter your CompuServe User ID and Password, and then click the Next button.

**7** When the It's Time to Publish! wizard appears, click the Next button.

Publishing Wizard connects to CompuServe and places your pages on
CompuServe's Web server.

**CAUTION**    **During this process, you will be assigned a URL for each of your
pages; make sure you write these URLs down!**

# Browsing Web pages of other CompuServe members

Your personal pages are placed on CompuServe's Our World Web site. You
can access Our World at http://ourworld.compuserve.com.

When you visit Our World's home page (shown in Fig. 25.5), click the Search
hyperlink to search for pages from other members. You can then search Our
World either by Query Form or from a unique World Map.

**Fig. 25.5**
CompuServe's Our
World home page.

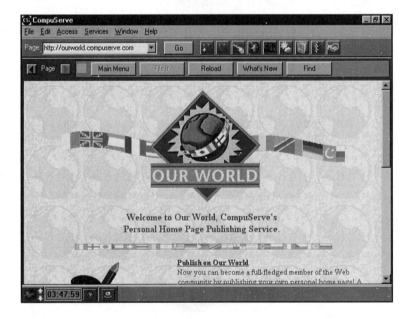

If you choose to search via Query Form, you can search by one or more of
the following criteria: First Name, Last Name, City, State, Country, Occupation, or Hobbies. For example, you could search for everyone named Smith

who lives in Illinois and has coin collecting as a hobby. When you click the Search button, CompuServe searches its personal Web pages and returns a list of those pages that match your criteria.

Searching via the World Map is a little different. You're essentially presented with the world map shown in Fig. 25.6. You click the region you want, and a more detailed map for that region appears.

**Fig. 25.6**
Searching Our World's World Map.

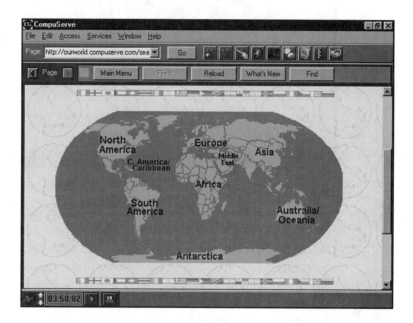

You keep clicking (and getting more localized maps) until you get to the state level. Then you'll receive a list of all personal pages created by members in the selected state. You can search for a specific member by positioning the cursor on an empty part of the page, clicking the *right* mouse button, and selecting the Find command from the resulting pop-up menu to search for names on the current page. When you find a page you want to view, you click on its link. It's as simple as that!

By the way, if you go to the Indiana page and search for Miller, you'll find my personal CompuServe page, shown in Fig. 25.7.

**Fig. 25.7**
The author's personal CompuServe home page (http://ourworld.compuserve.com:80/homepages/miller01/).

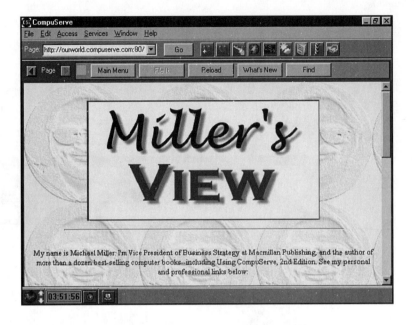

# Creating more sophisticated Web pages

If you want to create more sophisticated Web pages, you need to use an external HTML Editor. This is a software program that lets you create the HTML code behind Web pages. You can use a third-party HTML editor, and then use Publishing Wizard to place them on CompuServe's Web server. (For more information, see "Choosing an HTML editor" later in this chapter.)

## HTML basics

Before we talk about HTML Editors, you need to know a little bit about HTML itself. I can't teach you all there is to know about HTML in this space, but I can show you some HTML basics.

First, HTML is nothing more than text surrounded by codes. Each code turns on or off a particular attribute, such as boldface or italic text. All codes are in sets of "on/off" pairs; you turn "on" the code before the text you want to affect, and then turn "off" the code after the text.

One more thing about codes: they're all enclosed in angle brackets <like this>. An "off" code is merely the "on" code with a slash before it </like this>.

Let's look at some common HTML codes:

`<B>`**boldfaces text**`</B>`

`<I>`*italicizes text*`</I>`

`<U>`<u>underlines text</u>`</U>`

`<PRE>`displays text as "preformatted" for when you want to preserve line breaks and such`</PRE>`

`<TITLE>`formats text as the title for your page`</TITLE>`

`<H1>`formats text as a level-one heading`</H1>`

`<H2>`formats text as a level-two heading`</H2>`

`<H3>`formats text as a level-three heading`</H3>`

There are other codes that insert items into your page. These codes don't have "on/off" pairs; they're freestanding. These types of codes include:

`<P>` inserts a paragraph break

`<BR>` inserts a line break

`<HR>` inserts a horizontal rule

If you want to insert a graphic in your page, you need to know the address of that graphic (normally in the form of a Web page URL). You then use the following code, replacing "URL" with the true URL:

`<IMG  SCR="URL">`

Note that the location is enclosed in quotation marks. There is no "off" code for inserted graphics.

Finally, if you want to include a hyperlink to another Web page, you have to add the following codes before the linked text, replacing "URL" with the true URL:

`<A  HREF="URL">`

Then you have to turn "off" this link by using the following tag after the linked text:

`</A>`

Note that the URL is enclosed in quotation marks. Here's what a representative hyperlink code looks like:

```
<A HREF="http://www.mcp.com/people/miller/cis3top.htm">This links
to the Using CompuServe Page</A>
```

In addition to these codes, you need to start your document with an <HTML> code (to tell a Web browser that it will be reading an HTML document) and end it with an </HTML> "off" code. You also need to place a <BODY> code at the start of your page and a </BODY> "off" code at the end of your page.

These are only the basic HTML codes. There are also codes that designate the color and size of selected text, specify the background color or background graphic for a page, and even insert blinking and scrolling text. In addition, you can use external languages such as CGI, PERL, and Java to add deluxe features and applets to your pages. These techniques are beyond the scope of this chapter, however; you'll need a good book (like one from Que!) to learn these advanced techniques.

## Choosing an HTML editor

There are many different HTML editors to choose from. Some are commercial products (sold at your local software store); others are freeware or shareware products.

One of the best commercial products I've found is Microsoft's FrontPage. As you can see in Fig. 25.8, FrontPage is full of features (like many Microsoft products), and it hides the HTML code as you work in a "what you see is what you get" (WYSIWYG) mode. You can find more information about FrontPage at Microsoft's Web site (http://198.105.232.5/msoffice/frontpage/).

In terms of shareware/freeware programs, here are a few that I've used and can recommend:

- HotDog (download via FTP at ftp.mcp.com/pub/que/inetapps/html/hotdog/hstd13b1.exe)

- HTML Assistant (download via FTP at ftp.mcp.com/pub/que/inetapps/html/htmlasst/htmlasst.exe)

- HTML Easy! Pro (download via FTP at ftp.mcp.com/pub/que/inetapps/html/htmleasy/htmleasy.zip)

- HoTMetaL (download via FTP at ftp.mcp.com/pub/que/inetapps/html/softquad/hmfree2.exe)

- WebEdit (download via FTP at ftp.mcp.com/pub/que/inetapps/html/webedit/we14b2.zip)

- WebWizard (download via FTP at ftp.mcp.com/pub/que/inetapps/html/webwiza/webwiza.zip)

**Fig. 25.8**
Microsoft's FrontPage HTML editor.

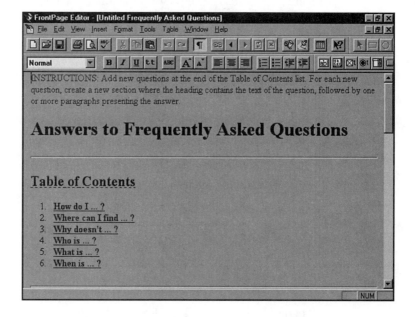

Any of these editors will do a good job for you. Some force you to edit raw HTML code, others insert the code automatically from pull-down menus, and others operate in pure WYSIWYG mode and keep the code hidden. Because each has its own way of doing things, you should check them all out to determine which one best meets your needs.

**TIP** **You can find these and other shareware/freeware HTML editors** listed in the Internet section of Que's Software Library (http://www.mcp.com/que/software/isoftwre.html).

# Publishing your new pages

Even though you've created your Web pages in a separate HTML editor, you still have to publish them. To do this, you have to launch Publishing Wizard separately; that is, you have to launch it from its icon in Windows, not from within Home Page Wizard.

As before, you'll see a series of "wizards" that will guide you through the publishing process. The steps for publishing independently created pages differ from those for the HPW-created variety. Follow these steps:

**1** When the Welcoming wizard appears, click the Next button to proceed.

**2** When the Selection Wizard appears, select Upload Files and click the Next button to proceed.

**3** When the Personal Information wizard appears, complete all relevant information and click the Next button to proceed.

**4** When the Directory Information wizard appears, complete all relevant information and click the Next button to proceed.

**5** When the File Upload Wizard appears, click the Next button to proceed.

**6** The next window is where you select which files to upload. Establish the directory the files are in via the top right pane; select the files themselves in the top left pane; then, with the files selected, click the Add button to add the files to your upload list (shown in the bottom pane). When all files have been added to the upload list, click the Next button to proceed.

**7** When the Home Page Selection wizard appears, select the file you want to be your "home" page. Click the Next button to proceed.

**8** When the Account Information wizard appears, enter your CompuServe User ID and Password, and then click the Next button to proceed.

**9** When the It's Time to Publish wizard appears, click the Next button.

Publishing Wizard connects to CompuServe and places your pages on CompuServe's Web server. Don't forget to write down the URLs for your new pages!

# HTML resources

If you're interested in learning more about HTML, there are lots of places to turn. You can find a lot of online help , right on the Web itself!

- Beginner's Guide to URLs (http://www.ncsa.uiuc.edu/demoweb/url-primer.html) is a guide to Web addresses from the folks at NCSA—where the first Web browser was created.

- Color Specifier (http://www.users.interport.net/~giant/COLOR/hype_color.html) lists all the codes you need to specify background colors for your Web page.

- Composing Good HTML (http://www.cs.cmu.edu/~tilt/cgh/) offers a solid guide to HTML from a graduate student at Carnegie Mellon University.

- Crash Course on Writing Documents for the Web (http://www.ziff.com/~eamonn/crash_course.html) is a good guide to Web page creation from the folks at PC Week Labs.

- Dos and Don'ts of Web Style (http://millkern.com/do-dont.html) provides some handy pointers for novice Web page designers.

- Elements of HTML Style (http://bookweb.cwis.uci.edu:8042/Staff/StyleGuide.html) is a takeoff of Strunk and White's *Elements of Style*, applied to Web pages.

- How Do They Do That with HTML? (http://www.nashville.net/~carl/htmlguide/index.html) offers some of the more unusual tricks used in Web page creation.

- HTML Documentation (http://www.utoronto.ca/webdocs/HTMLdocs/NewHTML/htmlindex.html) is one of the best online HTML resources I've found.

- Macmillan's HTML Workshop (http://www.mcp.com/general/workshop/) is a solid guide to online HTML resources from the folks who publish Que books.

- Special Characters in HTML (http://www.utoronto.ca/webdocs/HTMLdocs/NewHTML/entities.html) lists all the non-standard characters you can use in your Web documents.

- WebMaster Reference Library (http://www.webreference.com/) is a comprehensive information source for experienced Web page developers and administrators.

If this isn't enough, I can recommend a few good books on the subject: Que's *Special Edition Using HTML* and *HTML Visual Quick Reference* and Sams.net's *Teach Yourself Web Publishing with HTML*. Both of these are fine books that lead you from Web page basics to advanced HTML coding. (Que also has some fine books on CGI, PERL, and Java, if you want to get into the really heavy stuff.)

# Que CompuServe Directory

This directory represents a comprehensive listing of CompuServe services, along with the best of the Internet. If the entry represents a CompuServe service, the GO command is listed. If an entry represents an FTP site on the Internet, the address is preceded by the word "FTP." If the entry represents a site on the World Wide Web, the URL is preceded by the word "WEB."

Note, however, that keeping up with services on CompuServe and the Internet is a constant challenge. Every day new services and sites are added, and old ones are changed or shut down. For that reason, I can unfortunately make no claims to the accuracy or currency of these entries.

Also note that some services and sites can be classified several different ways. So you'll find some duplication of entries under different subjects. The directory contains the subject-related categories listed below.

# Accounting

**Accounting Vendor Forum**   Includes sections for major accounting programs.

> GO ACCOUNT

**ACIUS Forum**   Vendor forum.

> GO ACIUS

**DataEase International Forum**   Vendor forum.

> GO DATAEASE

**Intuit Forum**   Vendor forum for users of Quicken and QuickBooks.

> GO INTUIT

**Quicken Home Page**   Financial advice and support from Intuit, the publisher of Quicken.

> WEB http://www.intuit.com/
> quicken/

**TIMESLIPS Forum**   Vendor forum.

> GO TIMESLIPS

# Advertising

**Classified Ads**   Read or place classified advertisements.

> GO CLASSIFIEDS

# African-American Culture

### African-American Art and Culture Forum   Includes sections on art and cultural issues.

GO AFRO

### African-American Resources   Database and related areas with information on all aspects of African-American culture.

GO IRA

# Agriculture

### Agriculture Forum   For farmers and agriculturists.

GO AGFORUM

### Rural Living Forum   Issues unique to rural residents.

GO RURAL

# Airlines

### Air Canada Forum   Flight information and discussions.

GO AIRCANADA

### Air France   Information on Air France flights.

GO AF

### Air Line Pilots Association   Official service.

GO ALPA

### Air Travel Manager   Vendor forum for AirTM travel software.

GO AIRTM

### Air Traveler's Handbook   Basic info and links to other air travel resources on the Web.

WEB http://www.cs.cmu.edu/afs/
cs.cmu.edu/user/mkant/Public/
Travel/airfare.html

### Airlines of the Web   Links to all major U.S. and international airlines.

WEB http://haas.berkeley.edu/
~seidel/airline.html

### EAASY SABRE   American Airlines' travel reservation system.

GO SABRE

### Internet Travel Network   Online airline reservations.

WEB http://www.itn.net/

### Jeppesen's Aviation Weather Graphics   Radar, Lifted Index, and Convective Outlook charts; more than 60 different maps in all.

GO JEPP

### Official Airline Guide   Flight information.

GO OAG

### Travelocity   First-class site (run by the same folks who run EAASY SABRE) that lets you make airline, hotel, and auto rental reservations.

WEB http://www.travelocity.com/

**United Connection**   Online reservations system managed by United Airlines.

    GO UNITED

**WORLDSPAN Travelshopper**   Online reservations from Delta, Northwest, and TWA airlines.

    GO WORLDCIM

# Animals & Pets

**Acme Pet**   Comprehensive guide to pets on the Internet.

    WEB http://www.acmepet.com/

**Animal Forum**   Includes sections on ferrets, potbellied pigs, reptiles, parrots, wildlife, small mammals, insects, etc.

    GO ANIMALS

**Aquaria/Fish Forum**   Includes sections on freshwater and saltwater fish.

    GO FISHNET

**Cats Forum**   For cat lovers everywhere.

    GO CATS

**CyberPet**   Another good guide to pet resources on the Web.

    WEB http://www.cyberpet.com/
    cgibin/var/cyberpet/index1.htm

**Dogs Forum**   For dog fanciers.

    GO DOGS

**Fish Information Service (FINS)**   Fish on the Net.

    WEB http://www.actwin.com/fish/
    index.html

**Horses Forum**   For equestrians and horse lovers.

    GO HORSES

**Howell Book House**   The leading pet book publisher's home on the Web.

    WEB http://www.mcp.com//mgr/
    howell/

**Jack Hanna's Animal Adventures**   Animal fun from the TV show.

    GO JUNGLEJACK

**Pet Products/Reference Forum**   Customer support for pet products and services.

    GO PETPRO

**Pets News Clips**   News from the animal world.

    GO PETSNEWS

**PetsForum Group**   CompuServe's main area for pets and animals.

    GO PETSFORUM

**Time-Warner Dogs & Cats Forum** Includes sections on care, feeding, safety, training, etc.

    GO TWPETS

**Vet Care Forum**   Veterinary care issues.

    GO PETSVET

**ZooNet**   Guide to zoos on the Net.

    WEB http://www.mindspring.com/
    ~zoonet/zoonet.html

# Architecture

**Architecture Forum**   Includes sections on education, materials, design, CADD, project delivery, and so on.

    GO ARCH

# Art

**African-American Art and Culture Forum**   Includes sections on art and cultural issues.

    GO AFRO

**Ansel Adams Home Page**   Web base for the legendary photographer.

    WEB http://
    bookweb.cwis.uci.edu:8042/
    AdamsHome.html

**Artist Forum**   For artists and enthusiasts.

    GO ARTIST

**Fine Arts Forum**   Focuses on professional and classical art.

    GO FINEARTS

**Kalaidospace**   Supersite for art-related resources.

    WEB http://kspace.com/

**Metropolitan Museum of Art**   Online retailer.

    GO MMA

**Smithsonian**   Online version of the world's greatest museum.

    WEB http://www.si.edu/

**WebMuseum**   Interesting Web-based museum, based in France.

    WEB http://mistral.enst.fr/

# Australia

**Australian Associated Press Online**   Australian news.

    GO AAPONLINE

**Australian/New Zealand Research Centre**   Database of Australian information.

    GO ANZCOLIB

**Pacific Forum**   For residents and tourists.

    GO PACFORUM

**Pacific Vendor Forum**   Australian vendor support.

    GO PACVEN

# Automobiles

**American Racing Scene**   Top-notch Web site devoted to motor sports.

    WEB http://www.racecar.com/

**Automobile Forum**   Includes sections on auto industry news, insurance, safety, etc.

    GO CARS

**Automobile Magazine**   Online magazine.

    GO AUTOLIVE

**Automotive Information**   Main menu to CompuServe's auto-related services and information.

    GO AUTO

**AutoSite**   New car and used car showrooms on CompuServe; AutoSite lets you compare new car features and prices.

    GO AUTOSITE

**AutoSite**   Web-based new car and used car showrooms; AutoSite lets you compare new car features and prices.

    WEB http://www.autosite.com/

**CarWorld Connect**   Online British motoring magazine.

    GO CARWORLDCONNECT

**CarWorld Connect Forum**   Forum for the British motoring magazine.

    GO TALKCARWORLD

**Four Wheel Drive Forum**   For owners of 4WD vehicles.

    GO FOURWD

**Motor Sports Forum**   Includes sections on IndyCar, NASCAR, USAC, NHRA, Formula One, etc.

    GO RACING

**Motorcycle Forum**   For motorcyclists everywhere.

    GO RIDE

**MotorWeek Online**   Online motor sports magazine.

    GO MOTORWEEK

**New Car Showroom**   Database for comparison of different car models.

    GO NEWCAR

**Recreational Vehicle Forum**   For owners of RV vehicles.

    GO RVFORUM

**World Motoring News Forum**   News and discussions on F1, rally, and touring races.

    GO MOTORING

**Worldwide Car Network**   For enthusiasts of cars, motorcycles, trucks, etc.

    GO WWCAR

# Aviation

**Air Line Pilots Association**   Official service.

    GO ALPA

**Air Traffic Controller**   Online game.

    GO ATCONTROL

**Aviation Services**   Main menu to CompuServe's aviation services.

    GO FLY

**Aviation Special Interest Group**   Includes sections on safety, air traffic control, flying issues, etc.

    GO AVSIG

**Aviation Week Group**   Online magazine.

    GO AWG

**EMI Aviation Services**   For pilots and flight planners; includes weather briefings, flight plans, etc.

GO EMI

**Flight Simulation Forum**   For players of flight simulation games.

GO FSFORUM

**Jeppesen's Aviation Weather Graphics**
Radar, Lifted Index, and Convective Outlook charts; more than 60 maps in all.

GO JEPP

**Ninety Nines Forum**   Private forum of The Ninety-Nines, Inc., the International Organization of Women Pilots.

GO NINETYNINES

**NWS Aviation Weather**   Official aviation weather reports from the National Weather Service (NWS).

GO AWX

**Women in Aviation Forum**   For women in all fields of aviation and space endeavors.

GO WIAONLINE

# Belgium

**Belgium Forum**   For residents and tourists.

GO BELFORUM

# Benelux

**Microsoft Benelux**   Vendor forum for Microsoft's Benelux operations.

GO MSBEN

**Microsoft Benelux Forum**   Vendor forum for Microsoft's Benelux operations.

GO MSBDF

# Books

**Amazon.com Books**   Premier online bookstore.

WEB http://www.amazon.com/

**Book Preview Forum**   Previews of upcoming book releases.

GO PREVIEW

**Book Review Digest**   Reviews of more than 26,000 books.

GO BOOKREVIEW

**Books in Print**   Database of books distributed in the U.S.

GO BOOKS

**British Books in Print**   Database of books published in the U.K.

GO BBIP

**CompuBooks Online Bookstore**   Good online source for computer books.

WEB http://www.compubooks.com/

**Literary Forum**   For writers and readers.

GO LITFORUM

**Macmillan Computer Publishing**
Includes sections for Que, Sams, and other imprints; also includes large software library.

    GO MACMILLAN

**Macmillan Information SuperLibrary**
Includes online bookstore, software library, and monthly newsletter.

    WEB http://www.mcp.com

**Markt & Technik Forum**   German computer book publisher (sister company to Que).

    GO MTFORUM

**Markt & Technik Online**   German computer book publisher (sister company to Que).

    GO GERMUT

**Quality Paperback Book Club**   Online book club.

    GO QPB1

**Romance Forum**   Romance literature.

    GO ROMANCE

**Science Fiction and Fantasy Literature Forums**   Includes sections on science fiction, fantasy, and horror.

    GO SFLIT and GO SFLITTWO

**Small Computer Book Club**   Online book club.

    GO BK

**Technical Bookstores on the Net**   List of technical bookstores on the Net, provided by Macmillan Publishing.

    WEB http://www.mcp.com/general/
    techbook.html

**Time-Warner Authors Forum**   A gathering place for famous and would-be authors.

    GO TWAUTHORS

**Time-Warner Bookstore**   Online retailer.

    GO TWEP

**UK Book Reviews**   Reviews of British bestsellers.

    GO UKBREV

# Broadcasting

**Broadcast Professionals Forum**   Includes sections on television, radio, cable TV, audio, the FCC, etc.

    GO BPFORUM

**PTS Newsletter Database—Broadcast & Publishing Section**   Database of media-related newsletters.

    GO MEDIANEWS

**Society of Broadcast Engineers**   A place where professionals in the radio, TV, CATV, and audio industry share news and views.

    GO SBENET

# Business

**Basic Company Snapshot**  Essential company information.

```
GO BASCOMPAN
```

**Biz\*File**  Look up names, addresses, and phone numbers for businesses across the U.S.

```
GO BIZFILE
```

**BizTravel**  A good site for business travelers.

```
WEB http://www.biztravel.com/
guide/
```

**British Trade Marks**  Database of trade marks for U.K. companies.

```
GO UKTRADEMARK
```

**Business Database Plus**  Database of detailed company information.

```
GO BUSDB
```

**Business Wire, The**  Database of business press releases.

```
GO TBW
```

**Canadian Company Information**
Financial reports on Canadian companies.

```
GO COCAN
```

**Company Analyzer**  Comprehensive, one-stop shopping for company information.

```
GO ANALYZER
```

**Company Corporation, The**  Information on incorporating businesses.

```
GO CORP
```

**Company Screening**  Searches Disclosure database to identify investment candidates.

```
GO COSCREEN
```

**Disclosure**  Very comprehensive database with full financial and management information on more than 11,000 firms, compiled from 10K and other public reports. Recommended.

```
GO DISCLOSURE
```

**Dun and Bradstreet Information Services**  D&B information on the Web.

```
WEB http://www.dbisna.com/
```

**Dun's Canadian Market Identifiers**
Database of information on Canadian companies (from D&B).

```
GO DBCAN
```

**Dun's Electronic Business Directory**
Database of company information (from D&B).

```
GO DYP
```

**Dun's Market Identifiers**  Database of company information (from D&B).

```
GO DUNS
```

**E-SPAN**  Service for employee searching.

```
GO ESPAN
```

**Entrepreneur Magazine**  Online magazine, also known as the *Small Business Emporium*, with more than 165 guides for entrepreneurs and small businesses.

```
GO ENT
```

**Entrepreneur Small Business Square** The main area for *Entrepreneur Magazine's* online services—including the Franchise & Business Opportunities Database.

    GO ENTMAGAZINE

**Entrepreneurs on the Web** Good site for small businesses and entrepreneurs.

    WEB http://sashimi.wwa.com/
    ~notime/eotw/EOTW.html

**Entrepreneur's Small Business Forum** For entrepreneurs and small businesses (from *Entrepreneur Magazine*).

    GO USEN

**European Company Information** Financial reports on European companies.

    GO COEURO

**Executives Online Forum** Direct access to computer industry executives, part of ZDNet.

    GO ZNT:EXEC

**Federation of International Distributors Forum** Targeting members of the European Federation.

    GO FEDERATION

**German Company Information** Financial reports on German companies.

    GO COGERMAN

**Global Report** Database of company information (from Citibank).

    GO GLOREP

**Hoover's Company Database** Offering Company Profiles and Company Capsules.

    GO HOOVER

**Hoover's Online** Detailed company-specific information, similar to CompuServe's Hoover's database.

    WEB http://www.hoovers.com/

**I/B/E/S Earning Estimate Reports** Institutional Broker's Estimate System, representing a consensus of analysts' forecasts.

    GO IBES

**Ideas, Inventions, and Innovations Forum** Includes sections on creativity, research, new technology, funding, etc.

    GO INNOVATION

**Information Management Forum** Includes sections on professional development, desktop issues, network issues, host issues, etc.

    GO INFOMANAGE

**Information Please Business Almanac** Business almanac from the Information Please people.

    GO BIZALMANAC

**InvesText** Database of financial reports compiled by major Wall Street analysts.

    GO INVTEXT

**Management InfoCenter** A subset of IQuest that focuses on business management information.

    GO IQMANAGEMENT

**NewsNet**   Database of business news from major newsletters and news services.

    GO NN

**OTC NewsAlert**   News clipping service, featuring news from Reuters, Washington Post, etc.

    GO ENS

**Patent Research Center**   Database of U.S. patents.

    GO PATENT

**PR Newswire**   Compendium of press releases, updated daily.

    GO PRNEWS

**Selling**   Online magazine.

    GO SELLING

**SIC Codes**   Database of standard industrial classification (SIC) codes.

    GO SICCODE

**Small and Home Based Business Links**
Links to numerous Web-based resources for small businesses and home-based businesses.

    WEB http://www.ro.com/
    small_business/homebased.html

**SmartBiz: Small Business Supersite**   Lots of resources for small businesses.

    WEB http://www.smartbiz.com/

**Standard & Poor's Online**   Current business information on more than 5000 companies.

    GO S&P

**Thomas Register Online**   Database of information on more than 150,000 U.S. and Canadian companies.

    GO THOMAS

**TRADEMARKSCAN**   Databases containing state and USA trademark information.

    GO TRADERC

**TRW Business Credit Reports**   Database of credit information on more than 13 million businesses.

    GO TRWREPORTS

**UK Company Information**   Financial information on British companies.

    GO COUK

**UK Company Library**   Database of information on British companies.

    GO UKLIB

**UK Historical Stock Pricing**   Database of historical information on British stocks and bonds.

    GO UKPRICE

**UK Professionals Forum**   Includes sections on job opportunities, news, and professional groups.

    GO UKPROF

**Working-From-Home Forum**   Includes sections on taxes, equipment, consulting, writing, etc.

    GO WORK

# Canada

**Canada Forum**   For residents and tourists.

GO CANADA

**Canada Net Pages**   Comprehensive source for Canadian business and financial data.

WEB http://www.visions.com/

**Canadian Company Information** Financial reports on Canadian companies.

GO COCAN

**Dun's Canadian Market Identifiers** Database of information on Canadian companies (from D&B).

GO DBCAN

**Peterson's College Database**   Database with descriptions of more than 4,000 U.S. and Canadian colleges.

GO PETERSON

**Reuter's Canadian News Clips**   Canadian news.

GO RTCANADA

**Thomas Register Online**   Database of information on more than 150,000 U.S. and Canadian companies.

GO THOMAS

# Cards

**Collectibles Forum**   Includes sections on stamps, coins, autographs, books, music, sports cards, dolls, Star Trek, etc.

GO COLLECT

**Internet Gaming Zone**   Site for online Hearts, Bridge, Chess, and card games.

WEB http://www.zone.com/

**Play-by-Mail/Board/Card Games Forum**   The place to find other PBM gamers, board gamers, and card gamers.

GO PBMGAMES

**Trading Card Forum**   For sports and non-sports cards.

GO CARDS

# Careers

**America's Job Bank**   Online job searches.

WEB http://www.ajb.dni.us/

**Career Management Forum**   For finding, changing, and keeping jobs.

GO ESPAN

**E-SPAN**   Job searching on CompuServe.

GO ESPAN

**Kaplan**   Online test prep.

WEB http://www.kaplan.com/

**OWL Resume Workshop**   Improve your resume (from Purdue University).

WEB http://owl.trc.purdue.edu/
Files/Resume.html

# Celebrities

**Entertainment Drive Forum**   Includes sections on movies, television, music, people, etc.

    GO EDRIVE

**Fan Club Forums**   Multiple forums (FANACLUB, FANBCLUB, etc.), with sections for movie and music stars.

    GO FANCLUB

**Stein Online**   Eliot Stein's online talk show with celebrity guests.

    GO STEIN

# Chat, Conversations, and Surveys

**CompuServe Chat**   CompuServe's main Chat area.

    GO CHAT

**CompuServe Convention Center**   Online conferences

    GO CONVENTION

**Cupcake's Column**   The latest gossip from the world of CompuServe Chat, from Cupcake—the resident Chat columnist.

    GO CUPCAKE

**Online Surveys**   Take online surveys.

    GO SURVEY

**Participate**   This special forum lets you start and monitor discussions on any topic you choose.

    GO PARTI

**Speakeasy Forum**   A relaxed online meeting place, part of the ZDNet service.

    GO SPEAKEASY

**WorldsAway**   CompuServe's WorldsAway visual chat.

    GO WAW

# Comics

**Alternative Comix Forum**   For fans of non-mainstream comix.

    GO COMIX

**Comics Publishers Forum**   Information about major publishers of comic books, such as Marvel and DC Comics.

    GO COMICPUB

**Comics/Animation Forum**   CompuServe's main comics forum. Includes sections on reviews, news, and conventions; if you're lucky, you'll find some comics pros online here!

    GO COMIC

**DC Comics**   Home of Superman, Batman, and other famous comic book characters.

    WEB http://www.dccomics.com/

**Dilbert Zone**   Dilbert's very own home page, complete with daily comic strips.

    WEB http://www.unitedmedia.com/
    comics/dilbert/

**Funnies Forum**   Comic strips.

GO FUNFOR

**New Comic Book Releases**   Current comics release lists.

WEB http://www.america.net/
~cslepage/ncrl.html

**Snoopy Site**   Peanuts comics and art online.

GO SNOOPY

**Superman Radio Serial**   Listen to episodes from 1940s Superman radio serials, on your own PC.

WEB http://www.dccomics.com/
radio/index.html

# Communications

**European Community Telework Forum**   News and discussions on the Telework project.

GO ECTF

**Home Electronics and Communications Forum**   Focusing on small and personal electronics.

GO HOMELECT

**Telecommunications Forum**   Includes sections on long distance services, First Amendment rights, etc.

GO TELECO

**Telework Europa Forum**   News and discussions on the Telework project.

GO TWEUROPA

# CompuServe

**Access Numbers**   Look up CompuServe dial-in numbers.

GO PHONES

**Ask Customer Service**   The place to ask your questions about the CompuServe service.

GO QUESTIONS

**Billing Information**   Find out your current CompuServe bill.

GO BILLING

**Change Member Address Information**
The place to change your address.

GO ADDRESS

**Change Your Password**   The place to change your CompuServe password.

GO PASSWORD

**Command Summary**   An online quick reference to CompuServe's keyboard shortcuts.

GO COMMAND

**Common Questions**   A database of frequently asked questions about CompuServe.

GO QUESTIONS

**CompuServe Applications Forum**
Discussions on various CompuServe applications.

GO CSAPPS

**CompuServe Chat**   The place to talk to other members.

    GO CHAT

**CompuServe Community Center**   A central gathering place.

    GO CISCENTER

**CompuServe Convention Center**   Online conferences.

    GO CONVENTION

**CompuServe E-Mail**   CompuServe's e-mail center.

    GO MAIL

**CompuServe Electonic Mall**
CompuServe's main online shopping area.

    GO SHOPPING

**CompuServe Help Forum**   A forum dedicated to answering users' questions.

    GO HELPFORUM

**CompuServe Information Manager for Windows (WinCIM)**   The place to download/order new WinCIM software.

    GO WINCIM

**CompuServe Magazine**   Online magazine.

    GO COMPUMAG

**CompuServe Navigator for Windows Support Forum**   Support for CSNav.

    GO WCSNAVSUP

**CompuServe Navigator Information**   The place for CSNav information and software.

    GO CSNAV

**CompuServe Practice Forum**   A forum where you can practice your skills for free.

    GO PRACTICE

**CompuServe Software**   Order the latest CompuServe software, online.

    GO CISSOFT

**CompuServe Store**   Where you can order all sorts of CompuServe-related merchandise.

    GO ORDER

**CompuServeCD**   To order your CompuServeCD subscription.

    GO CCD

**CompuServe's Web Page**   CompuServe's main page on the Web.

    WEB http://www.compuserve.com

**Cupcake's Column**   The latest gossip from the world of CompuServe Chat, from Cupcake—the resident Chat columnist.

    GO CUPCAKE

**Customer Help Database**   Comprehensive database of problems and solutions.

    GO CSHELP

**Directory of Catalogs**   The place to order catalogs from CompuServe merchants.

    GO DTC

**Electronic Mall ELITE**   Special offers for shoppers on the Electronic Mall.

    GO ELITE

**Electronic Mall News**   News from CompuServe's Electronic Mall.

    GO EMN

**ExtraGrams**   To send SantaGrams, CongressGrams, CupidGrams, and CandidateGrams.

>  GO GRAMS

**Feedback to CompuServe**   Send e-mail to CompuServe personnel.

>  GO FEEDBACK

**Forums**   Gateway to CompuServe's numerous forums and communities.

>  GO FORUMS

**GO Commands**   Quick reference to the GO commands for all of CompuServe's services.

>  GO QUICK

**Home Page Wizard**   CompuServe's software for creating and publishing your own Web pages.

>  GO HPWIZ

**Index of Services**   Good list of what's where on CompuServe.

>  GO INDEX

**Internet Center**   The main menu for CompuServe's Internet services.

>  GO INTERNET

**Logon Instructions**   Instructions for logging onto the service.

>  GO LOGON

**Macintosh CIM Support Forum**   Official support for CompuServe's MacCIM software.

>  GO MCIMSUP

**MacNav Support Forum**   Official support for CompuServe's Macintosh Navigator software.

>  GO MNAVSUPPORT

**Mail Rates**   Find out the latest e-mail rates.

>  GO MAILRATES

**Member Assistance**   CompuServe's main help area.

>  GO HELP

**Member Directory**   Searchable directory of CompuServe members.

>  GO DIRECTORY

**Member Recommendation**   Recommend a friend to CompuServe and receive a usage credit.

>  GO FRIEND

**Membership Changes**   Change your membership information.

>  GO MEMBER

**NetLauncher Support Forum**   For support of CompuServe's NetLauncher software.

>  GO NLSUPPORT

**New Member Welcome Center**   Come here if you're new.

>  GO WELCOME

**Online Surveys**   Take online surveys.

>  GO SURVEY

**Online Today**   Daily computer news.

>  GO ONLINE

**Online Tour of CompuServe**   A guided tour of the CompuServe service.

    GO TOUR

**Our World**   Personal home pages from CompuServe members.

    WEB http://
    ourworld.compuserve.com

**Parental Controls Center**   For controlling access to parts of CompuServe and the Internet.

    GO CONTROLS

**Rates Information**   The latest pricing plans.

    GO RATES

**Review Charges**   Review your personal CompuServe charges.

    GO CHARGES

**Service Terms and Rules**   The "fine print" of the CompuServe service.

    GO RULES

**Support Directory**   Directory of CompuServe support services.

    GO SUPPORT

**U.S. Postal Service Mail**   To send snail mail via CompuServe.

    GO ASCIIMAIL

**User Profile**   Changes options for terminal connections.

    GO TERMINAL

**What's New**   CompuServe's current events, updated daily.

    GO NEW

**WinCIM Support Forum**   Official support for CompuServe's WinCIM software.

    GO WCIMSUP

**WorldsAway**   CompuServe's WorldsAway visual chat.

    GO WAW

**ZDNet Membership and Benefits**   Information about the ZDNet service.

    GO ZNT:ZIFFMEM

**ZDNet Support Forum**   Part of ZDNet.

    GO ZIFFHELP

# Computer Books

**Amazon.com Books**   Premier online bookstore.

    WEB http://www.amazon.com/

**BradyGAMES Gamer Connection**   Good place to exchange gaming tips and meet other online gamers, as well as to order books on the most popular games.

    WEB http://www.mcp.com/brady/
    connect/

**CompuBooks Online Bookstore**   Good online source for computer books.

    WEB http://www.compubooks.com/

**HTML Editors**   Archive of popular HTML editing software (from the Que Software Library).

```
WEB http://www.mcp.com/que/
software/isoftwre.html
```

**Macmillan Computer Publishing**   Includes sections for Que, Sams, and other imprints; also includes large software library.

```
GO MACMILLAN
```

**Macmillan Information SuperLibrary**   Includes online bookstore, software library, and monthly newsletter.

```
WEB http://www.mcp.com
```

**Macmillan Software Library**   FTP version of Macmillan's software archives.

```
FTP ftp.mcp.com
```

**Macmillan's HTML Workshop**   Solid guide to HTML resources.

```
WEB http://www.mcp.com/general/
workshop/
```

**Markt & Technik Forum**   German computer book publisher (sister company to Que).

```
GO MTFORUM
```

**Markt & Technik Online**   German computer book publisher (sister company to Que).

```
GO GERMUT
```

**Miller's View**   Home page of *Using CompuServe's* author.

```
WEB http://www.mcp.com/people/
miller/
```

**New Riders Official World Wide Web Yellow Pages**   Online version of the popular printed directory.

```
WEB http://www.mcp.com/nrp/
wwwyp/
```

**Small Computer Book Club**   Online book club.

```
GO BK
```

**SuperSeek**   Engine that searches multiple search engines (from Macmillan Publishing).

```
WEB http://www.superseek.com/
```

**Technical Bookstores on the Net**   List of technical bookstores on the Net (provided by Macmillan Publishing).

```
WEB http://www.mcp.com/general/
techbook.html
```

**Using CompuServe Home Page**   The Web page for this book; contains updates and information not in the printed book.

```
WEB http://www.mcp.com/people/
miller/cis3top.htm
```

**ZDNet Electronic Books**   Online retailer.

```
GO ZNT:EBOOKS
```

# Computer Hardware

**3Com Online Information Service Menu**
Vendor forum.

```
GO THREECOM
```

**Acer America**   Vendor forum.

```
GO ACER
```

**Ask3Com Forum**   Vendor forum.

GO ASKFORUM

**AST Forum**   Vendor forum.

GO ASTFORUM

**Cabletron Systems Forum**   Vendor forum.

GO CTRONFORUM

**Cabletron Systems Menu**   Vendor forum.

GO CTRON

**Canon Net**   Vendor forum.

GO CANON

**Canon Support Forum**   Vendor forum.

GO CAN-10

**CoCo Forum**   Vendor forum for support of Tandy's Color Computer.

GO COCO

**Compaq Forum**   Vendor forum.

GO CPQFORUM

**CompuAdd Forum**   Vendor forum.

GO COMPUADD

**Creative Labs**   Vendor forum.

GO BLASTER

**DEC PC Forum**   Vendor forum.

GO DECPC

**DEC Users Network Main Menu**   Main menu for DEC's various vendor forums.

GO DECUNET

**Dell Forum**   Vendor forum.

GO DELL

**Digital Equipment Corporation**   Vendor forum.

GO DEC

**Digital PC Integration Forum**   Vendor forum.

GO DECPCI

**Digital PC Store**   Vendor forum.

GO DD-31

**Eicon Technology Forum**   Vendor forum.

GO EICON

**Gateway 2000 Forum**   Vendor forum.

GO GATEWAY

**Hayes Forum**   Vendor forum.

GO HAYFORUM

**Hayes Online**   Vendor forum.

GO HAYES

**Hewlett-Packard Handhelds Forum** Vendor forum.

GO HPHAND

**Hewlett-Packard Omnibook Forum** Vendor forum.

GO HPOMNIBOOK

**Hewlett-Packard Peripherals Forum** Vendor forum.

GO HPPER

**Hewlett-Packard Specials**   Vendor forum with items not found in other HP forums.

GO HPSPEC

**Hewlett-Packard Systems Forum** Vendor forum.

GO HPSYS

**IBM** IBM's official site on the Web.

WEB http://www.ibm.com/

**IBM Applications Forum** Vendor forum.

GO IBMAPP

**IBM Communications Forum** Vendor forum.

GO IBMCOM

**IBM DB2 Database Forum** Vendor forum.

GO IBMDB2

**IBM Hardware Forum** Vendor forum.

GO IBMHW

**IBM ImagePlus Forum** Vendor forum.

GO IBMIMAGE

**IBM Languages Forum** Vendor forum that covers APL and APL2 languages.

GO IBMLANG

**IBM LMU2 Forum** Vendor forum.

GO LMUFORUM

**IBM New User's Forum** Vendor forum.

GO IBMNEW

**IBM Object Technology Forum** Vendor forum.

GO IBMOBJ

**IBM OS/2 Support Forum** Vendor forum.

GO OS2SUPPORT

**IBM OS/2 Users Forum** Vendor forum.

GO OS2USER

**IBM Personal Software Products** Vendor forum.

GO IBMPSP

**IBM PowerPC Forum** Vendor forum.

GO POWERPC

**IBM Programming Forum** Vendor forum; includes sections on C, C++, BASIC, etc.

GO IBMPRO

**IBM PSP Deutschland Forum** Vendor forum.

GO OS2UGER

**IBM Software Forum** Vendor forum.

GO IBMDESK

**IBM Storage Systems Forum** Vendor forum.

GO IBMSTORAGE

**IBM Systems/Utilities Forum** Vendor forum.

GO IBMSYS

**IBM ThinkPad Forum** Vendor forum.

GO THINKPAD

**IBM Users Network** Vendor forum.

GO IBMNET

**Intel Corporation** Vendor forum.

GO INTEL

**JDR Microdevices** Online retailer.

GO JDR

**Lexmark Forum**   Vendor forum.

GO LEXMARK

**Logitech Forum**   Vendor forum.

GO LOGITECH

**Media Vision Forum**   Vendor forum.

GO MEDIAVISION

**MicroWarehouse**   Online retailer.

GO MCW

**Mobile Computing**   Main menu for various vendors of mobile computing products.

GO MOBILE

**Modem Vendor Forum**   Vendor forum.

GO MODEMVENDOR

**NCR/ATT Forum**   Vendor forum.

GO NCRATT

**NeXT Forum**   Vendor forum.

GO NEXTFORUM

**Packard Bell Forum**   Vendor forum.

GO PACKARDBELL

**PC Plug and Play Forum**   Focusing on the hardware and software issues of Plug and Play.

GO PLUGPLAY

**PC Vendor Forums**   Multiple vendor forums (PCVENA, PCVENB, and so on).

GO PCVEN

**PEARL Forum**   Vendor forum.

GO PEARL

**Support Directory**   Database with more than a thousand computer-related vendors and merchants who support their products via CompuServe.

GO SUPPORT

**Tandy Model 100 Forum**   Vendor forum.

GO M100SIG

**Tandy Professional Forums**   Vendor forum.

GO TRS80PRO

**Texas Instruments Forum**   Vendor forum.

GO TIFORUM

**Texas Instruments News**   Vendor forum.

GO TINEWS

**Toshiba Forum**   Vendor forum.

GO TOSHIBA

**Toshiba GmbH Forum**   Vendor forum.

GO TOSHGER

**Ultimedia Hardware Plus Forum**   Vendor forum.

GO ULTIHW

**US Robotics France**   Vendor forum.

GO USFRANCE

**VAX Forum**   Vendor forum.

GO VAXFORUM

**Vobis AG Computer Forum**   Vendor forum.

GO VOBIS

**Wang Support Forum**   Vendor forum.

GO WANGFORUM

**Zenith Data Systems Forum**   Vendor forum.

GO ZENITH

# Computer Networking

**3Com Online Information Service Menu**   Vendor forum.

GO THREECOM

**APPC Info Exchange Forum**   Addressing Advanced Program-to-Program Communication.

GO APPCFORUM

**Ask3Com Forum**   Vendor forum.

GO ASKFORUM

**Banyan Forum**   Vendor forum.

GO BANFORUM

**Cabletron Systems Forum**   Vendor forum.

GO CTRONFORUM

**Cabletron Systems Menu**   Vendor forum.

GO CTRON

**Eicon Technology Forum**   Vendor forum.

GO EICON

**IBM LMU2 Forum**   Vendor forum.

GO LMUFORUM

**LAN Magazine**   Online magazine.

GO LANMAG

**LAN Technology Forum**   Online magazine.

GO LANTECH

**LAN Vendor Forum**   Vendor forums.

GO LANVEN

**NetWare Solutions**   Online magazine.

GO NWSOLUTIONS

**Novell Client Forum**   Vendor forum.

GO NOVCLIENT

**Novell Connectivity Forum**   Vendor forum.

GO NCONNECT

**Novell Developer Info Forum**   Vendor forum.

GO NDEVINFO

**Novell Developer Support Forum**   Vendor forum.

GO NDEVSUPPORT

**Novell DSG Forum**   Vendor forum.

GO DRFORUM

**Novell Files Database**   Vendor database.

GO NOVFILES

**Novell Information Forum**   Vendor forum.

GO NGENERAL

**Novell Library Forum**   Vendor software libraries.

GO NOVLIB

**Novell NetWare 2.x Forum**   Vendor forum.

GO NETW2X

**Novell NetWare 3.x Forum**   Vendor forum.

```
GO NETW3X
```

**Novell NetWare 4.x Forum**   Vendor forum.

```
GO NETW4X
```

**Novell NetWire**   The main menu for Novell's many areas on CompuServe.

```
GO NOVELL
```

**Novell Network Management Forum**   Vendor forum.

```
GO NOVMAN
```

**Novell OS/2 Forum**   Vendor forum.

```
GO NOVOS2
```

**Novell Technical Bulletin Database**   Vendor database.

```
GO NTB
```

**Novell Vendor Forums**   Multiple vendor forums (NOVENA, NOVENB, and so on).

```
GO NVEN
```

**Other Banyon Patchware Forum**   Vendor forum.

```
GO BANPATCH
```

**Saber Software**   Vendor forum.

```
GO SABERSOFT
```

**Standard Microsystems Forum**   Vendor forum.

```
GO SMC
```

**Symantec Network Products Forum**   Vendor forum.

```
GO SYMNET
```

**SynOptics Forum**   Vendor forum.

```
GO SYNOPTICS
```

**Thomas-Conrad Forum**   Vendor forum.

```
GO TCCFORUM
```

**UNIXWare Forum**   Vendor forum for Novell's UNIXWare operating system.

```
GO UNIXWARE
```

**Vines 4.x Patchware Forum**   Vendor forum from Banyan.

```
GO VINES4
```

**Vines 5.x Patchware Forum**   Vendor forum from Banyan.

```
GO VINES5
```

# Computer Programming

**Apple II Programmers' Forum**   Vendor forum.

```
GO APPROG
```

**BASIS International Forum**   Vendor forum.

```
GO BASIS
```

**Borland C++/DOS Forum**   Vendor forum.

```
GO BCPPDOS
```

**Borland C++/Windows/OS2 Forum**   Vendor forum.

```
GO BCPPWIN
```

**Borland dBASE/DOS Forum** Vendor forum.

   GO DBASE

**Borland dBASE/Windows Forum** Vendor forum.

   GO DBASEWIN

**Borland Development Tools Forum** Vendor forum.

   GO BDEVTOOLS

**Borland GmbH Forum** Vendor forum.

   GO BORGER

**Borland International** Gateway to Borland's various software and programming forums.

   GO BORLAND

**Borland Paradox/DOS Forum** Vendor forum.

   GO PDOXDOS

**Borland Paradox/Windows Forum** Vendor forum.

   GO PDOXWIN

**Borland Pascal Forum** Vendor forum.

   GO BPASCAL

**CA-Clipper Germany Forum** Vendor forum.

   GO CLIPGER

**CA Application Development Forum** Vendor forum.

   GO CAIDEV

**CA Clipper Forum** Vendor forum.

   GO CLIPPER

**CA Visual Objects Forum** Vendor forum.

   GO VOFORUM

**CASE-DCI Forum** Addressing the methods and tools used to improve the quality of software development.

   GO CASEFORUM

**Cobb Programming Forum** Part of ZDNet.

   GO ZNT:COBBPR

**Computer Database Plus** Online magazine.

   GO COMPDB

**CSI Forth Net Forum** Vendor forum.

   GO FORTH

**Data Access Corporation Forum** Vendor forum.

   GO DACCESS

**Data Based Advisor Forum** Online magazine.

   GO DBADVISOR

**DBMS Forum** Online magazine.

   GO DBMS

**Digitalk Action Requests Database** Vendor problem report database.

   GO DBDIGITALK

**Digitalk Forum** Vendor forum.

   GO DIGITALK

**Dr. Dobb's Forum**   Online magazine.

    GO DDJFORUM

**Game Developer's Forum**   For programmers developing new computer games.

    GO GAMDEV

**Gamelan**   Earthweb's giant Java directory and supersite.

    WEB http://www.gamelan.com/

**IBM Languages Forum**   Vendor forum that covers APL and APL2 languages.

    GO IBMLANG

**IBM Object Technology Forum**   Vendor forum.

    GO IBMOBJ

**IBM OS/2 Developers Forums**   Vendor forums.

    GO OS2DF1 and GO OS2DF2

**IBM Programming Forum**   Vendor forum; includes sections on C, C++, BASIC, etc.

    GO IBMPRO

**Internet Developer's Forum**   For developers of Web pages and Web sites.

    GO INETDE

**Java Support Forum**   For developers and users of Java applets.

    GO JAVAUSER

**Macintosh Developers Forum**   Vendor forum.

    GO MACDEV

**Microsoft 32-bit Languages Forum**   Vendor forum.

    GO MSLNG32

**Microsoft BASIC Forum**   Vendor forum.

    GO MSBASIC

**Microsoft Connection**   The main menu for Microsoft's numerous areas on CompuServe.

    GO MICROSOFT

**Microsoft DevCast Forum**   Vendor forum.

    GO DEVCAST

**Microsoft Developers Relations Forum**   Vendor forum.

    GO MSDR

**Microsoft Foundation Classes Forum**   Vendor forum.

    GO MSMFC

**Microsoft Fox Users Forum**   Vendor forum.

    GO FOXUSER

**Microsoft SQL Server Forum**   Vendor forum.

    GO MSSQL

**Microsoft Win32 Forum**   Vendor forum.

    GO MSWIN32

**Microsoft Windows Extensions Forum**   Vendor forum.

    GO WINEXT

**Microsoft Windows Objects Forum**   Vendor forum.

    GO WINOBJECTS

**Microsoft Windows SDK Forum**   Vendor forum.

GO WINSDK

**Newton Developers Forum**   For developers for Apple's Newton PDA.

GO NEWTDEV

**Oracle Forum**   Vendor forum.

GO ORACLE

**PC MagNet Programming Forum**   Part of ZDNet.

GO PROGRAMMING

**Powersoft Forum**   Vendor forum.

GO POWERSOFT

**Software Development Forum**   Online magazine.

GO SDFORUM

**Sybase Forum**   Vendor forum.

GO SYBASE

**Symantec Development Tools Forum**
Vendor forum.

GO SYMDEVTOOL

**Visual Basic Programmer's Journal**
Online magazine.

GO VBPJFO

# Computer Software

**7th Level**   Vendor forum.

GO SEVENTH

**ACIUS Forum**   **Vendor forum.**

GO ACIUS

**Adobe Forum**   Vendor forum.

GO ADOBE

**Agendus Quo Vadis**   Vendor forum.

GO QUOVADIS

**Air Travel Manager**   Vendor forum for AirTM travel software.

GO AIRTM

**Amiga File Finder**   File Finder for Amiga-format files on CompuServe.

GO AMIGAFF

**Amiga Vendor Forum**   Vendor forum.

GO AMIGAVENDOR

**Apple II Vendors' Forum**   Vendor forum.

GO APIIVEN

**ARN**   Vendor forum.

GO ARNFR

**Artisoft Forum**   Vendor forum.

GO ARTISOFT

**ASP Shareware Forum**   From the Association of Shareware Professionals (ASP).

GO ASPFORUM

**Autodesk AutoCAD Forum**   Vendor forum.

GO ACAD

**Autodesk Multimedia Forum**   Vendor forum; includes sections on 3D Studio.

GO ASOFT

**Autodesk Retail Products Forum** Vendor forum.

GO ARETAIL

**Banyan Forum** Vendor forum.

GO BANFORUM

**BASIS International Forum** Vendor forum.

GO BASIS

**Bendata Forum** Vendor forum (part of ZDNet).

GO ZNT:BENDATA

**Berkeley Systems (After Dark for Macintosh)** Vendor forum.

GO ADMAC

**Berkeley Systems (After Dark for Windows)** Vendor forum.

GO ADWIN

**Bloc Publishing** Vendor forum.

GO BLOCPUB

**Blyth Software Forum** Vendor forum.

GO BLYTH

**Borland Applications Forum** Vendor forum.

GO BORAPP

**Borland dBASE/DOS Forum** Vendor forum.

GO DBASE

**Borland dBASE/Windows Forum** Vendor forum.

GO DBASEWIN

**Borland GmbH Forum** Vendor forum.

GO BORGER

**Borland International** Gateway to Borland's various software and programming forums.

GO BORLAND

**Borland Paradox/DOS Forum** Vendor forum.

GO PDOXDOS

**Borland Paradox/Windows Forum** Vendor forum.

GO PDOXWIN

**Broderbund Software** Vendor forum.

GO BB

**CA-Clipper Germany Forum** Vendor forum.

GO CLIPGER

**CA-SimplyForum** Vendor forum.

GO SIMPLY

**CA Application Development Forum** Vendor forum.

GO CAIDEV

**CA Clipper Forum** Vendor forum.

GO CLIPPER

**CA Productivity Solutions Forum** Vendor forum.

GO CAIPRO

**CADD/CAM/CAE Vendor Forum** Vendor forum for CADD/CAM professionals.

GO CADVEN

**CASE-DCI Forum** Addresses the methods and tools used to improve the quality of software development.

> GO CASEFORUM

**CD-ROM Forum** Includes sections on CD-ROM technology, production, hardware, industry issues, etc.

> GO CDROM

**CD-ROM Vendors Forum** Vendor forum.

> GO CDVEN

**Cheyenne Software Forum** Vendor forum.

> GO CHEYENE

**Clarion Software Forum** Vendor forum.

> GO CLARION

**Claris Corporation Forum** Vendor forum.

> GO CLARIS

**Claris France Forum** Vendor forum.

> GO CLARFR

**Claris Macintosh Forum** Vendor forum.

> GO MACCLARIS

**Claris TechInfo Database** Vendor database.

> GO CLATECH

**Claris Windows Forum** Vendor forum.

> GO WINCLARIS

**Cobb Applications Forum** Part of ZDNet.

> GO ZNT:COBAPP

**Computer Associates GmbH Forum** Vendor forum.

> GO CAMICRO

**Computer Training Forum** Includes sections on CBT, training techniques, software, etc.

> GO DPTRAIN

**Corel Forum** Vendor forum.

> GO CORELAPPS

**CPV Datensysteme** Vendor forum.

> GO PCIND

**Crosstalk Forum** Vendor forum.

> GO XTALK

**CTOS/Pathway Forum** Vendor forum that supports the UniSys CTOS operating system.

> GO CTOS

**Da Vinci Forum** Vendor forum.

> GO DAVINCI

**DataEase International Forum** Vendor forum.

> GO DATAEASE

**Delrina Forums** Vendor forum.

> GO DELRINA

**Desktop Publishing Forum** Includes fonts, clip art, and DTP utilities.

> GO DTPFORUM

**DiagSoft QAPlus Forum** Vendor forum.

> GO DIAGSOFT

**Digital NT Forum**   Vendor forum for support of DEC's use of Windows NT.

    GO DECWNT

**Dr. Neuhaus Forum**   Vendor forum.

    GO NEUHAUS

**Dvorak Development Forum**   Vendor forum for users of NavCIS.

    GO DVORAK

**Engineering Automation Forum**   For CADD/CAM professionals.

    GO LEAP

**FAST Multimedia AG**   Vendor forum.

    GO MULTIBVEN

**Graphics File Finder**   File Finder for graphics files.

    GO GRAPHFF

**Graphics Vendor Forums**   Includes multiple forums (GRAPHAVEN, GRAPHBVEN, etc.).

    GO GRVEN

**Gupta Forum**   Vendor forum.

    GO GUPTAFORUM

**HTML Editors**   Archive of popular HTML editing software (from the Que Software Library).

    WEB http://www.mcp.com/que/
    software/isoftwre.html

**IBM Applications Forum**   Vendor forum.

    GO IBMAPP

**IBM DB2 Database Forum**   Vendor forum.

    GO IBMDB2

**IBM OS/2 ServicePak**   Vendor forum.

    GO OS2SERV

**IBM OS/2 Vendor Forums**   Vendor forums.

    GO OS2AVEN and GO OS2BVEN

**IBM Personal Software Products**   Vendor forum.

    GO IBMPSP

**IBM Software Forum**   Vendor forum.

    GO IBMDESK

**IBM Systems/Utilities Forum**   Vendor forum.

    GO IBMSYS

**Imperial College Archives**   Repository of software on the Internet.

    FTP ftp.doc.ic.ac.uk

**Informatique France Forum**   Vendor forum.

    GO INFOFR

**Internet Resources Forum**   Discussions about (and libraries full of) Internet-related software.

    GO INETRES

**Intuit Forum**   Vendor forum for users of Quicken and QuickBooks.

    GO INTUIT

**Jumbo!**   Large shareware/freeware archive.

    WEB http://www.jumbo.com/

**Le Bihan & Cie**   Vendor forum.

    GO LEBIHAN

**Lotus Communications Forum**   Vendor forum.

    GO LOTUSCOMM

**Lotus GmbH Forum**   Vendor forum.

    GO LOTGER

**Lotus Press Release Forum**   Vendor forum.

    GO LOTUSNEWS

**Lotus Spreadsheet Forum**   Vendor forum.

    GO LOTUSA

**Lotus Technical Library**   Vendor forum.

    GO LOTUSTECH

**Lotus Word Processing Forum**   Vendor forum.

    GO LOTUSWP

**Lotus Words & Pixels Forum**   Vendor forum.

    GO LOTUSB

**Macintosh Applications Forum**   Managed by the Macintosh Applications Users Group (MAUG).

    GO MACAP

**Macintosh File Finder**   File Finder for Macintosh-compatible files.

    GO MACFF

**Macintosh Vendor Forums**   Multiple vendor forums (MACAVEN, MACBVEN, and so on).

    GO MACVEN

**Macmillan Software Library**   FTP version of Macmillan's software archives.

    FTP ftp.mcp.com

**Macmillan Software Library**   Shareware and freeware, plus code and files from various Macmillan books.

    WEB http://www.mcp.com/softlib/
    software.html

**Macromedia Forum**   Vendor forum.

    GO MACROMEDIA

**MacWAREHOUSE**   Online retailer.

    GO MW

**McAfee Virus Forum**   Vendor forum.

    GO NCSAVIRUS

**Micrografx Forum**   Vendor forum.

    GO MICROGRAFX

**Microsoft**   Microsoft's official Web site.

    WEB http://www.microsoft.com

**Microsoft**   Official Microsoft utilities and information.

    FTP ftp.microsoft.com

**Microsoft Access Forum**   Vendor forum.

    GO MSACCESS

**Microsoft Applications Forum**   Vendor forum for Microsoft's consumer-oriented software.

    GO MSAPP

**Microsoft Benelux**   Vendor forum for Microsoft's Benelux operations.

    GO MSBEN

**Microsoft Benelux Forum**   Vendor forum for Microsoft's Benelux operations.

    GO MSBDF

**Microsoft Central Europe Forum**   Vendor forum for Microsoft's central European operations.

    GO MSCE

**Microsoft Central European Services** Vendor forum for Microsoft's central European operations.

    GO MSEURO

**Microsoft Connection**   The main menu for Microsoft's numerous areas on CompuServe.

    GO MICROSOFT

**Microsoft DOS Forum**   Vendor forum.

    GO MSDOS

**Microsoft Excel Forum**   Vendor forum.

    GO MSEXCEL

**Microsoft Fox Users Forum**   Vendor forum.

    GO FOXUSER

**Microsoft France**   Vendor forum for Microsoft's French operations.

    GO MSFRANCE

**Microsoft France Forum**   Vendor forum for Microsoft's French operations.

    GO MSFR

**Microsoft Home Products Forum**   Vendor forum in support of Microsoft's Home product line.

    GO MSHOME

**Microsoft Italy**   Vendor forum for Microsoft's Italian operations.

    GO MSITA

**Microsoft Italy Forum**   Vendor forum for Microsoft's Italian operations.

    GO MSITALY

**Microsoft Knowledge Base**   Database of information concerning operation of all of Microsoft's products; kind of an online help desk.

    GO MSKB

**Microsoft Mail and Workgroups Forum** Vendor forum.

    GO MSWGA

**Microsoft Sales and Information Forum** Vendor forum.

    GO MSIC

**Microsoft Software Library**   Vendor forum; the place to find official Microsoft software and utilities on CompuServe.

    GO MSL

**Microsoft SQL Server Forum**   Vendor forum.

    GO MSSQL

**Microsoft TechNet Forum**   Vendor forum.

    GO TNFORUM

**Microsoft Windows Forum**   Vendor forum.

    GO MSWIN

**Microsoft Windows Fun Forum**   Vendor forum.

    GO WINFUN

**Microsoft Windows News Forum**   Vendor forum.

    GO WINNEWS

**Microsoft Windows NT SNA Forum**
Vendor forum.

    GO MSSNA

**Microsoft Windows Shareware Forum**   Includes libraries full of Windows-compatible shareware programs.

    GO WINSHARE

**Microsoft Word Foroum**   Vendor forum.

    GO MSWORD

**MicroStation Forum**   Vendor forum.

    GO MSTATION

**MicroWarehouse**   Online retailer.

    GO MCW

**MIDI Vendor Forums**   Multiple vendor forums (MIDIAVEN, MIDIBVEN, and so on).

    GO MIDIVEN

**Netscape**   Official Netscape software; the place to download the latest version of the Netscape Navigator Web browser.

    FTP ftp.netscape.com

**Netscape User's Forum**   For users of Netcape's Navigator Web browser.

    GO NSUSER

**NeXT Forum**   Vendor forum.

    GO NEXTFORUM

**Oak**   Repository of software on the Internet.

    FTP oak.oakland.edu

**Oracle Forum**   Vendor forum.

    GO ORACLE

**Other Banyon Patchware Forum**   Vendor forum.

    GO BANPATCH

**Ozarks West Software**   Vendor forum for OzCIS autopilot software.

    GO OZCIS

**PC File Finder**   File Finder for IBM-compatible files.

    GO PCFF

**PC Fun Forum**   For support of DOS-compatible computer games.

    GO PCFUN

**PC MagNet Utilities/Tips Forum**   Part of ZDNet.

    GO TIPS

**PC Plug and Play Forum**   Focusing on the hardware and software issues of Plug and Play.

    GO PLUGPLAY

**PC Vendor Forums**   Multiple vendor forums (PCVENA, PCVENB, and so on).

    GO PCVEN

**Powersoft Forum**   Vendor forum.

    GO POWERSOFT

**Prisma GmbH Forum**   Vendor forum.

    GO PRISMA

**Public Brand Software Applications Forum**
Libraries full of shareware programs
(part of the ZDNet service).

    GO PBSAPPS

**Public Brand Software Home Forum**
Libraries full of shareware programs
(part of the ZDNet service).

    GO PBSHOME

**Qualitas**   Vendor forum.

    GO QUALITAS

**Quattro Pro Forum**   Vendor forum.

    GO QUATTROPRO

**Quicken Home Page**   Financial advice
and support from Intuit, the publisher of
Quicken.

    WEB http://www.intuit.com/
    quicken/

**Santa Cruz Operations Forum**   Vendor
forum.

    GO SCOFORUM

**Shareware Depot**   Online retailer.

    GO SD

**Shareware Registration**   Area where you
can register and pay for shareware software; payment is added to your monthly
CompuServe bill.

    GO SWREG

**shareware.com**   Biggest collection of
shareware and freeware on the Net (from
c|net).

    WEB http://www.shareware.com

**Sierra Online**   Vendor forum.

    GO SI

**Smith Micro Forum**   Vendor forum.

    GO SMITHMICRO

**Softdisk Publishing**   Vendor forum.

    GO SP

**SOFTEX**   Online software retailer.

    GO SOFTEX

**Software Center**   Libraries full of
shareware and freeware programs (part
of the ZDNet service).

    GO ZNT:CENTER

**Software Publishers Association Forum**
Online home of the SPA, the major software
industry trade association.

    GO SPAFORUM

**Software Publishing Corporation**   Vendor
forum.

    GO SPC

**Spinnaker Software Forum**   Vendor forum.

    GO SPINNAKER

**Stac Electronics Forum**   Vendor forum.

    GO STACKER

**SunSoft Forum**   Vendor forum.

    GO SUNSOFT

**Support Directory**    Database with more than a thousand computer-related vendors and merchants who support their products via CompuServe.

    GO SUPPORT

**Sybase Forum**    Vendor forum.

    GO SYBASE

**Symantec AntiVirus Forum**    Vendor forum.

    GO SYMVIRUS

**Symantec Applications Forum**    Vendor forum.

    GO SYMAPPS

**Symantec Central Point Software DOS Forum**    Vendor forum.

    GO SYMCPDOS

**Symantec Central Point Software Windows Forum**    Vendor forum.

    GO SYMCPWIN

**Symantec Fifth Generation Systems Forum**    Vendor forum.

    GO SYMFGS

**Symantec Norton Utilities Forum** Vendor forum.

    GO SYMUTIL

**TAPCIS Forum**    Forum for the TAPCIS autopilot program.

    GO TAPCIS

**TIMESLIPS Forum**    Vendor forum.

    GO TIMESLIPS

**Travel Software Support Forum**    Vendor forum.

    GO TSSFORUM

**UK Shareware Forum**    Libraries full of shareware programs from British developers.

    GO UKSHARE

**Ultimedia Tools Forums**    Multiple vendor forums (ULTIATOOLS, ULTIBTOOLS, and so on).

    GO ULTIATOOLS, GO ULTIBTOOLS, and
    GO ULTICTOOLS

**UNIX Forum**    Includes sections on networking, LINUX, communications, etc.

    GO UNIXFORUM

**UNIX Vendor Forum**    Vendor forum.

    GO UNIXAVEN

**UNIXWare Forum**    Vendor forum for Novell's UNIXWare operating system.

    GO UNIXWARE

**UserLand Forum**    Vendor forum.

    GO USERLAND

**Vines 4.x Patchware Forum**    Vendor forum from Banyan.

    GO VINES4

**Vines 5.x Patchware Forum**    Vendor forum from Banyan.

    GO VINES5

**Vobis AG Forum**    Vendor forum.

    GO VOBIS

**Walnut Creek Software**   Repository of software on the Internet.

    FTP ftp.cdrom.com

**Washington University at St. Louis**
Repository of software on the Internet.

    FTP wuarchive.wustl.edu

**Windows 3rd Party Support Forums**   Multiple vendor forums (WINAPA, WINAPB, etc.).

    GO WINAP

**Windows Games Forum**   For games on the Windows platform.

    GO WINGAMES

**Windows Magazine Online**   Online magazine.

    GO WINMAG

**Windows NT Forum**   Vendor forum.

    GO WINNT

**Windows Sources Forum**   Online magazine.

    GO WINSOURCES

**Windowshare France Forum**   French Windows shareware.

    GO WSHARE

**WinSite**   Large repository of Windows-compatible software on the Internet; formerly known as the CICA collection at Indiana University.

    FTP ftp.winsite.com

**Wolfram Research Forum**   Vendor forum for Wolfram's Mathematic program.

    GO WOLFRAM

**WordPerfect Files Forum**   Vendor forum.

    GO WPFILES

**WordPerfect GmbH Forum**   Vendor forum.

    GO WPGER

**WordPerfect Magazine**   Online magazine.

    GO WPMAG

**WordPerfect Users Forum**   Vendor forum.

    GO WPUSERS

**WordStar Forum**   Vendor forum.

    GO WORDSTAR

**WRQ/Reflection Forum**   Vendor forum.

    GO WRQFORUM

**WUGNET Forum**   Official forum of the Windows User Group Network (WUGNET).

    GO WUGNET

**ZDNet Designer Templates**   Downloadable spreadsheet and word processing templates (part of ZDNet).

    GO FORMS

**ZDNet File Finder**   File Finder for files on the ZDNet service.

    GO ZNT:ZFILEFINDER

**ZDNet FREE UTILS Forum**   Free downloadable software utilities (part of the ZDNet service).

    GO ZNT:FREEUTIL

**ZDNet Reviews Index**  Database of reviews from various Ziff-Davis computer magazines.

    GO ZIFFINDEX

**ZDNet/Mac Download Forum**  Top Macintosh shareware and freeware programs from the editors of MacWEEK and MacUser magazines (part of ZDNet).

    GO ZMC:DOWNTECH

**ZDNet/Mac File Finder**  File Finder for Macintosh-compatible files on the ZDNet service.

    GO ZMC:FILEFINDER

**Zshare Online Newsletter**  Monthly review of shareware programs (part of the ZDNet service).

    GO ZNT:ZSHARE

# Computers

**AI Expert Forum**  Magazine vendor forum.

    GO AIEXPERT

**Atari Computing Forum**  Vendor forum.

    GO ATARICOMP

**Benchmarks and Standards Forum**  Includes sections on performance analysis, productivity, etc.

    GO BENCHMARK

**c|net**  The most popular computer-related site on the Web; includes news and reviews, as well as additional information from the c|net central television show.

    WEB http://www.cnet.com/

**CADENCE Forum**  Online magazine.

    GO CADENCE

**Canopus Research Forum**  For discussion of computer industry trends and technologies.

    GO CANOPUS

**Computer Club Forum**  For users of old computers no longer supported by their manufacturers, including Kaypro, Adam, Timex/Sinclair, etc.

    GO CLUB

**Computer Library Online**  Database of information for computer users.

    GO COMPLIB

**Computer Life**  Online magazine (from ZDNet).

    GO LIFE

**Computer Shopper Magazine**  Online magazine (part of the ZDNet service).

    GO CSHOPPER

**Computers on Television Forum**  Includes sections on Computer Chronicles, Random Access, @Home, Business Computing, etc.

    GO PCTV

**Computers/Technology Menu**  Main menu for CompuServe's computer-related services.

    GO COMPUTERS

**CP/M Forum**  Support for the venerable old CP/M operating system.

    GO CPMFORUM

**Cyber Forum**   Includes sections on virtual reality, CyberArts, CyberLit, etc.

GO CYBERFORUM

**Deutsches Computer Forum**   German computing topics.

GO GERNET

**Electronic Frontier Foundation Forum**
Sponsored by the EFF, focusing on freedom of expression in digital media.

GO EFFSID

**Executives Online Forum**   Direct access to computer industry executives (part of ZDNet).

GO ZNT:EXEC

**Families and Computer Forum**   For family-oriented computing topics.

GO FAMCOM

**IBM New User's Forum**   Vendor forum.

GO IBMNEW

**BM Users Network**   Vendor forum.

GO IBMNET

**Information Management Forum**   Includes sections on professional development, desktop issues, network issues, host issues, etc.

GO INFOMANAGE

**Mac Zone/PC Zone**   Online retailer.

GO MZ-1

**Macmillan Computer Publishing**   Includes sections for Que, Sams, and other imprints; also includes large software library.

GO MACMILLAN

**Macmillan Information SuperLibrary**   Includes online bookstore, software library, and monthly newsletter.

WEB http://www.mcp.com

**Microsoft**   Microsoft's official Web site.

WEB http://www.microsoft.com

**Microsoft Connection**   The main menu for Microsoft's numerous areas on CompuServe.

GO MICROSOFT

**Microsoft Knowledge Base**   Database of information concerning operation of all of Microsoft's products; kind of an online help desk.

GO MSKB

**Mobile Computing**   Main menu for various vendors of mobile computing products.

GO MOBILE

**Newsbytes**   Daily computer news (part of the ZDNet service).

GO ZNT:NEWSBYTES

**Online Today**   Daily computer news.

GO ONLINE

**PC Catalog**   Online retailer.

GO PCA

**PC Computing**   Online magazine (part of the ZDNet service).

    GO PCCOMP

**PC Contact Forum**   Part of ZDNet.

    GO PCCONTACT

**PC Direct France Forum**   Online magazine.

    GO PCDFRA

**PC Magazine**   Online magazine.

    GO PCMAGAZINE

**PC MagNet Editorial Forum**   Part of ZDNet.

    GO EDITORIAL

**PC Plus/PC Answers Online**   Online magazines.

    GO PCPLUS

**PC Publications**   Subscription service for *PC Novice*, *PC Today*, and *PC Catalog* magazines.

    GO PCB

**PC Week Forum**   Online magazine (part of the ZDNet service).

    GO PCWEEK

**PC World Online**   Online magazine.

    GO PCWORLD

**Speakeasy Forum**   A relaxed online meeting place (part of the ZDNet service).

    GO SPEAKEASY

**UK Computing Forum**   Covering computer topics of interest to the United Kingdom.

    GO UKCOMP

**ZDNet**   Ziff-Davis' online service, accessible to CompuServe members.

    GO ZIFFNET

**ZDNet**   Web version of ZDNet; quite different from the service on CompuServe.

    WEB http://www.zdnet.com/

**Ziff Editor's Choice**   Database of Editor's Choice awards (part of ZDNet).

    GO ZNT:EDCHOICE

# Computers—Apple

**Apple II Programmers' Forum**   Vendor forum.

    GO APPROG

**Apple II Users' Forum**   Vendor forum.

    GO APUSER

**Apple II Vendors' Forum**   Vendor forum.

    GO APIIVEN

**Claris Macintosh Forum**   Vendor forum.

    GO MACCLARIS

**Mac Zone/PC Zone**   Online retailer.

    GO MZ-1

**Macintosh Applications Forum**   Managed by the Macintosh Applications Users Group (MAUG).

    GO MACAP

**Macintosh CIM Support Forum**   Official support for CompuServe's MacCIM software.

    GO MCIMSUP

**Macintosh Communications Forum** Vendor forum.

    GO MACCOM

**Macintosh Community Club Forum** Informal discussions hosted by the Macintosh Applications Users Group.

    GO MACCLUB

**Macintosh Developers Forum**   Vendor forum.

    GO MACDEV

**Macintosh Entertainment Forum**   Vendor forum.

    GO MACFUN

**Macintosh File Finder**   File Finder for Macintosh-compatible files.

    GO MACFF

**Macintosh Forums**   Main menu for CompuServe's Macintosh-related areas.

    GO MACINTOSH

**Macintosh Hardware Forum**   Vendor forum.

    GO MACHW

**Macintosh Hypertext Forum**   Vendor forum for hypertext, Hypertalk, and HyperCard.

    GO MACHYPER

**Macintosh Multimedia Forum**   Vendor forum.

    GO MACMULTI

**Macintosh New Users Help Forum**   Vendor forum.

    GO MACNEW

**Macintosh Systems Forum**   Vendor forum.

    GO MACSYS

**Macintosh Vendor Forums**   Multiple vendor forums (MACAVEN, MACBVEN, and so on).

    GO MACVEN

**MacNav Support Forum**   Official support for CompuServe's Macintosh Navigator software.

    GO MNAVSUPPORT

**MacUser/MacWEEK Index**   Index of stories from MacUser and MacWEEK magazines (part of ZDNet).

    GO ZNT:ZMACINDEX

**MacWAREHOUSE**   Online retailer.

    GO MW

**Newton Developers Forum**   For developers for Apple's Newton PDA.

    GO NEWTDEV

**ZDNet/Mac**   ZDNet's Macintosh resources; also known as Zmac.

    GO ZMAC

**ZDNet/Mac Download Forum** Top Macintosh shareware and freeware programs from the editors of *MacWEEK* and *MacUser* magazines (part of ZDNet).

```
GO ZMC:DOWNTECH
```

**ZDNet/Mac File Finder** File Finder for Macintosh-compatible files on the ZDNet service.

```
GO ZMC:FILEFINDER
```

# Computers— Commodore

**Amiga Arts Forum** Vendor forum.

```
GO AMIGAARTS
```

**Amiga File Finder** File Finder for Amiga-format files on CompuServe.

```
GO AMIGAFF
```

**Amiga Tech Forum** Vendor forum for technical users and programmers.

```
GO AMIGATECH
```

**Amiga User Forum** Vendor forum.

```
GO AMIGAUSER
```

**Amiga Vendor Forum** Vendor forum.

```
GO AMIGAVENDOR
```

**CBM Service Forum** For users of Commodore computers.

```
GO CBMSERVICE
```

**Commodore Applications Forum** For users of Commodore computers.

```
GO CBMAPP
```

**Commodore Art/Games Forum** For users of Commodore computers.

```
GO CBMART
```

**Commodore Business Machines Menu** Main area for Commodore computers.

```
GO CBMNEWS
```

**Commodore/Amiga Forums Menu** Main area for Amiga computers.

```
GO CBMNET
```

# Computers— Communications

**CompuServe E-Mail** CompuServe's e-mail center.

```
GO MAIL
```

**Da Vinci Forum** Vendor forum.

```
GO DAVINCI
```

**Delrina Forums** Vendor forum.

```
GO DELRINA
```

**Dr. Neuhaus Forum** Vendor forum.

```
GO NEUHAUS
```

**E-Mail Essential Information** How to send e-mail to users on commercial services and the Internet.

```
WEB http://www.mcp.com/people/
miller/emailadd.htm
```

**ExtraGrams** To send SantaGrams, CongressGrams, CupidGrams, and CandidateGrams.

```
GO GRAMS
```

**Hayes Forum**   Vendor forum.

    GO HAYFORUM

**Hayes Online**   Vendor forum.

    GO HAYES

**IBM Communications Forum**   Vendor forum.

    GO IBMCOM

**Macintosh Communications Forum** Vendor forum.

    GO MACCOM

**Microsoft Mail and Workgroups Forum** Vendor forum.

    GO MSWGA

**Modem Vendor Forum**   Vendor forum.

    GO MODEMVENDOR

**Telecommunications Forum**   Includes sections on long distance services, First Amendment rights, etc.

    GO TELECO

**U.S. Postal Service Mail**   To send snail mail via CompuServe.

    GO ASCIIMAIL

**UK Communications Forum**   Communications information and discussions with a British flavor.

    GO UKCOMMS

# Computers— Multimedia

**Autodesk Multimedia Forum**   Vendor forum that includes sections on 3D Studio.

    GO ASOFT

**CD-ROM Forum**   Includes sections on CD-ROM technology, production, hardware, industry issues, etc.

    GO CDROM

**CD-ROM Vendors Forum**   Vendor forum.

    GO CDVEN

**FAST Multimedia AG**   Vendor forum.

    GO MULTIBVEN

**Macintosh Multimedia Forum**   Vendor forum.

    GO MACMULTI

**Macromedia Forum**   Vendor forum.

    GO MACROMEDIA

**Microsoft Windows Multimedia Forum** Vendor forum.

    GO WINMM

**Multimedia Forum**   Includes sections on video, audio, animation, interface design, etc.

    GO MULTIMEDIA

**Multimedia Vendor Forums**   Multiple vendor forums.

    GO MULTIVEN and GO MULTIBVEN

**Multimedia World**   Online magazine.

GO MMWORLD

# Computers—OS/2

**Borland C++/Windows/OS2 Forum**   Vendor forum.

GO BCPPWIN

**Golden CommPass Support**   Support for the OS/2 autopilot program.

GO GCPSUPPORT

**IBM OS/2 Developers Forums**   Vendor forums.

GO OS2DF1 and GO OS2DF2

**IBM OS/2 ServicePak**   Vendor forum.

GO OS2SERV

**IBM OS/2 Support Forum**   Vendor forum.

GO OS2SUPPORT

**IBM OS/2 Users Forum**   Vendor forum.

GO OS2USER

**IBM OS/2 Vendor Forums**   Vendor forums.

GO OS2AVEN and GO OS2BVEN

**Novell OS/2 Forum**   Vendor forum.

GO NOVOS2

# Consumer Electronics

**Appliance Forum**   For large and small appliances, from washers and dryers to vacuum cleaners.

GO APPLIANCE

**Consumer Electronics Audio Forum** For audiophiles.

GO CEAUDIO

**Consumer Electronics Network**   Gateway to CompuServe's various consumer electronics areas.

GO CENET

**Consumer Electronics Vendor Forum** Vendor forum.

GO CEVENDOR

**Consumer Electronics Video Forum** For videophiles.

GO CEVIDEO

**Escort Store, The**   Online retailer.

GO ESCORT

**Heath Company, The**   Online retailer.

GO HEATH

**Home Electronics and Communications Forum**   Focusing on small and personal electronics.

GO HOMELECT

**Ken Crane's Laserdisc Superstore**   Online laserdisc retailer.

    WEB http://www.kencranes.com/
    laserdiscs/

**Laser's Edge, The**   Online retailer of laserdiscs.

    GO LE

**Siemens Automation**   Vendor forum.

    GO SIEAUT

**Sight and Sound Forum**   Includes sections on audio/video equipment.

    GO SSFORUM

# Crime & Public Safety

**Safetynet Forum**   Includes sections on crime, firefighting, public safety, etc.

    GO SAFETYNET

**Time-Warner Crime Forum**   Includes sections on vice, murder, theft, fraud, terrorism, etc.

    GO TWCRIME

# Current Events & Issues

**America Vote's National Town Hall**   A way to send Washington your opinions on issues of the day; also provides information on Congressional bills and related issues.

    WEB http://www.americavote.com/
    vote

**CNN Forum**   CNN's forum on CompuServe.

    GO CNNFORUM

**Global Crisis Forum**   Discussions about the latest global hotspots and events.

    GO CRISIS

**Issues Forum**   Includes sections on culture, Canadian issues, politics, religion, and Rush Limbaugh.

    GO ISSUESFORUM

**JFK Assassination Forum**   Includes sections on transcripts, books, articles, organized crime, Jack Ruby, etc.

    GO JFKFORUM

**National Public Radio**   Includes daily news and conferences.

    GO NPR

**Online Issues Forum**   Discussions about censorship and other online issues.

    GO OLISSU

**Political Debate Forum**   Includes areas for both Democrats and Republicans.

    GO POLITICS

**Religious Issues Forum**   Lively discussions on current religious issues.

    GO RELISSUES

**Rush Limbaugh's Download Area**   Files of interest to Dittoheads.

    GO RUSHDL

**Yahoo's Society and Culture Index** List of sites focusing on current events and societal/cultural issues.

    WEB http://www.yahoo.com/
    Society_and_Culture/

# Education

**College and Adult Student Forum** For older students.

    GO STUFOB

**College and University Home Pages** List of colleges on the Web.

    WEB http://www.mit.edu:8001/
    people/cdemello/univ.html

**Collegiate Connections** Gateway to a variety of services and areas of interest to current and potential college students, including areas for college search, college sports, university information, funding & finances, and alumni.

    GO COLLEGE

**Computer Training Forum** Includes sections on CBT, training techniques, software, etc.

    GO DPTRAIN

**Dissertation Abstracts** Database of academic dissertations; includes doctorial dissertations from 1861 and masters theses since 1962.

    GO DISSERTATION

**Education Forum** Includes sections on home schooling, sex education, colleges, etc.

    GO EDFORUM

**Education Research Forum** Sponsored by the American Educational Research Association.

    GO EDRESEARCH

**Education Week** Online educational newspaper.

    GO EWE

**ERIC (Education Resources Information Center)** Database of education-related articles.

    GO ERIC

**Foreign Language Forum** Includes sections on French, German, Spanish, Italian, etc.

    GO FLEFO

**IBM Special Needs Forum** Software for students with special educational needs

    GO IBMSPEC

**International WWW School Registry** List of schools (at all levels) on the Internet.

    WEB http://web66.coled.umn.edu/
    schools.html

**Kids Students Forum** For younger students.

    GO STUFOC

**Peterson's College Database** Database with descriptions of more than 4,000 U.S. and Canadian colleges.

    GO PETERSON

**Smithsonian** Online version of the world's greatest museum.

    WEB http://www.si.edu/

**Space in the Classroom**   Sponsored by the United States Space Foundation.

    GO USSF

**Students Forum**   Gateway to multiple forums (such as STUFOA, STUFOB). Includes sections for grade schoolers, middle schoolers, high schoolers, and college students.

    GO STUFO

**SunSite**   University of North Carolina's FTP site, a good place to find academic information.

    FTP sunsite.unc.edu

**Teens Student Forum**   For high school and middle school students.

    GO STUFOA

**Trinity Delta**   Private online service for Trinity College.

    GO TDELTA

**Trinity Delta Forum**   CompuServe area for Trinity College.

    GO TRINITY

**University of Phoenix**   Information about the University of Phoenix' online curriculum.

    GO UP

# Engineering

**CADD/CAM/CAE Vendor Forum**   Vendor forum for CADD/CAM professionals.

    GO CADVEN

**Ei Compendex Plus**   Abstracts and articles from engineering literature.

    GO COMPENDEX

**Engineering Automation Forum**   For CADD/CAM professionals.

    GO LEAP

# Entertainment

**Associated Press Online**   Entertainment news.

    GO APO

**BIZ!**   Online entertainment site.

    WEB http://www.bizmag.com/

**Comedy Central**   Online version of the hit cable channel, includes sections for Politically Incorrect, Stand-Up Online, and Quick Laughs.

    GO COMEDY

**Entertainment Drive Forum** CompuServe's main entertainment area. Includes sections on movies, television, music, people, etc.

    GO EDrive

**Entertainment Weekly**   Online entertainment magazine.

    WEB http://www.pathfinder.com//
    ew/Welcome.html

**Fan Club Forums**   Multiple forums (FANACLUB, FANBCLUB, etc.) with sections for movie and music stars.

    GO FANCLUB

**Hollywood Hotline**  The latest entertainment industry news.

    GO HOLLYWOOD

**Marilyn Beck's Hollywood**  Daily observations on Hollywood from columnists Marilyn Beck and Stacy Jenel Smith.

    GO BECK

**Mr. Showbiz**  Supersite for entertainment-related resources.

    WEB http://web3.starwave.com/
    showbiz/

**Music and Performing Arts Forum**
Includes sections on music, dance, drama, etc.

    GO MUSICARTS

**Paramount Pictures**  Online home of Paramount, movies and television.

    WEB http://www.paramount.com/

**Playbill Online Forum**  Theater information and discussions; from the Broadway and London stages.

    GO PLAYBILL

**Show Business/Media Forum**  Includes sections on movies, radio, television, theater, music, etc.

    GO SHOWBIZ

**SHOWBIZQUIZ**  Entertainment-oriented trivia game.

    GO SBQ

**Stein Online**  Eliot Stein's online talkshow, with celebrity guests.

    GO STEIN

**Time-Warner Pathfinder**  Supersite containing various Time-Warner properties, including magazines (*TIME, Life, Entertainment Weekly, People, Money, Sports Illustrated, Vibe, Fortune*), Time-Warner books, Warner Bros. movies and music, HBO, and more. Recommended.

    WEB http://www.pathfinder.com/

**UK Entertainment Reviews**  Reviews of Britsh films, theatre, videos, and soap operas.

    GO UKENT

**UK Theatre Reviews**  Reviews from the U.K. stage.

    GO UKTHEATRE

**UK What's On Guide**  Comprehensive guide to British entertainment and events.

    GO UKWO

**Yahoo's Entertainment Index**  Master list of Internet entertainment resources.

    WEB http://www.yahoo.com/
    Entertainment/

**Youth Entertainment Drive**  Version of EDrive for kids and teens; includes sections on television, movies & videos, pop culture, music & bands, games, computers/internet, sports & hobbies, etc.

    GO YDRIVE

# Europe

**EUROMALL**  Web-based shopping mall for European merchants.

    WEB http://www.internet-
    eireann.ie/Euromall/

**European Community Telework Forum**   News and discussions on the Telework project.

    GO ECTF

**European Company Information** Financial reports on European companies.

    GO COEURO

**European Forum**   For residents and tourists.

    GO EURFORUM

**European Railway Schedule**   Schedules for continental rail travel.

    GO RAILWAY

**European Research Centre**   Database of European information.

    GO EUROLIB

**Federation of Interational Distributors Forum**   Targeting members of the European Federation.

    GO FEDERATION

**International Sportswire Feed** International sports news and scores.

    GO DSPORT

**Microsoft Central Europe Forum**   Vendor forum for Microsoft's central European operations.

    GO MSCE

**Microsoft Central European Services** Vendor forum for Microsoft's central European operations.

    GO MSEURO

**Musik Europe Alive**   The European music scene.

    GO MUSIK

**Telework Europa Forum**   News and discussions on the Telework project.

    GO TWEUROPA

**World Community Forum**   Unique multilanguage forum.

    GO WCOMMUNITY

**World Motoring News Forum**   News and discussions on F1, rally, and touring races.

    GO MOTORING

# Family Issues

**America's Funniest Home Videos**   Fun from the hit TV show.

    GO HOMEVIDEOS

**Christian Fellowship Forum**   A family-oriented gathering place.

    GO FELLOWSHIP

**Computrace**   Service that researches background and current information on more than 100 million living and deceased U.S. citizens.

    GO TRACE

**Families and Computer Forum**   For family-oriented computing topics.

    GO FAMCOM

**Family Medicine Internet Sites**   List of family-oriented medical sites on the Web.

```
WEB http://
mir.med.ucalgary.ca:70/1/family
```

**Family Services Forum**   Includes sections on pregnancy/birth, newborns/infants, daycare, grade schoolers, adoption, extended family, family abuse, separation/divorce, etc.

```
GO MYFAMILY
```

**Family World**   Good family-oriented site.

```
WEB http://family.com/
homepage.html
```

**Genealogy Forum**   CompuServe's main genealogy area; a good place to start to trace your family roots.

```
GO ROOTS
```

**Genealogy Support Forum**   Access to major genealogy service providers, such as Brothers Keeper, Comm Soft, The Family Edge, Leister Productions, The New England Historic Genealogical Society, and Wholly Genes Software.

```
GO GENSUP
```

**Missing Children Forum**   Sponsored by the National Center for Missing and Exploited Children; includes information about and pictures of missing children.

```
GO MISSING
```

**Parent Soup**   Good family-oriented site.

```
WEB http://www.parentsoup.com/
```

**Parent's Place**   Online parenting resource center.

```
WEB http://www.parentsplace.com/
```

# File Finders

**Adult File Finder**   File Finder for files with adult content.

```
GO ADULTFF
```

**Amiga File Finder**   File Finder for Amiga-format files on CompuServe.

```
GO AMIGAFF
```

**Games File Finder**   File Finder for games files.

```
GO GAMESFF
```

**Graphics File Finder**   File Finder for graphics files.

```
GO GRAPHFF
```

**Macintosh File Finder**   File Finder for Macintosh-compatible files.

```
GO MACFF
```

**PC File Finder**   File Finder for IBM-compatible files.

```
GO PCFF
```

**ZDNet File Finder**   File Finder for files on the ZDNet service.

```
GO ZNT:ZFILEFINDER
```

**ZDNet/Mac File Finder**   File Finder for Macintosh-compatible files on the ZDNet service.

```
GO ZMC:FILEFINDER
```

# Food & Drink

**Adventures in Food**   Online retailer.

GO AIF

**Bacchus Wine and Beer Forum**   Includes sections on wine tasting, brewing, etc.

GO WINEFORUM

**Better Homes Kitchen Forum**   For cooks (from the Better Homes & Garden people).

GO BHKFORUM

**Cook's Online Forum**   Includes sections about meats, herbs and spices, ethnic recipes, vegetarian cooking, etc.

GO COOKS

**Dinner on Us Club**   Discount dining club.

GO DINE

**Good Pub Guide**   Database guide to British pubs.

GO UKPUBS

**Omaha Steaks International**   Online retailer.

GO OS

**Time-Warner Lifestyle Forum**   Includes sections on travel/places, food/drink/ parties, sports/hobbies, appearance, relationships, etc.

GO TWLIFE

**Vegetarian Forum**   Recipes and issues of interest to vegetarians.

GO VEGETARIAN

**Virginia Diner**   Online retailer.

GO DINER

**Wine—the Interactive Gourmet**   Good culinary site.

WEB http://www.cuisine.com/

**Zagat Restaurant Guide**   Thousands of restaurant reviews for more than 20 cities.

GO ZAGAT

# France

**Agendus Quo Vadis**   Vendor forum.

GO QUOVADIS

**Air France**   Information on Air France flights.

GO AF

**ARN**   Vendor forum.

GO ARNFR

**Associated Press France en Ligne**   French news.

GO APFRANCE

**Claris France Forum**   Vendor forum.

GO CLARFR

**France Cinema Forum**   French films.

GO CINEFORUM

**France Forum**   For residents and tourists.

GO FRFORUM

**Informatique France Forum**   Vendor forum.

GO INFOFR

**Le Bihan & Cie**   Vendor forum.

    GO LEBIHAN

**Le Monde**   Online French newspaper.

    GO LME

**Microsoft France**   Vendor forum for Microsoft's French operations.

    GO MSFRANCE

**Microsoft France Forum**   Vendor forum for Microsoft's French operations.

    GO MSFR

**PC Direct France Forum**   Online magazine.

    GO PCDFRA

**US Robotics France**   Vendor forum.

    GO USFRANCE

**WebMuseum**   Interesting Web-based museum (based in France).

    WEB http://mistral.enst.fr/

**Windowshare France Forum**   French Windows shareware.

    GO WSHARE

# Games

**7th Level**   Vendor forum.

    GO SEVENTH

**Action Games Forum**   Focusing on shoot-em-ups like DOOM and Descent.

    GO ACTION

**Air Traffic Controller**   Online game.

    GO ATCONTROL

**Astrology Calculator**   Online astrological charting.

    GO ASTROLOGY

**Biorhythms**   Online biorhythm charting.

    GO BIORHYTHM

**BlackDragon**   Online adventure game.

    GO BLACKDRAGON

**BradyGAMES Gamer Connection**   Good place to exchange gaming tips and meet other online gamers, as well as order books on the most popular games.

    WEB http://www.mcp.com/brady/
    connect/

**Bridge Forum**   For Bridge players.

    GO BRIDGE

**British Legends**   Online adventure game.

    GO LEGENDS

**Broderbund Software**   Vendor forum.

    GO BB

**Cardiff's MUD Page**   Comprehensive list of Net-based MUDs and MOOs.

    WEB http://arachnid.cm.cf.ac.uk/
    User/Andrew.Wilson/MUDlist/

**CastleQuest**   Online adventure game.

    GO CQUEST

**Chess Forum**   For Chess players of all skill levels.

GO CHESSFORUM

**Classic Adventure**   Online adventure game.

GO CLADVENT

**Commodore Art/Games Forum**   For users of Commodore computers.

GO CBMART

**Computer Gaming World**   Online magazine.

GO CGWMAGAZINE

**E*TRADE Stock Market Game**   Online game modeled on current financial markets.

GO ETGAME

**EA Online**   Official site for Electronic Arts.

WEB http://www.ea.com/

**Electronic Gamer**   Online magazine.

GO EGAMER

**Electronic Gamer Archives**   Repository of reviews and step-by-step walk throughs for the most popular computer games.

GO TEG

**Enhanced Adventure**   Advanced version of the classic adventure game.

GO ENADVENT

**Epic MegaGames**   Games you can download.

GO EPIC

**Epic MegaGames Forum**   Includes discussions on Epic's downloadable games.

GO EPICFO

**Fantasy Basketball**   Fantasy basketball leagues online.

GO FASTBREAK

**Fantasy Football League**   Play fantasy football online.

GO SIFFL

**Fantasy/Role-Playing Adventure Games**   Includes games like British Legends and Island of Kesmai.

GO ADVENT

**Flight Simulation Forum**   For players of flight simulation games.

GO FSFORUM

**Game Developer's Forum**   For programmers developing new computer games.

GO GAMDEV

**Game Forums and News**   Main menu for all of CompuServe's game-related forums; includes the latest gaming news.

GO GAMECON

**Game Gallery**   Web-based game site.

WEB http://www.gamegallery.com/

**Game Publisher Beta Forum**   Where game publishers test their upcoming games.

GO GAMBETA

**Games Domain**   Links to hundreds of Net-based game sites, walkthroughs, home pages, electronic magazines, and MUDs.

WEB http://www.gamesdomain.com/

**Games File Finder**   File Finder for games files.

    GO GAMESFF

**Games Publishers Forums**   Includes multiple forums (GAMAPUB, GAMBPUB, and so on).

    GO GAMPUB

**Games Site**   Youth-oriented game center.

    GO GMS

**Hangman**   Online game.

    GO HANGMAN

**Hot Games Download Area**   Hot PC games available for downloading.

    GO HOTGAMES

**Interactive Magic Gaming**   Site for Magic: The Gathering.

    WEB http://www.imagicgames.com/

**Internet Gaming Zone**   Site for online Hearts, Bridge, Chess, and card games.

    WEB http://www.zone.com/

**Island of Kesmai**   Online adventure game.

    GO ISLAND

**Just for Laffs**   Online joke contest for kids.

    GO JFL

**Macintosh Entertainment Forum**   Vendor forum.

    GO MACFUN

**MegaWars I and III**   Online adventure games.

    GO MEGA1 and GO MEGA3

**Microsoft Home Products Forum**   Vendor forum in support of Microsoft's Home product line.

    GO MSHOME

**Microsoft Windows Fun Forum**   Vendor forum.

    GO WINFUN

**Modem-to-Modem Challenge Board**   Worldwide database of MTM game players.

    GO MTMCHALLENGE

**Modem-to-Modem Games Support**   Support for modem-to-modem games.

    GO MTMGAMES

**Modem-to-Modem Gaming Lobby**   The place to find other modem-to-modem gamers.

    GO MTMLOBBY

**Modem Games/Games Challenge Forum**   Includes sections on various multiplayer games that can be played via modem.

    GO MODEMGAMES

**MUDs**   Information about MUDs and MOOs.

    WEB http://
    draco.centerline.com:8080/
    ~franl/mud.html

**Multi-Player Games Forum**   Forum for various multiplayer games.

GO MPGAMES

**New Games City**   Complete listing of game-related areas on CompuServe.

GO GAMES

**Nintendo Online**   Vendor forum.

GO NINTENDO

**Nintendo Power**   Nintendo's supersite on the Web.

WEB http://www.nintendo.com

**NUKE**   Perhaps the best site on the Net for game information. Recommended.

WEB http://www.nuke.com/

**Outland Online Games**   A place to play graphical real-time games with other gamers.

WEB http://www.outland.com/

**PC Fun Forum**   For support of DOS-compatible computer games.

GO PCFUN

**PC World Entertainment Forum**   Online magazine with coverage of state-of-the-art multimedia games.

GO GAMING

**Play-by-Mail/Board/Card Games Forum**   The place to find other PBM gamers, board gamers, and card gamers.

GO PBMGAMES

**Role-Playing Games Forum**   The hangout for RPGers, with sections for advanced dungeons and dragons, fantasy, heroes, science fiction, and other types of role-playing games.

GO RPGAMES

**Science Trivia Quiz**   Online trivia game.

GO SCITRIVIA

**Sega Forum**   Vendor forum.

GO SEGA

**SHOWBIZQUIZ**   Entertainment-oriented trivia game.

GO SBQ

**Sierra Online**   Vendor forum.

GO SI

**SNIPER!**   Online combat game.

GO SNIPER

**Sports Simulation Forum**   For players of sports simulation games.

GO SPRTSIMS

**STAGEII**   Online trivia game.

GO STAGEII

**The Multiple Choice**   Online trivia game.

GO TMC

**Trading Card Forum**   For sports and non-sports cards.

GO CARDS

**Trivia Games**   Complete listing of CompuServe's trivia games.

GO TTGAMES

**Video Games Forum**   Includes sections for Sega, Nintendo, Playstation, 3DO, etc.

GO VIDGAM

**Video Games Publishers Forum**   Vendor forum.

GO VIDAPUB

**Virtual Vegas**   Vegas-style gambling, online.

WEB http://www.virtualvegas.com/

**Whiz Quiz**   Online trivia game from Grolier's.

GO WHIZ

**Windows Games Forum**   For games on the Windows platform.

GO WINGAMES

**Yahoo's Games Index**   A big list of game-related sources on the Internet.

WEB http://www.yahoo.com/Enter-tainment/Games/

**You Guessed It!**   Online trivia game.

GO YGI

**Yoyodyne Entertainment**   Online games for kids.

GO YOY

**Zarf's List of Interactive Games on the Web**   Comprehensive list of all sorts of Web-based games, from online chess and trivia quizzes to MUDs and MUSHes.

WEB http://www.leftfoot.com/games.html

# Gardening

**Burpee**   Official Burpee Web site.

WEB http://garden.burpee.com/

**Gardening Forum**   Managed by *National Gardening* Magazine.

GO GARDENING

**GardenNet**   Good general gardening site.

WEB http://www.olympus.net/gardens/home.htm

# Gay & Lesbian Issues

**PRIDE! Central**   For gay and lesbian members.

GO PRIDE

# Genealogy

**Computrace**   Service that researches background and current information on more than 100 million living and deceased U.S. citizens.

GO TRACE

**Genealogy Forum**   CompuServe's main genealogy area.

GO ROOTS

**Genealogy Support Forum**   Access to major genealogy service providers, such as Brothers Keeper, Comm Soft, The Family Edge, Leister Productions, The New England Historic Genealogical Society, and Wholly Genes Software.

GO GENSUP

# Germany

**BertelsmannUnivsallexikon** Bertelsmann's German-language encyclopedia, online.

GO BEPLEXIKON

**Borland GmbH Forum** Vendor forum.

GO BORGER

**CA-Clipper Germany Forum** Vendor forum.

GO CLIPGER

**Computer Associates GmbH Forum** Vendor forum.

GO CAMICRO

**CPV Datensysteme** Vendor forum.

GO PCIND

**DER SPIEGEL Forum** Online magazine.

GO SPIEGEL

**Deutsches Computer Forum** German computing topics.

GO GERNET

**Deutsches Film Forum** German films.

GO FILME

**Deutschland Online Forum** For residents and tourists.

GO GERLINE

**DPA-Kurznachrichtendfiendst** German news.

GO DPANEWS

**Dr. Neuhaus Forum** Vendor forum.

GO NEUHAUS

**FAST Multimedia AG** Vendor forum.

GO MULTIBVEN

**German Company Information** Financial reports on German companies.

GO COGERMAN

**German Research Centre** Database of German information.

GO GERLIB

**IBM PSP Deutschland Forum** Vendor forum.

GO OS2UGER

**Lotus GmbH Forum** Vendor forum.

GO LOTGER

**Magna Media Forum** Online magazines, including *Computer Persoenlich* and *PC Magazine*.

GO MAGNA

**Markt & Technik Forum** German computer book publisher (sister company to Que).

GO MTFORUM

**Markt & Technik Online** German computer book publisher (sister company to Que).

GO GERMUT

**Neue Zurcher Zeitung** Online German newspaper.

GO ZUERCHER

**PC Direkt Forum** Online magazine.

GO PCDIREKT

**PC Professionell Forum** Online magazine.

GO PCPRO

**PEARL Forum** Vendor forum.

GO PEARL

**Prisma GmbH Forum** Vendor forum.

GO PRISMA

**Siemens Automation** Vendor forum.

GO SIEAUT

**Toshiba GmbH Forum** Vendor forum.

GO TOSHGER

**Vobis AG Computer Forum** Vendor forum.

GO VOBIS

**Vobis AG Forum** Vendor forum.

GO VOBIS

**Windows Deutschland Forum** Online magazine.

GO GERWIN

**WordPerfect GmbH Forum** Vendor forum.

GO WPGER

# Government

**CapWeb** An unauthorized—but comprehensive—guide to the U.S. Congress.

WEB http://policy.net/capweb/

**CONGRESSGrams** Send e-mail to your congressmen and senators.

GO GRAMS

**Contacting Congress** An independent site at the University of Minnesota that lists contact information for all members of Congress.

WEB http://ast1.spa.umn.edu/
juan/congress.html

**Department of State Advisories** Advisories and warnings for Americans traveling abroad.

GO STATE

**Electronic Democracy Forum** Where you can read and discuss Newt Gingrich's Contract with America.

WEB http://
edf.www.media.mit.edu/

**Information USA** Information about various government services.

GO INFOUSA

**IRS Online** A good source for tax information and downloadable forms.

WEB http://www.irs.ustreas.gov/
prod/

**IRS Tax Forms and Documents**
Downloadable and printable IRS tax forms complete with instructions.

    GO TAXFORMS

**Library of Congress**   Good source for government and other information.

    WEB http://www.loc.gov

**Library of Congress: Federal Government Page**   Links to Members of Congress Database of names, addresses, and other information about members of the Senate and the House of Representatives.

    WEB http://lcweb.loc.gov/global/
    legislative/congress.html

**Presidential Mail**   Send e-mail to the President.

    GO PRESMAIL

**Thomas: Legislative Information on the Internet**   Contains the full text of legislation before the House and Senate.

    WEB http://thomas.loc.gov/

**House of Representatives**   The place to find your congressperson online.

    WEB http://www.house.gov

**Senate**   A gopher server for the Senate.

    WEB http://www.senate.gov:70/

**Visa Advisors**   Service offering assistance in obtaining passports and visas.

    GO VISA

**White House**   The President's official Web site.

    WEB http://www.whitehouse.gov/

**White House Forum**   Libraries contain files provided by the White House.

    GO WHITEHOUSE

**Yahoo's Government Resources Index**
Master list of government-related resources on the Net.

    WEB http://www.yahoo.com/
    Government/

# Graphics

**Adobe Forum**   Vendor forum.

    GO ADOBE

**Adult File Finder**   File Finder for files with adult content.

    GO ADULTFF

**Amiga Arts Forum**   Vendor forum.

    GO AMIGAARTS

**Archive Photos Forum**   Historical photographs and drawings.

    GO ARCHIVE

**Autodesk AutoCAD Forum**   Vendor forum.

    GO ACAD

**Autodesk Multimedia Forum**   Vendor forum that includes sections on 3D Studio.

    GO ASOFT

**Autodesk Retail Products Forum**   Vendor forum.

    GO ARETAIL

**CADD/CAM/CAE Vendor Forum**   Vendor forum for CADD/CAM professionals.

    GO CADVEN

**CADENCE Forum**   Online magazine.

    GO CADENCE

**Commodore Art/Games Forum**   For users of Commodore computers.

    GO CBMART

**Computer Art Forum**   Featuring computer-generated images.

    GO COMART

**Corbis**   Photo archive on the Web.

    WEB http://www.corbis.com

**Corel Forum**   Vendor forum.

    GO CORELAPPS

**Desktop Publishing Forum**   Includes fonts, clip art, and DTP utilities.

    GO DTPFORUM

**Engineering Automation Forum**   For CADD/CAM professionals.

    GO LEAP

**FontBank Online**   Downloadable fonts for desktop publishing and word processing.

    GO FONTBANK

**Glamour Graphics Forum**   Libraries full of fashion and glamour photography; some adult content.

    GO GLAMOUR

**GO GRAPHICS Tutorial**   Tutorial for CompuServe's GO GRAPHICS areas.

    GO PIC

**Graphics Corner Forum**   CompuServe's primary collection of GIF and JPG images.

    GO CORNER

**Graphics Developers Forum**   Includes sections on fractals, ray tracing, 3D, animation, morphing, etc.

    GO GRAPHDEV

**Graphics File Finder**   File Finder for graphics files.

    GO GRAPHFF

**Graphics Forums**   Main area for CompuServe's graphics.

    GO GRAPHICS

**Graphics Gallery Forum**   Graphics collections.

    GO GALLERY

**Graphics Plus Forum**   High-resolution graphics files.

    GO GRAPHPLUS

**Graphics Showcase**   Highlights of individual contributions to CompuServe's graphics forums.

    GO GRFSHOW

**Graphics Support Forum**   Features software and utilities for viewing, downloading, converting, and printing GIF and JPG format graphics.

    GO GRAPHSUPPORT

**Graphics Vendor Forums**   Includes multiple forums (GRAPHAVEN, GRAPHBVEN, etc.)

    GO GRVEN

**Graphics Visual Index Forum**   Previews of images in CompuServe's graphics forums that use low-resolution thumbnails.

    GO GRFINDEX

**Human Form Photo Forum**   Photography of the human body, including swimsuit and lingerie photos; includes adult content.

    GO PHOTOHUMAN

**IBM ImagePlus Forum**   Vendor forum.

    GO IBMIMAGE

**Kodak CD Forum**   Vendor forum.

    GO KODAK

**Liaison International**   A Photo archive on the Web.

    WEB http://www.liaisonintl.com

**Words & Pixels Forum**   Vendor forum.

    GO LOTUSB

**Micrografx Forum**   Vendor forum.

    GO MICROGRAFX

**MicroStation Forum**   Vendor forum.

    GO MSTATION

**Muse**   Photo archive on the Web.

    WEB http://www.weststock.com

**PhotoDisc**   15,000 pictures in an online archive.

    WEB http://www.photodisc.com

**Picture Network International** Photographcs, clip art, illustrations, and sound effects archive.

    WEB http://
    www.publishersdepot.com

**Quick Picture Forum**   Low-resolution graphics files and clip art.

    GO QPICS

**Yahoo Image Surfer**   Yahoo's index of graphics on the Net; it uses a unique thumbnail preview.

    WEB http://isurf.yahoo.com/

# Health & Fitness

**American Medical Association**   Official site of the AMA.

    WEB http://www.ama-assn.org/

**Ample Living Forum**   For people of size.

    GO AMPLE

**Attention Deficit Disorder Forum**   For those coping with ADD.

    GO ADD

**Biorhythms**   Online biorhythm charting.

    GO BIORHYTHM

**CCML AIDS Articles** Articles from the Comprehensive Core Medical Library.

    GO CCMLAIDS

**Consumer Reports Complete Drug Reference** Database on more than 700 prescription and over-the-counter medicines.

    GO DRUGS

**Diabetes Forum** Includes sections on hypoglycemics, insulin, oral medications, diet, exercise, etc.

    GO DIABETES

**Disabilities Forum** Includes sections on developmental disabilities, emotional disturbances, hearing impairments, etc.

    GO DISABILITIES

**Family Medicine Internet Sites** List of family-oriented medical sites on the Web.

    WEB http://
    mir.med.ucalgary.ca:70/1/family

**Handicapped User's Database** Information relevant to handicapped individuals.

    GO HANDICAPPED

**Health and Fitness Forum** Includes sections on mental health, addiction/recovery, family health, exercise & fitness, nutrition, martial arts, and self-help.

    GO GOODHEALTH

**Health and Vitamin Express** Online retailer.

    GO HVE-1

**Health Database Plus** Database of articles related to health care, disease prevention, fitness, nutrition, substance abuse, etc.

    GO HLTDB

**Health World Online** Online health resource.

    WEB http://www.healthy.net/

**Health/Fitness Service** Gateway to CompuServe's health-related services.

    GO FITNESS

**HealthGate** Online health resource.

    WEB http://www.healthgate.com/

**HealthNet** Health news and information; includes the HealthNet Reference Library and Sports Medicine.

    GO HNT

**HealthNet** Online health resource.

    WEB http://www.health-net.com/

**Healthtouch** Online health resource.

    WEB http://www.healthtouch.com/

**Human Sexuality Databank** Database of information on sex-related topics.

    GO HUMAN

**Internet Health Resources** List of health resources on the Internet.

    WEB http://www.ihr.com/

**Multimedia Medical Reference Library**
Database of health information; research
your own condition.

```
WEB http://www.tiac.net/users/
jtward/images.html
```

**Natural Medicine Forum**   Includes
sections on herbs and plants, diet and
exercise, women's health, chiropractic,
natural foods, etc.

```
GO HOLISTIC
```

**New Age Forums**   Multiple forums
(NEWAAGE, NEWBAGE, etc.).

```
GO NEWAGE
```

**Online Health Network**   Online health
resource.

```
WEB http://healthnet.ivi.com/
```

**PaperChase**   Access to the National
Library of Medicine's MEDLINE database
of biomedical literature.

```
GO PCH
```

**Physicians Data Query**   Access to four
databases from the National Cancer
Institute.

```
GO PDQ
```

**Public Health Forum**   Focuses on public
health issues.

```
GO PUBHLTH
```

**Rare Diseases Database**   Developed by the
National Organization for Rare Diseases
(NORD).

```
GO NORD
```

**Sundown Vitamins**   Online retailer.

```
GO SDV
```

**Survivors Forum**   Support services for
trauma survivors and their families and
caregivers.

```
GO SAFEPLACE
```

**Vegetarian Forum**   Recipes and issues for
vegetarians to digest.

```
GO VEGETARIAN
```

# History

**History Forum**   For students and history
buffs.

```
GO PAST
```

**Living History Forum**   Devoted to the re-
enactment of selected historical periods.

```
GO LIVING
```

# Hobbies

**Antique Forum**   For antique collectors.

```
GO ANTIQUES
```

**Artist Forum**   For artists and enthusiasts.

```
GO ARTIST
```

**Collectibles Forum**   Includes sections on
stamps, coins, autographs, books, music,
sports cards, dolls, Star Trek, etc.

```
GO COLLECT
```

**Comics/Animation Forum**   Includes sections on reviews, news, and conventions.

    GO COMIC

**Crafts Forum**   Includes sections on knitting, weaving, woodworking, quilting, etc.

    GO CRAFTS

**Dolls Forum**   For doll collectors.

    GO DOLLS

**HamNet Forum**   Includes sections on amateur radio, shortwave radio, satellite television, morse code, the FCC, etc.

    GO HAMNET

**Ideas, Inventions, and Innovations Forum**   Includes sections on creativity, research, new technology, funding, etc.

    GO INNOVATION

**Time-Warner Lifestyle Forum**   Includes sections on travel/places, food/drink/parties, sports/hobbies, appearance, relationships, etc.

    GO TWLIFE

**TrainNet Forum**   For model railroaders and fans of real trains.

    GO TRAINNET

**Yahoo's Hobbies and Crafts Index**
Master list of hobby/craft resources on the Internet.

    WEB http://
    www.yahoo.com/Entertainment/
    Hobbies_and_Crafts/

# Home & Leisure

**Appliance Forum**   For large and small appliances, everything from washers and dryers to vacuum cleaners.

    GO APPLIANCE

**Family Handyman Forum**   Includes sections on woodworking, remodeling, home repair, plumbing, painting, etc.

    GO HANDYMAN

**Gardening Forum**   Managed by National Gardening Magazine.

    GO GARDENING

**Home Forum**   Includes sections on security, home building, interior furnishing, lighting, etc.

    GO HOME

**Homefinder by AMS**   Online retailer.

    GO HF

**HomeValue Report**   Lets you determine the current value of any property in the U.S.

    GO DHV-1

**Mortgage Calculator**   Online tool for calculating mortgage rates.

    GO HOM-17

**Mortgage Strategies**   Online report: how to save on your mortgage interest.

    WEB http://www.ais.net:80/
    netmall/mortgage/mortgage.html

**Rural Living Forum**   Issues relevant to rural residents.

GO RURAL

**Time-Warner Dwellings Forum**   Topics of interest for homeowners.

GO DWELLINGS

**Time-Warner Home Forum**   Home improvement information; this forum covers the designing, building, restoring, renovating, and repairing of homes.

GO HOMING

**Time-Warner Lifestyle Forum**   Includes sections on travel/places, food/drink/parties, sports/hobbies, appearance, relationships, etc.

GO TWLIFE

**Working-From-Home Forum**   Includes sections on taxes, equipment, consulting, writing, etc.

GO WORK

# Hong Kong

**Hong Kong Forum**   For residents and tourists.

GO HONGKONG

# Hotels

**ABC Worldwide Hotel Guide**   Listings of over 60,000 hotels worldwide.

GO ABC

**Hotel Guide**   Web guide to hotels around the world.

WEB http://www.hotelguide.ch/

**Inn and Lodging Forum**   Includes sections on innkeeping, bed & breakfasts, elegant hotels, etc.

GO INNFORUM

**Lanier Bed & Breakfast Database**   Data on more than 9000 North American inns.

GO INNS

**TravelData Guide to Bed & Breakfast Inns**   Listing of thousands of bed & breakfast inns across America.

WEB http://www.ultranet.com/biz/inns/

**TravelWeb**   Information and reservations for most major hotel chains.

WEB http://www.travelweb.com/

**UK Accomodations & Travel Services**   Services provided by the UK Automobile Association.

GO UKACCOMODATION

**WORLDSPAN Travelshopper**   Online reservations from Delta, Northwest, and TWA airlines.

GO WORLDCIM

# Internet

**Alta Vista**   Web-based search engine.

WEB http://www.altavista.digital.com/

**Archie FTP and Gopher Search**   Search for available FTP and Gopher sites.

> WEB http://www-ns.rutgers.edu/
> htbin/archie/

**Around the World in 80 Clicks**   Clickable map of the world; there are Web sites in each hotlinked region.

> WEB http://www.coolsite.com/
> arworld.html

**Beginner's Guide to URLs**   HTML resource.

> WEB http://www.ncsa.uiuc.edu/
> demoweb/url-primer.html

**Best of British Web Sites**   Best Web sites in the U.K.

> WEB http://www.vnu.co.uk/vnu/
> pcw/bob.html

**Big Eye**   List of five-star Web sites.

> WEB http://
> emporium.turnpike.net/E/
> emailclub/goodurls.htm

**c|net**   Most popular computer-related site on the Web.

> WEB http://www.cnet.com/

**Color Specifier**   HTML resource.

> WEB http://
> www.users.interport.net/~giant/
> COLOR/hype_color.html

**Composing Good HTML**   HTML resource.

> WEB http://www.cs.cmu.edu/~tilt/
> cgh/

**CompuServe E-Mail**   CompuServe's e-mail center.

> GO MAIL

**Cool Site of the Day**   Best of the Web highlighted daily.

> WEB http://www.infi.net/
> cool.html

**Crash Course on Writing Documents for the Web**   HTML resource.

> WEB http://www.ziff.com/~eamonn/
> crash_course.html

**CUSI**   Configurable Unified Search Index; a Web-based search engine.

> WEB http://www.eecs.nwu.edu/
> susi/cusi.html

**Do's and Don'ts of Web Style**   HTML resource.

> WEB http://millkern.com/
> do-dont.html

**E-Mail Essential Information**   How to send e-mail to users on commercial services and the Internet.

> WEB http://www.mcp.com/people/
> miller/emailadd.htm

**Elements of HTML Style**   HTML resource.

> WEB http://
> bookweb.cwis.uci.edu:8042/Staff/
> StyleGuide.html

**Excite**   Web-based search engine.

> WEB http://www.excite.com/

**FAQ Lists**   Archive of frequently asked questions lists.

> FTP rtfm.mit.edu

**FTP**   File transfer protocol for downloading files from the Internet.

> GO FTP

**Gamelan**   Earthweb's giant Java directory and supersite.

```
WEB http://www.gamelan.com/
```

**Home Page Wizard**   CompuServe's software for creating and publishing your own Web pages.

```
GO HPWIZ
```

**HotBot**   Web-based search engine.

```
WEB http://www.hotbot.com/
```

**How Do They Do That with HTML?**   HTML resource.

```
WEB http://www.nashville.net/
~carl/htmlguide/index.html
```

**HTML Documentation**   One of the best HTML resources available.

```
WEB http://www.utoronto.ca/
webdocs/HTMLdocs/NewHTML/
htmlindex.html
```

**HTML Editors**   Archive of popular HTML editing software, from the Que Software Library.

```
WEB http://www.mcp.com/que/
software/isoftwre.html
```

**iGuide**   A TV Guide for the Net.

```
WEB http://www.iguide.com/
index.sml
```

**InfoSeek**   Web-based search engine.

```
WEB http://guide.infoseek.com/NS
```

**Internet Developer's Forum**   For developers of Web pages and Web sites.

```
GO INETDE
```

**Internet Center**   The main menu for CompuServe's Internet services.

```
GO INTERNET
```

**Internet Commerce Forum**   For those using the Internet for business purposes.

```
GO INETCO
```

**Internet Controls**   Limit access to selected Internet sites.

```
GO PATROL
```

**Internet Magazine Forum**   Online magazine.

```
GO INTMAG
```

**Internet New Users Forum**   For new Internet users.

```
GO INETNEW
```

**Internet Publishing Forum**   For those publishing content on the Internet.

```
GO INETPUB
```

**Internet Resources Forum**   Establishes discussions and libraries for Internet-related software.

```
GO INETRES
```

**Internet WebMasters Forum**   For WebMasters and site administrators.

```
GO INETWEB
```

**Internet Welcome Center**   A good starting place for Internet users.

```
GO INETWC
```

**InternetWorld Magazine Forum**   Online magazine.

    GO IWORLD

**InterNIC**   Collections of all important Internet documents and information.

    FTP ds.internic.net

**Java Support Forum**   For developers and users of Java applets.

    GO JAVAUSER

**Lycos**   Web-based search engine.

    WEB http://www.lycos.com

**Macmillan's HTML Workshop**   Solid guide to HTML resources.

    WEB http://www.mcp.com/general/
    workshop/

**McKinley Magellan**   Web-based directory.

    WEB http://www.mckinley.com/

**Mother-of-all BBs**   Monster list of Web locations.

    WEB http://www.cs.colorado.edu/
    homes/mcbryan/public_html/bb/
    summary.html

**NetGuide**   Online magazine.

    GO NETGUIDE

**NetLauncher Support Forum**   For support of CompuServe's NetLauncher software.

    GO NLSUPPORT

**Netscape**   Official Netscape site; the place to download the latest version of Netscape Navigator.

    FTP ftp.netscape.com

**Netscape User's Forum**   For users of Netcape's Navigator Web browser.

    GO NSUSER

**New Riders Official World Wide Web Yellow Pages**   Online version of the popular printed directory.

    WEB http://www.mcp.com/nrp/
    wwwyp/

**Newbie's Guides to the Net**   Contains guides and hotlists for new Net users.

    WEB http://ug.cs.dal.ca:3400/
    franklin.html

**Online Issues Forum**   Discussions about censorship and other online issues.

    GO OLISSU

**Onramp Access**   Good places for new Net users to start.

    WEB http://onr.com/

**Our World**   Personal home pages from CompuServe members.

    WEB http://
    ourworld.compuserve.com

**Parental Controls Center**   For controlling access to parts of CompuServe and the Internet.

    GO CONTROLS

**Scout Report**   Weekly list of newly announced Internet resources.

    WEB http://rs.internic.net/
    scout_report-index.html

**Search.com**  List of all major search engines, from c|net.

WEB http://www.search.com/

**Special Characters in HTML**  HTML resource.

WEB http://www.utoronto.ca/
webdocs/HTMLdocs/NewHTML/
entities.html

**Starting Point**  A great starting point for Web exploration, with lists of sites arranged into categories.

WEB http://www.stpt.com/

**Submit It!**  Service that lists your Web pages with various search engines and directories

WEB http://www.submit-it.com/

**SuperSeek**  One engine that searches multiple search engines; it's from Macmillan Publishing.

WEB http://www.superseek.com/

**Telnet**  For accessing remote computers in command-line mode.

GO TELNET

**TradeWinds Galaxy**  Supersite with good search tools.

WEB http://www.einet.net

**Ultimate Guide to Internet Service Providers**  Listing of ISPs from c|net.

WEB http://www.cnet.com/Content/
Reviews/Compare/ISP/

**URouLette**  Click to this site and get randomly spun to another site somewhere on the Web.

WEB http://kuhttp.cc.ukans.edu/
cwis/organizations/kucia/
uroulette/uroulette

**Useless WWW Pages**  The worst of the Web.

WEB http://www.primus.com/staff/
paulp/useless.html

**USENET Newsgroup Archives**  Archive of newsgroup articles, hosted by the University of Birmingham (U.K.).

FTP ftp.cs.bham.ac.uk

**USENET Newsgroups**  CompuServe's gateway to USENET, including newsreader software.

GO USENET

**UUNet NetNews**  Central distribution site for netnews traffic.

FTP ftp.uu.net

**Web Central**  A listing of popular sites on the Web—plus libraries full of the latest Web browsers.

GO WEBCENTRAL

**WebCrawler**  Search engine operated by CompuServe's chief competitor, America Online.

WEB http://webcrawler.com

### WebMaster Reference Library
Comprehensive resource for experienced Web developers and administrators.

```
WEB http://
www.webreference.com/
```

**WireTap**   Eclectic collection of interesting documents.

```
FTP wiretap.spies.com
```

**WWW Virtual Library**   Established list of Web sites.

```
WEB http://www.w3.org/
hypertext/DataSources/
bySubject/Overview.html
```

**Yahoo!**   One of the top Internet directories.

```
WEB http://www.yahoo.com
```

**Yahoo! Image Surfer**   Yahoo's index of graphics on the Net; it uses a unique thumbnail preview.

```
WEB http://isurf.yahoo.com/
```

**Yahooligans!**   Yahoo's directory of kid-friendly sites.

```
WEB http://www.yahooligans.com/
```

# Ireland

**Northern Ireland News**   News from the Emerald Isle.

```
GO NIRELAND
```

# Israel

**Israel Forum**   For residents and tourists.

```
GO ISRAEL
```

**Jerusalem Post**   Online Israli newspaper.

```
GO JERUSALEM
```

**Jewish CyberCenter**   Main menu for CompuServe's Jewish-related areas.

```
GO JWS
```

# Italy

**Il Sole 24 Ore**   Covering Italian financial, industrial, and economic information.

```
GO ILSOLE
```

**Italian Forum**   For residents and tourists

```
GO ITALFO
```

**Microsoft Italy**   Vendor forum, for Microsoft's Italian operations.

```
GO MSITA
```

**Microsoft Italy Forum**   Vendor forum, for Microsoft's Italian operations.

```
GO MSITALY
```

**Mondo Economico/L'Impresa**   Online Italian newspaper.

```
GO MONDOECO
```

# Japan

**Japan Forum**   For residents and tourists.

```
GO JAPAN
```

# Kids

**Animal Forum**   Includes sections on ferrets, potbellied pigs, reptiles, parrots, wildlife, small mammals, insects, etc.

    GO ANIMALS

**Best Sites for Children**   List of kid-friendly Web sites.

    WEB http://www.cochran.com:80/
    theosite/ksites.html

**Dinosaur Forum**   Includes discussions of interest to both the professional and the layperson; great for kids!

    GO DINO

**Frost's Summer Camp Guide**   Online guide to summer camps.

    GO FRO

**Games Site**   Youth-oriented game center.

    GO GMS

**Jack Hanna's Animal Adventures**   Animal fun from the TV show.

    GO JUNGLEJACK

**Just for Laffs**   Online joke contest for kids.

    GO JFL

**Kid Central**   CompuServe's gateway to areas of interest to kids.

    GO KID

**Kids Students Forum**   For younger students.

    GO STUFOC

**KidsNet**   Various CompuServe services just for kids.

    GO KIDSNET

**Missing Children Forum**   Sponsored by the National Center for Missing and Exploited Children; includes information about and pictures of missing children.

    GO MISSING

**My Virtual Reference Desk**   Reference information for children.

    WEB http://www.refdesk.com/

**Outdoors Kids Forum**   Outdoor fun.

    GO OUTKIDS

**Scouting Forum**   Scouting program discussions and news.

    GO SCOUTING

**Snoopy Site**   Peanuts comics and art online.

    GO SNOOPY

**Teens Student Forum**   For high school and middle school students.

    GO STUFOA

**Trading Card Forum**   For sports and other cards.

    GO CARDS

**Yahooligans!**   Yahoo's directory of kid-friendly sites.

    WEB http://www.yahooligans.com/

**Youth Entertainment Drive**   Version of EDrive for kids and teens; includes sections on television, movies & videos, pop culture, music & bands, games, computers/Internet, sports & hobbies, etc.

    GO YDRIVE

**Yoyodyne Entertainment**   Online games for kids.

    GO YOY

# Latin America

**Latin American Forum**   For residents and tourists.

    GO FORLATIN

**Microsoft Spain/Latin America**   Vendor forum.

    GO MSSPAIN

**Microsoft Spain/Latin America Forum**   Vendor forum.

    GO MSSP

# Law

**Cornell University Law School Archives**   Legal documents on the Internet.

    FTP ftp.law.cornell.edu

**Court Reporters Forum**   For court reporters and related professionals.

    GO CRFORUM

**Legal Forum**   For both attorneys and the layperson.

    GO LAWSIG

**Legal Research Center**   Access to various legal databases, including American Banker, Congressional Information Service, Criminal Justice Periodical Index, Legal Resource Index, National Criminal Justice Reference Service, and Tax Notes Today.

    GO LEGALRC

**Patent Research Center**   Database of U.S. patents.

    GO PATENT

**Seamless WebSite**   Law and legal resources on the Web.

    WEB http://starbase.ingress.com/
    tsw/

# Magazines

**Advertising Age**   Online marketing magazine.

    WEB http://www.adage.com/

**AI Expert Forum**   Magazine vendor forum.

    GO AIEXPERT

**Automobile Magazine**   Online magazine.

    GO AUTOLIVE

**Aviation Week Group**   Online magazine.

    GO AWG

**CADENCE Forum**   Online magazine.

    GO CADENCE

**CarWorld Connect**   Online British motoring magazine.

    GO CARWORLDCONNECT

**CarWorld Connect Forum**   Forum for the British motoring magazine.

    GO TALKCARWORLD

**CCM Online**   Online version of Christian music magazine.

    GO CCMUSIC

**Cobb Applications Forum**   Part of ZDNet.

    GO ZNT:COBAPP

**Cobb Programming Forum**   Part of ZDNet.

    GO ZNT:COBBPR

**CompuServe Magazine**   Online magazine.

    GO COMPUMAG

**Computer Database Plus**   Online magazine.

    GO COMPDB

**Computer Gaming World**   Online magazine.

    GO CGWMAGAZINE

**Computer Life**   Online magazine.

    GO LIFE

**Computer Shopper Magazine**   Online magazine; part of the ZDNet service.

    GO CSHOPPER

**Conde Nast Traveler**   Online travel magazine.

    WEB http://www.cntraveler.com/

**Consumer Reports**   Online magazine.

    GO CONSUMER

**Consumer Reports Complete Drug Reference**   Database on more than 700 prescription and over-the-counter medicines.

    GO DRUGS

**Data Based Advisor Forum**   Online magazine.

    GO DBADVISOR

**DBMS Forum**   Online magazine.

    GO DBMS

**DER SPIEGEL Forum**   Online magazine.

    GO SPIEGEL

**Dr. Dobb's Forum**   Online magazine.

    GO DDJFORUM

**Electronic Gamer**   Online magazine.

    GO EGAMER

**Electronic Newsstand**   Listing of electronic newspapers and magazines on the Internet.

    WEB http://www.enews.com/

**Entertainment Weekly**   Online entertainment magazine.

    WEB http://www.pathfinder.com/
    ew/Welcome.html

**Small Business Forum**   For entrepreneurs and small businesses, from *Entrepreneur Magazine*.

    GO USEN

**FHM Connect** Online version of British men's magazine.

GO FHMCONNECT

**FHM Connect Forum** Forum for *FHM* magazine.

GO TALKFHM

**FORBES** Online magazine.

GO FORBES

**Fortean Times** Online magazine of the paranormal; lots of UFOs, aliens, ghosts, etc.

WEB http:// alpha.mic.dundee.ac.uk/ft/

**FORTUNE Magazine** Online magazine.

GO FORTUNE

**HotWired** Online version of *Wired* magazine.

WEB http://www.hotwired.com/

**IndustryWeek Interactive** Online magazine.

GO INDWEEK

**Internet Magazine Forum** Online magazine.

GO INTMAG

**InternetWorld Magazine Forum** Online magazine.

GO IWORLD

**Kiplinger Online** Online magazine.

WEB http://www.kiplinger.com/

**LAN Magazine** Online magazine.

GO LANMAG

**Macleans Online** Online magazine.

GO MACLEANS

**MacUser/MacWEEK Index** Index of stories from *MacUser* and *MacWEEK* magazines, part of ZDNet.

GO ZNT:ZMACINDEX

**Magazine Database Plus** Database of articles from major magazines.

GO MAGDB

**Magna Media Forum** Online magazines, including *Computer Persoenlich* and *PC Magazin*.

GO MAGNA

**Money Magazine** Online magazine.

GO MONEY

**Money Magazine's FundWatch Online** Database that lets you analyze and screen more than 1900 mutual funds.

GO MONEYMAG

**MotorWeek Online** Online motor sports magazine.

GO MOTORWEEK

**Multimedia World** Online magazine.

GO MMWORLD

**National Geographic Online** Online magazine.

GO NATIONALGEOGRAPHIC

**NetGuide**   Online magazine.

```
GO NETGUIDE
```

**NetWare Solutions**   Online magazine.

```
GO NWSOLUTIONS
```

**New York Magazine**   Online magazine.

```
GO NYMAG
```

**News Source USA**   Database of articles from major U.S. newspapers and magazines.

```
GO NEWSLIB
```

**PC Computing**   Online magazine, part of the ZDNet service.

```
GO PCCOMP
```

**PC Direct France Forum**   Online magazine.

```
GO PCDFRA
```

**PC Direct UK Magazine Forum**   Online magazine; part of the ZDNet service.

```
GO PCDUK
```

**PC Direkt Forum**   Online magazine.

```
GO PCDIREKT
```

**PC Magazine**   Online magazine.

```
GO PCMAGAZINE
```

**PC Magazine UK Forum**   Online magazine; part of the ZDNet service.

```
GO PCUKFORUM
```

**PC Magazine UK Online**   Online magazine; part of the ZDNet service.

```
GO PCUKONLINE
```

**PC MagNet Editorial Forum**   Part of ZDNet.

```
GO EDITORIAL
```

**PC MagNet Programming Forum**   Part of ZDNet.

```
GO PROGRAMMING
```

**PC MagNet Utilities/Tips Forum**   Part of ZDNet.

```
GO TIPS
```

**PC Plus/PC Answers Online**   Online magazines.

```
GO PCPLUS
```

**PC Professionell Forum**   Online magazine.

```
GO PCPRO
```

**PC Publications**   Subscription service for *PC Novice*, *PC Today*, and *PC Catalog* magazines.

```
GO PCB
```

**PC Week Forum**   Online magazine, part of the ZDNet service.

```
GO PCWEEK
```

**PC World Entertainment Forum**   Online magazine with coverage of state-of-the-art multimedia games.

```
GO GAMING
```

**PC World Online**   Online magazine.

```
GO PCWORLD
```

**People Magazine Online**   Online magazine.

```
GO PEOPLE
```

**Playboy**   The famous men's magazine online.

    GO PLAYBOY

**Playboy Forum**   The forum for *Playboy* magazine.

    GO PLAYFORUM

**Reserve Officers Association**   Online military magazine.

    GO MIL-401

**Selling**   Online magazine.

    GO SELLING

**Sky & Telescope**   Online magazine.

    GO SKYTEL

**Software Development Forum**   Online magazine.

    GO SDFORUM

**Sports Illustrated**   Online magazine that serves as CompuServe's main sports area.

    GO SPORTS

**Sports Illustrated Online**   Online magazine.

    GO SIMAGAZINE

**Stars and Stripes**   Online military magazine.

    GO MIL-300

**Time-Warner Pathfinder**   Supersite containing various Time-Warner properties including magazines, Time-Warner books, Warner Bros. movies and music, HBO, and more. Recommended.

    WEB http://www.pathfinder.com/

**Time News Center**   News from *TIME* magazine, plus breaking news from the Associated Press.

    GO TIME

**UK Computer Shopper Forum**   Online magazine.

    GO UKSHOPPER

**Veterans of Foreign Wars**   Online military magazine.

    GO MIL-500

**Vietnam Veterans of America**   Online military magazine.

    GO MIL-420

**Visual Basic Programmer's Journal**   Online magazine.

    GO VBPJFO

**Vogel**   Online magazine.

    GO VOGEL

**Windows Deutschland Forum**   Online magazine.

    GO GERWIN

**Windows Magazine Online**   Online magazine.

    GO WINMAG

**Windows Sources Forum**   Online magazine.

    GO WINSOURCES

**WordPerfect Magazine** Online magazine.

GO WPMAG

**ZDNet** Web version of ZDNet—quite different from the service on CompuServe.

WEB http://www.zdnet.com/

**Ziff Editor's Choice** Database of Editor's Choice awards; part of ZDNet.

GO ZNT:EDCHOICE

**Zshare Online Newsletter** Monthly review of shareware programs; part of the ZDNet service.

GO ZNT:ZSHARE

# Maps

**Around the World in 80 Clicks** Clickable map of the world with hotlinked Web sites in each region.

WEB http://www.coolsite.com/
arworld.html

**Lycos Road Map** Instant Web-based mapping service—enter your information, and it draws a detailed map.

WEB http://www.proximus.com/
lycos/

**MAGELLAN Geographix** Online mapping.

GO MAGELLAN

# Marketing

**Advertising Age** Online marketing magazine.

WEB http://www.adage.com/

**PR and Marketing Forum** Includes sections on public relations, advertising, research, etc.

GO PRSIG

# Masonry

**Masonry Forum** Topics of interest to Freemasons.

GO MASONRY

# Mexico

**Mexico Forum** For residents and tourists.

GO MEXICO

**Mexico Interest Forum** Items of interest to residents and travelers.

GO HOM-213

**Mexico Travel & Culture Forum** Discussions of interest to tourists.

GO MEXTRAVEL

**Televisa Noticias** Mexican news.

GO TEV

# Military

**All Things Military** Main menu to CompuServe's military-related services.

GO MILITARY

**Buddy Search** Search for current and past members of the military.

GO MIL-200

**Civil War Forum**   For Civil War buffs.

    GO CIVILWAR

**Military and Vet Affairs News**   News of interest to American veterans and current military.

    GO MIL-100

**Military Forum**   Includes sections on veterans, Vietnam, WWII, military history, reunions, Civil War, etc.

    GO MILFORUM

**Military Multimedia Forum**   Military pictures and sounds.

    GO MILGRAPHICS

**Military Organizations Forum**   Includes sections on ROA, VFW, VVA, Marine Corps League, Civil Air Patrol, etc.

    GO MILORGAN

**Reserve Officers Association**   Online military magazine.

    GO MIL-401

**Stars and Stripes**   Online military magazine.

    GO MIL-300

**Veterans of Foreign Wars**   Online military magazine.

    GO MIL-500

**Vietnam Veterans of America**   Online military magazine.

    GO MIL-420

# Movies

**All-Movie Guide**   Comprehensive movie database from the folks who brought you the All-Music Guide.

    GO ALLMOVIE

**Archive Films Forum**   Downloadable historical videos in AVI format; over 14,000 hours of footage from newsreels, silent films, Hollywood features and documentaries .

    GO ARCFILM

**Deutsches Film Forum**   German films.

    GO FILME

**Entertainment Drive Forum**   Includes sections on movies, television, music, people, etc.

    GO EDRIVE

**Film.com**   Good movie site.

    WEB http://www.film.com/

**Firefly**   Find others who share your taste in movies and music—interactively.

    WEB http://www.ffly.com/

**France Cinema Forum**   French films.

    GO CINEFORUM

**Hollywood Hotline**   The latest entertainment industry news.

    GO HOLLYWOOD

**Hollywood Online**   Good movie site.

    WEB http://www.hollywood.com/

**Hollywood Online Forum**  Movie information and discussions.

    GO FLICKS

**Internet Movie Database**  Comprehensive database of movies, actors, directors, etc.

    WEB http://www.cm.cf.ac.uk/
    movies

**Ken Crane's Laserdisc Superstore**  Online laserdisc retailer.

    WEB http://www.kencranes.com/
    laserdiscs/

**Laser's Edge, The**  Online laserdisc retailer.

    GO LE

**Magill's Survey of Cinema**
Comprehensive database of film-related articles dating back to 1902.

    GO MAGILL

**Movie Reviews**  Gateway to CompuServe's various movie review features.

    GO MOVIES

**Movie Web**  Good movie site.

    WEB http://movieweb.com/movie/
    movie.html

**Paramount Pictures**  Online home of Paramount—movies and television.

    WEB http://www.paramount.com/

**Roger Ebert's Movie Reviews**  Database of movie reviews from the guy with the big thumb.

    GO EBERT

**Science Fiction and Fantasy Media Forums**  All forms of SF and fantasy are represented here, from current TV shows and movies to classic SF like Star Wars, Star Trek, and Doctor Who.

    GO SFMEDIA1 and GO SFMEDIA2

**ScreenScene**  Main menu to CompuServe's movie and TV areas.

    GO SCENE

**Time-Warner Pathfinder**  Supersite containing various Time-Warner properties, including magazines (*TIME, Life, Entertainment Weekly, People, Money, Sports Illustrated, Vibe, Fortune*), Time-Warner books, Warner Bros. movies and music, HBO, and more. Recommended.

    WEB http://www.pathfinder.com/

**UK Film Reviews**  Reviews of movies currently playing in Britain.

    GO UKFILMS

**UK Video Reviews**  Reviews of current British videotape releases.

    GO UKVIDEO

# Music

**All-Music Guide**  Comprehensive database of albums and artists.

    GO AMGTOP

**All-Music Guide Forum**  Providing help and discussions on the All-Music Guide database.

    GO AMGOP

**American Oldies Diner**   For fans of the oldies.

    GO OLDIES

**Billboard Online**   Online version of the music industry magazine.

    WEB http://www.billboard-
    online.com/

**CCM Online**   Online version of Christian music magazine.

    GO CCMUSIC

**CDNow!**   Online retailer of music CDs and tapes.

    WEB http://www.cdnow.com/

**Country Connection**   Premier site for country music.

    WEB http://digiserve.com/
    country/

**Electric Soul Forum**   Soul music online.

    GO SOUL

**Firefly**   Find others who share your taste in movies and music—interactively.

    WEB http://www.ffly.com/

**Grammys**   Site devoted to the Grammy awards.

    GO GRAMMY

**Internet Music World**   Good music site.

    WEB http://mozart.mw3.com:80/
    imw/

**Jazz Beat Forum**   For online jazzers.

    GO JAZZ

**Metaverse**   Supersite for music and counterculture.

    WEB http://www.metaverse.com/
    index.html

**MIDI Vendor Forums**   Multiple vendor forums (MIDIAVEN, MIDIBVEN, etc.)

    GO MIDIVEN

**MIDI/Music Forum**   Includes large software library of music files.

    GO MIDIFORUM

**Music and Performing Arts Forum**   Includes sections on music, dance, drama, etc.

    GO MUSICARTS

**Music Hall**   Gateway to CompuServe's music-related areas.

    GO MUSIC

**Music In(ter)Action Forum**   New music, electronic music, and experimental music.

    GO IMUSIC

**Music Industry Forum**   For music industry professionals.

    GO INMUSIC

**Music Vendor Forum**   Vendor forum.

    GO MUSICVEN

**Music/Arts Forum**   Includes sections on classical/opera, blues, jazz, shows, pop/rock, religious music, etc.

    GO MUSICARTS

**Musik Europe Alive** The European music scene.

GO MUSIK

**Recording Industry Forum** News from commercial and independent record labels.

GO RECORD

**Rock Online Forum** Rock & roll online.

GO ROCKONLINE

**Rocknet** The latest news in rock and lists of the top releases.

GO ROCK

**Rocknet Forum** Includes reviews of concerts and albums.

GO ROCKNET

**Ticketmaster Online** Order tickets for upcoming concerts, online.

WEB http://www.ticketmaster.com/

**TV Bytes** Comprehensive database of television theme songs, playable over the Web.

WEB http://www.tvtrecords.com/ tvbytes/

**UK Music Forum** Music in the U.K.

GO UKMUSIC

**Virgin Megastores** Online retailer; the largest record store in the world.

GO VIRGIN

**Warner Bros. Song Preview** Song clips, release dates, and tour dates for major Warner Bros. Records artists.

GO WBPREVIEW

**Wired on Country Forum** For fans of country music.

GO COUNTRY

# Netherlands

**Netherlands Forum** For residents and tourists.

GO NLFORUM

# News

**Archive Photos Forum** Historical photographs and drawings.

GO ARCHIVE

**Associated Press France en Ligne** French news.

GO APFRANCE

**Associated Press Online** General news coverage.

GO APO

**Business Wire, The** Database of business press releases.

GO TBW

**ClariNet** Access to all the news in ClariNet newsgroups.

WEB http://www.clarinet.com/

**CNN Forum** CNN's forum on CompuServe.

GO CNNFORUM

**CNN Interactive** Online version of the Cable News Network.

    GO CNN

**CNN Web** CNN's Web-based service.

    WEB http://www.cnn.com/

**CNNfn** Online version of the cable financial news network.

    WEB http://cnnfn.com/

**Commercial News Services on the Internet** Listing of major news services on the Web.

    WEB http://www.jou.ufl.edu/
    commres/webjou.htm

**DPA-Kurznachrichtendfiendst** German news.

    GO DPANEWS

**Executive News Service** CompuServe's customizable news area.

    GO ENS

**Focus on the News** Full-service news area.

    GO BAD

**National Public Radio** Includes daily news and conferences.

    GO NPR

**New York NewsLink Forum** New York-area news and information from Gannett Suburban Newspapers.

    GO NEWYORK

**News** CompuServe's main News menu and a gateway to other news services online.

    GO NEWS

**News-A-Tron** Daily financial news.

    GO NAT

**News Source USA** Database of articles from major U.S. newspapers and magazines.

    GO NEWSLIB

**Newsbytes** Daily computer news, part of the ZDNet service.

    GO ZNT:NEWSBYTES

**NewsGrid** Stories from wire services worldwide.

    GO NEWSGRID

**NewsNet** Database of business news from major newsletters and news services.

    GO NN

**Northern Ireland News** News from the Emerald Isle.

    GO NIRELAND

**Online Today** Daily computer news.

    GO ONLINE

**OTC NewsAlert** News clipping service featuring news from Reuters, Washington Post, etc.

    GO ENS

**PA News Online** British news.

    GO PAO

**PR Newswire** Compendium of press releases, updated daily.

GO PRNEWS

**Reuter's Canadian News Clips** Canadian news.

GO RTCANADA

**Reuters News Pictures Forum** News photographs from Reuters.

GO NEWSPI

**Reuter's UK News Clips** British news.

GO UKREUTERS

**Televisa Noticias** Mexican news.

GO TEV

**Time News Center** News from *TIME* magazine and breaking news from the Associated Press.

GO TIME

**UK News Clips** Current U.K. news from the PA News service.

GO UKNEWS

**UUNet NetNews** Central distribution site for netnews traffic.

FTP ftp.uu.net

**What's New** Events and news about CompuServe.

GO NEW

**Yahoo's News Index** List of hundreds of online news sources.

WEB http://www.yahoo.com/News/

# Newspapers

**Australian Associated Press Online** Australian news.

GO AAPONLINE

**Detroit Free Press** Online newspaper.

GO DETROIT

**Detroit Free Press Store** Subscription service for the Detroit Free Press; also includes books and other merchandise.

GO DFM-1

**Education Week** Online educational newspaper.

GO EWE

**Electronic Newsstand** Listing of electronic newspapers and magazines on the Internet.

WEB http://www.enews.com/

**Florida Today Forum** Online newspaper.

GO FLATODAY

**Il Sole 24 Ore** Online Italian newspaper.

GO ILSOLE

**Jerusalem Post** Online Israli newspaper.

GO JERUSALEM

**Le Monde** Online French newspaper.

GO LME

**Mondo Economico/L'Impresa** Online Italian newspaper.

GO MONDOECO

**Neue Zurcher Zeitung**   Online German newspaper.

GO ZUERCHER

**New York NewsLink Forum**   New York-area news and information from Gannett Suburban Newspapers.

GO NEWYORK

**New York Times on the Web**   Online newspaper.

WEB http://www.nytimes.com/

**News Source USA**   Database of articles from major U.S. newspapers and magazines.

GO NEWSLIB

**Newspaper Archives**   Database of stories from major U.S. and U.K. newspapers.

GO NEWSARCHIVE

**Newspapers on the Net**   Listing of Web-based newspapers from the Newspaper Association of American (NAA).

WEB http://www.infi.net/naa/

**Syndicated Columns**   Database of recent columns from more than a dozen newspaper journalists, this forum includes the Gadget Guru, Joyce Jillson's Horoscope, Marilyn Beck, and Stacy Smith's Hollywood.

GO COLUMNS

**UK Newspaper Library**   Database of stories from major U.K. newspapers.

GO UKPAPERS

**USA Today**   Online version of USA's newspaper.

WEB http://www.usatoday.com/

**Wall Street Journal on the Web**   Online newspaper that includes the continually updated Money & Investing Update.

WEB http:///www.wsj.com/

# Paranormal

**Encounters Forum**   Includes video clips, interviews, news reports, and discussions about UFO sightings.

GO ENCOUNTERS

**Fortean Times**   Online magazine of the paranormal; lots of UFOs, aliens, ghosts, etc.

WEB http://
alpha.mic.dundee.ac.uk/ft/

**JFK Assassination Forum**   Includes sections on transcripts, books, articles, organized crime, Jack Ruby, etc.

GO JFKFORUM

**Mysteries Forum**   For paranormal and conspiracy buffs; sections on the JFK assassination, government secrecy, crimes and trials, alternative science, natural oddities, etc.

GO MYSTERIES

**UFO Forum**   Aliens, abductions, encounters, theories; you name it, they're all here.

GO UFOFORUM

**UFO Page**   UFOs on the Net.

> WEB http://www.schmitzware.com/
> ufo.html

# Photography

**Ansel Adams Home Page**   Web site for the legendary photographer.

> WEB http://
> bookweb.cwis.uci.edu:8042/
> AdamsHome.html

**Archive Photos Forum**   Historical photographs and drawings.

> GO ARCHIVE

**Corbis**   Photo archive on the Web.

> WEB http://www.corbis.com

**FocalPoint f/8**   Premier Web site for photographers.

> WEB http://www.f8.com/

**Glamour Graphics Forum**   Libraries full of fashion and glamour photography; some adult content.

> GO GLAMOUR

**Graphics Corner Forum**   CompuServe's primary collection of GIF and JPG images.

> GO CORNER

**Graphics Gallery Forum**   Graphics collections.

> GO GALLERY

**Graphics Plus Forum**   High-resolution graphics files.

> GO GRAPHPLUS

**Human Form Photo Forum**   Photographs of the human form, including swimsuit and lingerie photos; includes adult content.

> GO PHOTOHUMAN

**Kodak CD Forum**   Vendor forum.

> GO KODAK

**Liaison International**   Photo archive on the Web.

> WEB http://www.liaisonintl.com

**Muse**   Photo archive on the Web.

> WEB http://www.weststock.com

**PhotoDisc**   15,000 pictures in an online archive.

> WEB http://www.photodisc.com

**Photography Forum**   For amateur and professional photographers.

> GO PHOTOFORUM

**Picture Network International** Photographics, clip art, illustrations, and sound effects archive.

> WEB http://
> www.publishersdepot.com

**Reuters News Pictures Forum**   News photographs from Reuters.

> GO NEWSPI

# Politics

**AllPolitics**   Great political information site, jointly run by CNN and TIME.

> WEB http://allpolitics.com/

**America Vote's National Town Hall** A way to send Washington your opinions on issues of the day.

    WEB http://www.americavote.com/
    vote

**American Voter '96** Web site devoted to the 1996 election.

    WEB http://voter96.cqalert.com/

**CapWeb** An unauthorized but comprehensive guide to the U.S. Congress.

    WEB http://policy.net/capweb/

**CBS Campaign '96** CBS News' official Web site for the 1996 elections.

    WEB http://www.cbsnews.com/
    campaign96/

**Democratic Forum** For members of the Democratic Party.

    GO DEMOCRAT

**Electronic Democracy Forum** Where you can read and discuss Newt Gingrich's Contract with America.

    WEB http://
    edf.www.media.mit.edu/

**Political Action Resources** A great page of political information and links (U.S. information from Korea).

    WEB http://kimsoft.com/
    kimpol.htm

**Political Debate Forum** Includes areas for both Democrats and Republicans.

    GO POLITICS

**Republican Forum** For members of the GOP.

    GO REPUBLICAN

**Rush Limbaugh's Download Area** Files of interest to Dittoheads.

    GO RUSHDL

**WebActive** A good site for Web-based political activism.

    WEB http://www.webactive.com/

**Yahoo's Politics Index** Massive listing of political sites on the Net.

    WEB http://www.yahoo.com/
    Politics/

# Publishing

**Comics Publishers Forum** Information about major publishers of comic books, such as Marvel and DC Comics.

    GO COMICPUB

**Cowles/SIMBA Media Daily** A daily online newsletter reporting on the publishing and media businesses.

    GO MEDIADAILY

**Internet Publishing Forum** For those publishing content on the Internet.

    GO INETPUB

**PRC Database Publishing Services** Online manufacturer specializing in publishing needs.

    GO PRC

**PTS Newsletter Database, Broadcast &
Publishing Section** Database of media-
related newsletters.

GO MEDIANEWS

# Radio

**Broadcast Professionals Forum** Includes
sections on television, radio, cable TV,
audio, the FCC, etc.

GO BPFORUM

**National Public Radio** Includes daily
news and conferences.

GO NPR

**Superman Radio Serial** Listen to episodes
from 1940s Superman radio serials on your
own PC.

WEB http://www.dccomics.com/
radio/index.html

# Recreation

**AA Golf** British golf information.

GO UKGOLF

**Camping Forum** For campers.

GO CAMPING

**Complete Guide to America's National
Parks** News and information from the
National Park Service.

GO PARKS

**Cycling Forum** For bicyclists.

GO CYCLING

**Firearms Forum** For gun lovers.

GO FIREARMS

**Fishing Forum** For fishermen of all types.

GO FISHING

**Golf Guide Online** From the Lanier Golf
Database, a comprehensive listing of more
than 12,000 golf courses across the U.S. and
1,200 more courses worldwide.

GO GLF

**Great Outdoor Recreation Pages (GORP)**
Terrific source for information on outdoor
activities.

WEB http://www.gorp.com/

**Hunting Forum** Topics relevant to gun and
bow hunters.

GO HUNTING

**Nudist & Naturist Forum** For the clothing-
free among us.

GO NUDIST

**Outdoors Forum** Includes sections on
fishing, hunting, camping, cycling, birding,
boating, scouting, nudism, etc.

GO OUTDOORS

**Outdoors Kids Forum** Outdoor fun.

GO OUTKIDS

**Outdoors News Clips** News on environmental and outdoors activities.

GO OUTNEWS

**Recreational Vehicle Forum** For RV owners.

GO RVFORUM

**Sail Racing Forum** Includes sections about inshore, offshore, and other types of racing.

GO SAILRACE

**Sailing Forum** Includes sections on weather survival, safety, folklore, etc.

GO SAILING

**Sailing Reception Area** Main sailing area.

GO SAIL

**Scouting Forum** Scouting program discussions and news.

GO SCOUTING

**SCUBA Forum** Includes sections on equipment, dive sites, etc.

GO DIVING

**Skiing Forum** For snow skiers everywhere.

GO SKIING

**Tennis Forum** For tennis players and fans.

GO TENNIS

# Reference

**American Heritage Dictionary** Online dictionary.

GO DICTIONARY

**AT&T's 800 Directory** Database of toll-free numbers across the U.S.

WEB http://att.net/dir800/

**BertelsmannUnivsallexikon** Bertelsmann's German-language encyclopedia online.

GO BEPLEXIKON

**Biography Research Center** Biographical information on international business executives and other professionals.

GO BIOGRAPHY

**Biz*File** Look up names, addresses, and phone numbers for businesses across the U.S.

GO BIZFILE

**Computer Library Online** Database of information for computer users.

GO COMPLIB

**Electric Library** Good Web-based encyclopedia and database of information.

WEB http://www.elibrary.com/

**Encyclopedia Britannica Online** Web-based version of EB.

WEB http://www.eb.com/

**Grolier's Academic American Encyclopedia** Online encyclopedia.

GO GROLIERS

**Hutchinson Encyclopedia** Online encyclopedia.

GO HUTCHINSON

**Information Please Almanac** General-interest almanac.

   GO GENALMANAC

**Information Please Business Almanac** Business almanac, from the Information Please people.

   GO BIZALMANAC

**Information Please Sports Almanac** Sports almanac, from the Information Please people.

   GO APTALMANAC

**Information USA** Information about various government services.

   GO INFOUSA

**My Virtual Reference Desk** Reference information for children.

   WEB http://www.refdesk.com/

**Phone*File** Look up personal names, addresses, and phone numbers across the U.S.

   GO PHONEFILE

**Smithsonian** Online version of the world's greatest museum.

   WEB http://www.si.edu/

**Yahoo's Reference Index** Listing of reference resources on the Web.

   WEB http://www.yahoo.com/
   Reference/

# Religion

**Catholic Online Forum** Catholic issues and discussions.

   GO CATHOLIC

**CCM Online** Online version of Christian music magazine.

   GO CCMUSIC

**Christian City** Major area for Christian interests, including books and music.

   GO CHRISTIAN

**Christian City Forum** Includes sections on singles issues, teen's club, home schoolers, bible roundtable, families & kids, etc.

   GO CCITY

**Christian Fellowship Forum** A family-oriented gathering place.

   GO FELLOWSHIP

**Christian Interactive Network** Gateway to a variety of Christian and family-value areas on CompuServe.

   GO CIN

**Jewish CyberCenter** Main menu for CompuServe's Jewish-related areas.

   GO JWS

**Jewish Forum** Covers topics of interest to Jewish CompuServe members.

   GO JEWISH

**Jewish Singles**   Includes sections on single life, online dating, sexuality, women's issues, men's issues, etc.

    GO MAZALT

**New Age Forum**   Multiple forums (NEWAAGE, NEWBAGE, etc.).

    GO NEWAGE

**Religion Forum**   With sections for all major religions.

    GO RELIGION

**Religious Issues Forum**   Lively discussions on current religious issues.

    GO RELISSUES

**SDAs Online**   For members of the Seventh-Day Adventist church.

    GO SDA

**Taoism Home Page**   For Taoists.

    WEB www.cnu.edu/~patrcik/
    taoism.html

**The Holy See**   The Vatican, online.

    WEB http://www.vatican.va/

**Trinity Delta**   Private online service for Trinity College.

    GO TDELTA

**Trinity Delta Forum**   CompuServe area for Trinity College.

    GO TRINITY

**Worship Center**   A resource for church leadership and lay participants.

    GO WORSHIP

# Research

**AT&T's 800 Directory**   Database of toll-free numbers across the U.S.

    WEB http://att.net/dir800/

**Australian/New Zealand Research Centre**   Database of Australian information.

    GO ANZCOLIB

**Basic Company Snapshot**   Essential company information.

    GO BASCOMPAN

**Biography Research Center**   Biographical information on international business executives and other professionals.

    GO BIOGRAPHY

**Biz*File**   Look up names, addresses, and phone numbers for businesses across the U.S.

    GO BIZFILE

**Business Database Plus**   Database of detailed company information.

    GO BUSDB

**Canadian Company Information**   Financial reports on Canadian companies.

    GO COCAN

**Census Bureau Online Service**   A selection of statistical reports.

    GO CENDATA

**Company Analyzer** Comprehensive, one-stop shopping for company information.

```
GO ANALYZER
```

**Company Screening** Searches Disclosure database to identify investment candidates.

```
GO COSCREEN
```

**Disclosure** Very comprehensive database with full financial and management information on more than 11,000 firms, compiled from 10K and other public reports. Recommended.

```
GO DISCLOSURE
```

**Dissertation Abstracts** Database of academic dissertations; includes doctoral dissertations from 1861 and masters theses since 1962.

```
GO DISSERTATION
```

**Dun and Bradstreet Information Services** D&B information on the Web.

```
WEB http://www.dbisna.com/
```

**Dun's Canadian Market Identifiers** Database of information on Canadian companies, from D&B.

```
GO DBCAN
```

**Dun's Electronic Business Directory** Database of company information, from D&B.

```
GO DYP
```

**Dun's Market Identifiers** Database of company information, from D&B.

```
GO DUNS
```

**Education Research Forum** Sponsored by the American Educational Research Association.

```
GO EDRESEARCH
```

**Ei Compendex Plus** Abstracts and articles from engineering literature.

```
GO COMPENDEX
```

**ERIC (Education Resources Information Center)** Database of education-related articles.

```
GO ERIC
```

**European Company Information** Financial reports on European companies.

```
GO COEURO
```

**European Research Centre** Database of European information.

```
GO EUROLIB
```

**German Company Information** Financial reports on German companies.

```
GO COGERMAN
```

**German Research Centre** Database of German information.

```
GO GERLIB
```

**Global Report** Database of company information, from Citibank.

```
GO GLOREP
```

**Hoover's Company Database** Offering Company Profiles and Company Capsules.

```
GO HOOVER
```

**Hoover's Online**   Detailed company-specific information, similar to CompuServe's Hoover's database.

    WEB http://www.hoovers.com/

**I/B/E/S Earning Estimate Reports**   Institutional Broker's Estimate System, representing a consensus of analysts' forecasts.

    GO IBES

**IQuest**   CompuServe's major research database; you can look here for just about anything. Recommended.

    GO IQUEST

**Knowledge Index**   Database of articles from major journals. Accessible only during "off" hours.

    GO KI

**Library of Congress**   Good source for government and other information.

    WEB http://www.loc.gov

**Magazine Database Plus**   Database of articles from major magazines.

    GO MAGDB

**Management InfoCenter**   A subset of IQuest that focuses on business management information.

    GO IQMANAGEMENT

**Patent Research Center**   Database of U.S. patents.

    GO PATENT

**Phone*File**   Look up personal names, addresses, and phone numbers across the U.S.

    GO PHONEFILE

**Standard & Poor's Online**   Current business information on more than 5000 companies.

    GO S&P

**State and County Demographics**   Database of state and county demographic information.

    GO DEMOGRAPHICS

**SUPERSITE Demographics**   Database of demographics information; very sophisticated search capabilities.

    GO SUPERSITE

**Thomas Register Online**   Database of information on more than 150,000 U.S. and Canadian companies.

    GO THOMAS

**TRADEMARKSCAN**   Databases containing state and USA trademark information.

    GO TRADERC

**UK Company Information**   Financial information on British companies.

    GO COUK

**UK Company Library**   Database of information on British companies.

    GO UKLIB

# Restaurants

**AA Restaurants**   British restaurant information.

    GO UKREST

**CitySavvy**   Insider's guides to entertainment and dining in major U.S. cities.

    WEB http://www.cais.net/
    citysavvy/

**Good Pub Guide**   Database guide to British pubs.

    GO UKPUBS

**Zagat Restaurant Guide**   Thousands of restaurant reviews for more than 20 cities.

    GO ZAGAT

# Science

**Astronomy Forum**   For amateur and professional astronomers.

    GO ASTROFORUM

**Dinosaur Forum**   Includes discussions of interest to both the professional and the layperson; great for kids!

    GO DINO

**Earth Forum**   Includes sections on climate, water, forest, recycling, energy, population, Greenpeace, etc.

    GO EARTH

**Science Trivia Quiz**   Online trivia game.

    GO SCITRIVIA

**Science/Math Education Forum**   For science educators and students; includes practice problems for science and math college boards.

    GO SCIENCE

**Space Exploration Forum**   Includes information on earth observation, the planets, the sun, the moon, etc.

    GO SPACEX

**Space Flight Forum**   Includes sections on the Space Shuttle, space stations, new technology, etc.

    GO SPACEFLIGHT

**Space/Astronomy Forum**   Includes information on sunspots, solar flares, NASA activities, space technology, and space shuttle schedules.

    GO SPACE

# Science Fiction

**Collectibles Forum**   Includes sections on stamps, coins, autographs, books, music, sports cards, dolls, Star Trek, etc.

    GO COLLECT

**Science Fiction and Fantasy Literature Forums**   Includes sections on science fiction, fantasy, and horror.

    GO SFLIT and GO SFLITTWO

**Science Fiction and Fantasy Media Forums**   All forms of SF and fantasy are represented here, from current TV shows and movies, to classic SF like Star Wars, Star Trek, and Doctor Who.

GO SFMEDIA1 and GO SFMEDIA2

**Star Trek**   Paramount's official page for TV and movie versions of Star Trek.

WEB http://www.paramount.com/
Splash.html

**Star Trek Resources**   List of Star Trek sites on the Internet.

WEB http://www.astro.nwu.edu/
lentz/sci-fi/star-trek/
home-st.html

# Security

**McAfee Virus Forum**   Vendor forum.

GO NCSAVIRUS

**National Computer Security Association**   Official forum of the NCSA.

GO NCSA

**Symantec AntiVirus Forum**   Vendor forum.

GO SYMVIRUS

# Seniors

**American Association of Retired People (AARP)**   Official online area for the AARP.

GO AARP

**Retirement Living Forum**   Includes sections on food, housing, family, etc.

GO RETIREMENT

# Sexuality & Adult Topics

**Adult File Finder**   File Finder for files with adult content.

GO ADULTFF

**FHM Connect**   Online version of the British men's magazine.

GO FHMCONNECT

**FHM Connect Forum**   Forum for *FHM* magazine.

GO TALKFHM

**HSX Adult Forum**   Adult topics, with files closed to the general public.

GO HSX200

**HSX Open Forum**   Similar to HSX100 without the adult files.

GO HSX100

**Human Sexuality Databank**   Database of information on sex-related topics.

GO HUMAN

**Nudist & Naturist Forum**   For the naked among us.

GO NUDIST

**Playboy**   The famous men's magazine online.

GO PLAYBOY

**Playboy Forum**   The forum for *Playboy* magazine.

GO PLAYFORUM

# Shopping

**800 Flowers**   Online retailer.

GO FGS

**Absolut Museum, The**   Online manufacturer.

GO ABS

**Adventures in Food**   Online retailer.

GO AIF

**Airline Services Unlimited**   Online retailer.

GO ASU-1

**Alaska Peddler**   Online retailer.

GO ALASKA

**Amazon.com Books**   Premier online bookstore.

WEB http://www.amazon.com/

**Americana Clothing**   Online retailer.

GO AC

**AutoSite**   New car and used car showrooms on CompuServe.

GO AUTOSITE

**AutoSite**   Lets you compare new car features and prices.

WEB http://www.autosite.com/

**Branch Mall**   Web-based shopping mall.

WEB http://branch.com:1080/

**Brooks Brothers Online Store**   Online retailer.

GO BR

**CDNow!**   Online retailer of music CDs and tapes.

WEB http://www.cdnow.com/

**Classified Ads**   Read or place classified advertisements.

GO CLASSIFIEDS

**Commercial Services on the Net**   Open Market's directory of commercial services, products, and information on the Internet.

WEB http://www.directory.net/

**CompuBooks Online Bookstore**   Good online source for computer books.

WEB http://www.compubooks.com/

**CompuServe Electonic Mall**
CompuServe's main online shopping area.

GO SHOPPING

**CompuServe Store**   Where you can order all sorts of CompuServe-related merchandise.

GO ORDER

**Consumer Forum**   Includes sections on banking, bargains, coupons, complaints, rights, and ripoffs.

GO CONSUMER

**Consumer Reports**   Online magazine.

GO CONSUMER

**Detroit Free Press Store**   Subscription service for the *Detroit Free Press* that also includes books and other merchandise.

GO DFM-1

**Dial-A-Mattress**   Online retailer.

GO BEDS

**Dinner on Us Club**   Discount dining club.

GO DINE

**Directory of Catalogs**   The place to order catalogs from CompuServe merchants.

GO DTC

**Electronic Mall ELITE**   Special offers for shoppers on the Electronic Mall.

GO ELITE

**Electronic Mall News**   News from CompuServe's Electronic Mall.

GO EMN

**Escort Store, The**   Online retailer.

GO ESCORT

**EUROMALL**   Web-based shopping mall for European merchants.

WEB http://
www.internet-eireann.ie/
Euromall/

**Figi's Inc.**   Online retailer.

GO FIGIS

**FTD Online**   Online retailer.

GO FTD

**Gift Sender, The**   Online retailer.

GO GIFT

**Hall of Malls**   Listing of dozens of online malls.

WEB http://nsns.com/MouseTracks/
HallofMalls.html

**Health and Vitamin Express**   Online retailer.

GO HVE-1

**Heath Company, The**   Online retailer.

GO HEATH

**Homefinder by AMS**   Online retailer.

GO HF

**Interflora**   Online retailer.

GO UKINTERFLORA

**Internet Mall**   Web-based shopping mall.

WEB http://
www.internet-mall.com/

**Internet Shopping Network**   Web-based shopping mall.

WEB http://www.internet.net/

**JC Penney**   Online retailer.

GO JCPENNEY

**JDR Microdevices**   Online retailer.

GO JDR

**Ken Crane's Laserdisc Superstore**   Online laserdisc retailer.

WEB http://www.kencranes.com/
laserdiscs/

**Laser's Edge, The**   Online laserdisc retailer.

    GO LE

**Mac Zone/PC Zone**   Online retailer.

    GO MZ-1

**MacWAREHOUSE**   Online retailer.

    GO MW

**marketplaceMCI**   Web-based shopping mall hosted by MCI.

    WEB http://www2.pcy.mci.net/
    marketplace/index.html

**Metropolitan Museum of Art**   Online retailer.

    GO MMA

**MicroWarehouse**   Online retailer.

    GO MCW

**New Car Showroom**   Database for comparison of different car models.

    GO NEWCAR

**Omaha Steaks International**   Online retailer.

    GO OS

**PC Catalog**   Online retailer.

    GO PCA

**PC Publications**   Subscription service for *PC Novice*, *PC Today*, and *PC Catalog* magazines.

    GO PCB

**PRC Database Publishing Services**   Online manufacturer, specializing in publishing needs.

    GO PRC

**Quality Paperback Book Club**   Online book club.

    GO QPB1

**Sears**   Online retailer.

    GO SEARS

**Seattle Film Works**   Online retailer.

    GO SFW-1

**Shareware Depot**   Online retailer.

    GO SD

**Shoppers Advantage Club**   Online shopper's discount club.

    GO SAC

**Small Computer Book Club**   Online book club.

    GO BK

**SOFTEX**   Online retailer.

    GO SOFTEX

**Sundown Vitamins**   Online retailer.

    GO SDV

**Sunglasses/Shavers & More**   Online retailer.

    GO SN

**Technical Bookstores on the Net**  List of technical bookstores on the Net provided by Macmillan Publishing.

    WEB http://www.mcp.com/general/
    techbook.html

**The Store**  Online retailer.

    GO STORE

**Ticketmaster Online**  Order tickets for upcoming concerts, online.

    WEB http://www.ticketmaster.com/

**Time-Warner Bookstore**  Online retailer.

    GO TWEP

**Travelers Advantage**  Online travel club.

    GO TRAVADV

**Virgin Megastores**  Online retailer; the largest record store in the world.

    GO VIRGIN

**Virginia Diner**  Online retailer.

    GO DINER

**Walter Knoll Florist**  Online retailer.

    GO WK

**Yahoo's Products and Services Index**
Comprehensive list of businesses on the Net.

    WEB http://
    www.yahoo.com/Business/
    Products_and_Services/

**ZDNet Electronic Books**  Online retailer.

    GO ZNT:EBOOKS

# Space

**Astronomy Forum**  For amateur and professional astronomers.

    GO ASTROFORUM

**NASA**  Official NASA Web site.

    WEB http://www.nasa.gov

**NASA Hubble Space Telescope Electronic Information**  Stunning photographs from the Hubble telescope.

    WEB http://marvel.stsci.edu/
    top.html

**NASA News and Information**  News, schedules, and photos from NASA.

    GO NASA

**Sky & Telescope**  Online magazine.

    GO SKYTEL

**Space Exploration Forum**  Includes information on earth observation, the planets, the sun, the moon, etc.

    GO SPACEX

**Space Flight Forum**  Includes sections on the Space Shuttle, space stations, new technology, etc.

    GO SPACEFLIGHT

**Space in the Classroom**  Sponsored by the United States Space Foundation.

    GO USSF

**Space/Astronomy Forum**  Includes information on sunspots, solar flares, NASA activities, space technology, and so on.

    GO SPACE

# Spain

**Microsoft Spain/Latin America**   Vendor forum.

    GO MSSPAIN

**Microsoft Spain/Latin America Forum**
Vendor forum.

    GO MSSP

**Spanish Forum**   For residents and tourists.

    GO SPFORUM

# Sports

**American Racing Scene**   Top-notch Web site devoted to motor sports.

    WEB http://www.racecar.com/

**America's Cup Forum**   Info on the America's Cup competition.

    GO AMERICASCUP

**Associated Press Online**   Up-to-the-minute sports news.

    GO APO

**Baseball**   News, scores, stats, and links.

    GO SIBASEBALL

**College Basketball**   News, scores, stats, and links.

    GO SICBASKETBALL

**College Football**   News, scores, stats, and links.

    GO SICFOOTBALL

**ESPNet SportsZone**   The most comprehensive and most in-depth sports site on the Web.

    WEB http://
    espnet.sportszone.com/

**Fantasy Basketball**   Fantasy basketball leagues online.

    GO FASTBREAK

**Fantasy Football League**   Play fantasy football online.

    GO SIFFL

**Golf Guide Online**   From the Lanier Golf Database, a comprehensive listing of more than 12,000 golf courses across the U.S. and 1,200 more courses worldwide.

    GO GLF

**Information Please Sports Almanac**
Sports almanac, from the Information Please people.

    GO APTALMANAC

**International Sportswire Feed**
International sports news and scores.

    GO DSPORT

**MLB@BAT**   Web site for major league baseball.

    WEB http://
    www.majorleaguebaseball.com/

**Motor Sports Forum**   Includes sections on IndyCar, NASCAR, USAC, NHRA, Formula One, etc.

    GO RACING

**MotorWeek Online** Online motor sports magazine.

    GO MOTORWEEK

**Nando Sports Server** Good all-around sports service on the Web.

    WEB http://www.nando.net/
    SportServer/

**NBA.com** Web site for NBA basketball.

    WEB http://www.nba.com/

**NBC Sports** Good Web-based sports site run by NBC Sports.

    WEB http://www.nbc.com/sports/
    index.html

**NCAA Collegiate Sports Network** Statistics and scores for major college sports.

    GO NCAA

**Professional Basketball** News, scores, stats, and links.

    GO SIPBASKETBALL

**Professional Football** News, scores, stats, and links.

    GO SIPFOOTBALL

**Professional Hockey** News, scores, stats, and links.

    GO SIPHOCKEY

**Sports Forum** Includes sections on football, baseball, hockey, basketball, etc.

    GO FANS

**Sports Illustrated** CompuServe's main sports area, run by Sports Illustrated.

    GO SPORTS

**Sports Illustrated Online** Online sports magazine.

    GO SIMAGAZINE

**Sports Simulation Forum** For players of sports simulation games.

    GO SPRTSIMS

**SportsLine USA** Comprehensive sports-oriented Web site.

    WEB http://www.sportsline.com/

**Team NFL** Web site for NFL football.

    WEB http://nflhome.com/

**Tennis Forum** For tennis players and fans.

    GO TENNIS

**UK Sports Clips** News on British sports, including football, cricket, snooker, and rugby.

    GO UKSPORTS

# Stocks, Bonds, and Personal Finance

**American Stock Exchange** News and information on all listed companies.

    WEB http://www.amex.com/

**Basic Company Snapshot** Essential company information.

    GO BASCOMPAN

**Bonds Listing**   Listings and ratings from S&P and Moody's.

    GO BONDS

**Business Database Plus**   Database of detailed company information.

    GO BUSDB

**Canada Net Pages**   Comprehensive source for Canadian business and financial data.

    WEB http://www.visions.com/

**Ceres Securities**   Online brokerage.

    WEB http://www.ceres.com

**Charles Schwab & Company, Inc.**   Online brokerage.

    WEB http://www.schwab.com

**CNNfn**   Online version of the cable financial news network.

    WEB http://cnnfn.com/

**Company Analyzer**   Comprehensive, one-stop shopping for company information.

    GO ANALYZER

**Company Screening**   Searches Disclosure database to identify investment candidates.

    GO COSCREEN

**Current Market SNAPSHOT**   One-page report of statistics and key indicators of the current market.

    GO SNAPSHOT

**Detailed Issue Examination**   Detailed analysis of stock/bond performance.

    GO EXAMINE

**Disclosure**   Very comprehensive database with full financial and management information on more than 11,000 firms, compiled from 10K and other public reports. Recommended.

    GO DISCLOSURE

**Dividends and Splits**   Information about dividends, bond interest, and splits.

    GO DIVIDENDS

**Dreyfus Corporation**   Information on selecting mutual funds.

    GO DR

**Ebroker**   Online brokerage.

    WEB http://www.ebroker.com

**E*TRADE**   The Web version of the E*TRADE service offered on CompuServe.

    WEB http://www.etrade.com

**E*TRADE Securities**   Online trading.

    GO ETRADE

**E*TRADE Stock Market Game**   Online game, modeled on current financial markets.

    GO ETGAME

**Finance**   CompuServe's main menu for stock market and personal finance services.

    GO FINANCE

**FinanCenter**   Online personal finance resource center. Recommended.

    WEB http://www.financenter.com/
    resources/

**Financial Forecasts**   Gateway to various financial analysis, including I/B/E/S Earnings Estimate, S&P Online, InvesText, etc.

GO EARNINGS

**Financial Forums**   Main area for CompuServe's financial services.

GO FINFORUM

**Financial Information Link Library**   List of links to financial sites around the world.

WEB http://www.mbnet.ca:80/
~russell/

**FORBES**   Online magazine.

GO FORBES

**FORTUNE Magazine**   Online magazine.

GO FORTUNE

**Hoover's Company Database**   Offering Company Profiles and Company Capsules.

GO HOOVER

**Hoover's Online**   Detailed company-specific information, similar to CompuServe's Hoover's database.

WEB http://www.hoovers.com/

**Institutional Brokers Estimate Service Earning Estimate Reports**   Representing a consensus of analysts' forecasts.

GO IBES

**InvesText**   Database of financial reports compiled by major Wall Street analysts.

GO INVTEXT

**InvestGrow**   Online investment center.

WEB http://www.investgrow.com/
index.shtml

**Issue Pricing History**   Day-by-day, week-by-week, or month-by-month history of an issue's pricing.

GO PRICES

**Kiplinger Online**   Online magazine.

WEB http://www.kiplinger.com/

**Lombard Securities**   Online brokerage.

WEB http://www.lombard.com

**Market Highlights**   Current stock quotes.

GO MARKET

**Money Magazine**   Online magazine.

GO MONEY

**Money Magazine's FundWatch Online**   Database that lets you analyze and screen more than 1900 mutual funds.

GO FUNDWATCH

**MoneyAdvisor**   Web-based personal finance site.

WEB http://www.moneyadvisor.com/

**Mortgage Calculator**   Online tool for calculating mortgage rates.

GO HOM-17

**Mortgage Strategies**   Online report: how to save on your mortgage interest.

WEB http://www.ais.net:80/
netmall/mortgage/mortgage.html

**NETworth**   GALT Technologies' in-depth information on more than 5000 mutual funds.

    WEB http://networth/galt.com/

**New Stocks Daily**   Analysis of new stock offerings.

    WEB http://www.dma.net/dom/

**News-A-Tron**   Daily financial news.

    GO NAT

**PAWWS Financial Network**   Providing a variety of online quotes, charts, and financial information.

    WEB http://pawws.secapl.com/

**PC Quote**   Real-time securities quotations and news.

    WEB http://ds9.spacecom.com/
    Participants/pcquote/

**Portfolio Valuation**   Tracks the value of your portfolio.

    GO PORT

**Pricing Statistics**   Snapshot of price and volume performance of an issue over a given period.

    GO PRISTATS

**Quicken Home Page**   Financial advice and support from Intuit, the publisher of Quicken.

    WEB http://www.intuit.com/
    quicken/

**QuickWay**   Online brokerage service provided by Quick & Reilly.

    GO QWK

**Quote.Com**   Up-to-date financial market data, as well as business news, market analysis, and commentary.

    WEB http://www.quote.com/

**Securities Screening**   Microquotes database of stock performance.

    GO SCREEN

**Securities Symbols Lookup**   Look up issues by name or ticker symbol.

    GO SYMBOLS

**Single Issue Price History**   Database of stock and bond pricing.

    GO PRICES

**Standard & Poor's Online**   Current business information on more than 5,000 companies.

    GO S&P

**StockTracker**   Third-party software for tracking stock-market information.

    GO STOCKTRADER

**Ticker/Symbol Lookup**   Look up stocks by name or ticker symbol.

    GO LOOKUP

**UK Historical Stock Pricing**   Database of historical information on British stocks and bonds.

    GO UKPRICE

**UK Issue Lookup**   Look up information for British stocks.

    GO SEDOL

**Vestor Stock Recommendation**  Unique service that helps you make investment decisions.

    GO VESTOR

**Wall Street Journal on the Web**  Online newspaper; includes the continually updated Money & Investing Update.

    WEB http:///www.wsj.com/

# Sweden

**Microsoft Sweden Forum**  Vendor forum for Microsoft's Swedish operations.

    GO MSSWE

# Taxes

**Electronic Tax Return Filing**  File your taxes online via this service.

    GO TAXRETURN

**Essential Tax Links**  Links to numerous Web-based tax resources.

    WEB http://www.el.com/ToTheWeb/
    Taxes/

**H&R Block**  Online tax information.

    GO HRB

**Forum**  Vendor forum, for users of Quicken and QuickBooks.

    GO INTUIT

**Intuit Personal Tax Forum**  Vendor forum, for users of TurboTax software.

    GO INVIT

**IRS Online**  Good source for tax information and downloadable forms.

    WEB http://www.irs.ustreas.gov/
    prod/

**IRS Tax Forms and Documents**  Downloadable and printable IRS tax forms, complete with instructions.

    GO TAXFORMS

**Legal Research Center**  Access to various legal databases, including American Banker, Congressional Information Service, Criminal Justice Periodical Index, Legal Resource Index, National Criminal Justice Reference Service, and Tax Notes Today.

    GO LEGALRC

# Television

**America's Funniest Home Videos**  Fun from the hit TV show.

    GO HOMEVIDEOS

**Broadcast Professionals Forum**  Includes sections on television, radio, cable TV, audio, the FCC, etc.

    GO BPFORUM

**CBS Campaign '96**  CBS News' official Web site for the 1996 elections.

    WEB http://www.cbsnews.com/
    campaign96/

**CNN Forum**  CNN's forum on CompuServe.

    GO CNNFORUM

**CNN Interactive**  Online version of the
Cable News Network.

 GO CNN

**CNN TalkBack Live Forum**  Talk back to
CNN right here.

 GO TALKBACK

**CNN Web**  CNN's Web-based service.

 WEB http://www.cnn.com/

**CNNfn**  Online version of the cable
financial news network.

 WEB http://cnnfn.com/

**Comedy Central**  Online version of the
hit cable channel; it includes Politically
Incorrect, Stand-Up Online, and Quick
Laughs.

 GO COMEDY

**Computers on Television Forum**  Includes
sections on Computer Chronicles, Random
Access, @Home, Business Computing, etc.

 GO PCTV

**ETV Forum**  EDrive's TV forum.

 GO ETV

**Jack Hanna's Animal Adventures**  Animal
fun from the TV show.

 GO JUNGLEJACK

**NBC Sports**  Good Web-based sports site
run by NBC Sports.

 WEB http://www.nbc.com/sports/
 index.html

**Science Fiction and Fantasy Media Forums**
All forms of SF and fantasy are represented
here, from current TV shows and movies to
classic SF like Star Wars, Star Trek, and
Doctor Who.

 GO SFMEDIA1 and GO SFMEDIA2

**ScreenScene**  Main menu to CompuServe's
movie and TV areas.

 GO SCENE

**Soap Opera Forum**  Discuss your favorite
soaps online.

 GO SOAPFORUM

**Soap Opera Summaries**  Summaries and
news from daytime and primetime TV soap
operas.

 GO SOAPS

**Star Trek**  Paramount's official page for TV
and movie versions of Star Trek.

 WEB http://www.paramount.com/
 Splash.html

**TV Bytes**  Comprehensive database of
television theme songs, playable over the
Web.

 WEB http://www.tvtrecords.com/
 tvbytes/

**TV Host**  Online TV schedules.

 WEB http://www.tvhost.com/
 ~tvhost/

**TV Net**  Good TV site.

 WEB http://www.tvnet.com/
 TVnet.html

**TV Zone Forum** Television news, information, and discussions.

GO TVZONE

**UK TV Soap Previews** Previewing British soaps.

GO UKSOAPS

**Weather Channel Forum** The cable weather channel online.

GO TWCFORUM

# Testing

**Intelligence Test** Online IQ test.

GO TMC-101

**Kaplan** Online test prep.

WEB http://www.kaplan.com/

**Mensa Forum** For current and would-be Mensa members.

GO MENSA

**Personality Profile** Online personality quizzes.

GO TMC-90

**Science/Math Education Forum** For science educators and students; includes practice problems for science and math college boards

GO SCIENCE

# Travel

**AA Days Out** British travel activities.

GO UKDAYSOUT

**AA Restaurants** British restaurant information.

GO UKREST

**AA Roadwatch** Real-time information on British road conditions.

GO AAROADWATCH

**ABC Worldwide Hotel Guide** Listings of over 60,000 hotels worldwide.

GO ABC

**Adventures in Travel** Articles about worldwide travel.

GO AIT

**Air Canada Forum** Flight information and discussions.

GO AIRCANADA

**Air France** Information on Air France flights.

GO AF

**Air Travel Manager** Vendor forum, for AirTM travel software.

GO AIRTM

**Air Traveler's Handbook** Basic info and links to other air travel resourses on the Web.

WEB http://www.cs.cmu.edu/afs/
cs.cmu.edu/user/mkant/Public/
Travel/airfare.html

**Airline Services Unlimited**   Online retailer.

```
GO ASU-1
```

**Airlines of the Web**   Links to all major U.S. and international airlines.

```
WEB http://haas.berkeley.edu/
~seidel/airline.html
```

**BizTravel**   A good site for business travelers.

```
WEB http://www.biztravel.com/
guide/
```

**Caribbean Travel Forum**   Discussions of interest to tourists.

```
GO CARIBFORUM
```

**City.Net**   A comprehensive guide to cities around the world.

```
WEB http://www.city.net/
```

**CitySavvy**   Insider's guides to entertainment and dining in major U.S. cities.

```
WEB http://www.cais.net/
citysavvy/
```

**Complete Guide to America's National Parks**   News and information from the National Park Service.

```
GO PARKS
```

**Conde Nast Traveler**   Online travel magazine.

```
WEB http://www.cntraveler.com/
```

**Department of State Advisories**
Advisories and warnings for Americans traveling abroad.

```
GO STATE
```

**EAASY SABRE**   American Airlines' travel reservation system.

```
GO SABRE
```

**European Railway Schedule**   Schedules for continental rail travel.

```
GO RAILWAY
```

**Foreign Language Forum**   Includes sections on French, German, Spanish, Italian, etc.

```
GO FLEFO
```

**GNN Travel Resource Center**   One of the Web's premier travel-related sites, from the Global Network.

```
WEB http://gnn.com/meta/travel/
index.html
```

**Golf Guide Online**   From the Lanier Golf Database, a comprehensive listing of more than 12,000 golf courses across the U.S. and 1,200 more courses worldwide.

```
GO GLF
```

**Hotel Guide**   Web-based guide to hotels around the world.

```
WEB http://www.hotelguide.ch/
```

**Inn and Lodging Forum**   Includes sections on innkeeping, bed & breakfasts, elegant hotels, etc.

```
GO INNFORUM
```

**Internet Travel Network**   Online airline reservations.

```
WEB http://www.itn.net/
```

**Lanier Bed & Breakfast Database**   Data on more than 9000 North American inns.

    GO INNS

**Lycos Road Map**   Instant Web-based mapping service; enter your information and a detailed map will be drawn.

    WEB http://www.proximus.com/
    lycos/

**Macmillan Travel**   Home of Frommer's travel guides.

    WEB http://www.mcp.com/mgr/
    travel/

**MAGELLAN Geographix**   Online mapping.

    GO MAGELLAN

**Mexico Interest Forum**   Items of interest to residents and travelers.

    GO HOM-213

**Mexico Travel & Culture Forum**
Discussions of interest to tourists.

    GO MEXTRAVEL

**Official Airline Guide**   Flight information.

    GO OAG

**Ohio Travel Forum**   Discussions for tourists.

    GO OHIO

**Outdoors News Clips**   News on environmental and outdoors activities.

    GO OUTNEWS

**State Travel Tourism Forum**   Discussions of interest to tourists, organized by state.

    GO USTOUR

**Subway Navigator**   Unique site that displays subway routes in cities around the world.

    WEB http://
    metro.jussieu.fr:10001/bin/
    cities/english

**Travel**   CompuServe's main travel area, where you can access a variety of travel-related services and forums.

    GO TRAVEL

**Travel Britain Online**   Information on British travel.

    GO TBONLINE

**Travel Forum**   Includes sections on restaurants, hotels, cruises, customs, etc.

    GO TRAVSIG

**Travel Software Support Forum**   Vendor forum.

    GO TSSFORUM

**Travel Weekly**   Good source for up-to-the-minute travel news.

    WEB http://www.traveler.net/

**TravelData Guide to Bed & Breakfast Inns**   Lists thousands of bed & breakfast inns across America.

    WEB http://www.ultranet.com/biz/
    inns/

**Travelers Advantage**   Online travel club.

    GO TRAVADV

**Travelocity**   First-class site run by the same folks who run EAASY SABRE; it lets you make airline, hotel, and auto rental reservations.

    WEB http://www.travelocity.com/

**TravelWeb**   Information and reservations for most major hotel chains.

    WEB http://www.travelweb.com/

**UK Accomodations & Travel Services** Services provided by the UK Automobile Association.

    GO UKACCOMODATION

**United Connection**   Online reservations system, managed by United Airlines.

    GO UNITED

**USA CityLink Project**   A listing of Web pages for selected U.S. cities and states.

    WEB http://www.NeoSoft.com:80/
    citylink/

**Virtual Tourist II**   Map-based interface to City.Net. Highly recommended.

    WEB http://wings.buffalo.edu/
    world/vt2/

**Visa Advisors**   Offers assistance in obtaining passports and visas.

    GO VISA

**West Coast Travel**   Travel guide to western U.S. destinations.

    GO WESTCOAST

**WORLDSPAN Travelshopper**   Online reservations from Delta, Northwest, and TWA airlines.

    GO WORLDCIM

**Zagat Restaurant Guide**   Thousands of restaurant reviews for more than 20 cities.

    GO ZAGAT

# United Kingdom

**AA Days Out**   British travel activities.

    GO UKDAYSOUT

**AA Golf**   British golf information.

    GO UKGOLF

**AA Restaurants**   British restaurant information.

    GO UKREST

**AA Roadwatch**   Real-time information on British road conditions.

    GO AAROADWATCH

**Best of British Web Sites**   Best Web sites in the U.K.

    WEB http://www.vnu.co.uk/vnu/
    pcw/bob.html

**British Books in Print**   Database of books published in the U.K.

    GO BBIP

**British Trade Marks**   Trade mark database for U.K. businesses.

    GO UKTRADEMARK

**CarWorld Connect**   Online British motoring magazine.

    GO CARWORLDCONNECT

**CarWorld Connect Forum**   Forum for the British motoring magazine.

    GO TALKCARWORLD

**FHM Connect**   Online version of British men's magazine.

GO FHMCONNECT

**FHM Connect Forum**   Forum for *FHM* magazine.

GO TALKFHM

**Good Pub Guide**   Database guide to British pubs.

GO UKPUBS

**Imperial College Archives**   Repository of software on the Internet.

FTP ftp.doc.ic.ac.uk

**Interflora**   Online retailer.

GO UKINTERFLORA

**Newspaper Archives**   Database of stories from major U.S. and U.K. newspapers.

GO NEWSARCHIVE

**PA News Online**   British news.

GO PAO

**PC Direct UK Magazine Forum**   Online magazine; part of the ZDNet service.

GO PCDUK

**PC Magazine UK Forum**   Online magazine; part of the ZDNet service.

GO PCUKFORUM

**PC Magazine UK Online**   Online magazine; part of the ZDNet service.

GO PCUKONLINE

**PC Plus/PC Answers Online**   Online magazines.

GO PCPLUS

**Reuter's UK News Clips**   British news.

GO UKREUTERS

**Travel Britain Online**   Information on British travel.

GO TBONLINE

**UK Accomodations & Travel Services**   Services provided by the UK Automobile Association.

GO UKACCOMODATION

**UK Book Reviews**   Reviews of British bestsellers.

GO UKBREV

**UK Communications Forum**   Communications information and discussions with a British flavor.

GO UKCOMMS

**UK Company Information**   Financial information on British companies.

GO COUK

**UK Company Library**   Database of information British companies.

GO UKLIB

**UK Computer Shopper Forum**   Online magazine.

GO UKSHOPPER

**UK Computing Forum**   Covering computer topics of interest to the United Kingdom.

GO UKCOMP

**UK Entertainment Reviews**   Reviews of British films, theatre, videos, and soap operas.

GO UKENT

**UK Film Reviews**   Reviews of movies currently playing in Britain.

   GO UKFILMS

**UK Forum**   For residents and tourists.

   GO UKFORUM

**UK Historical Stock Pricing**   Database of historical information on British stocks and bonds.

   GO UKPRICE

**UK Issue Lookup**   Look up information for British stocks.

   GO SEDOL

**UK Music Forum**   Music in the U.K.

   GO UKMUSIC

**UK News Clips**   Current U.K. news from the PA News service.

   GO UKNEWS

**UK Newspaper Library**   Database of stories from major U.K. newspapers.

   GO UKPAPERS

**UK Professionals Forum**   Includes sections on job opportunities, news, and professional groups.

   GO UKPROF

**UK Research Centre**   Database of British information.

   GO UKLIB

**UK Shareware Forum**   Libraries full of shareware programs from British developers.

   GO UKSHARE

**UK Sports Clips**   News on British sports, including football, cricket, snooker, and rugby.

   GO UKSPORTS

**UK Theatre Reviews**   Reviews from the U.K. stage.

   GO UKTHEATRE

**UK TV Soap Previews**   Previewing British soaps.

   GO UKSOAPS

**UK Video Reviews**   Reviews of current British videotape releases.

   GO UKVIDEO

**UK Weather**   Weather from the British Isles.

   GO UKWEATHER

**UK What's On Guide**   Comprehensive guide to British entertainment and events.

   GO UKWO

**USENET Newsgroup Archives**   Archive of newsgroup articles, hosted by the University of Birmingham (U.K.).

   FTP ftp.cs.bham.ac.uk

# U.S. Locales

**Alaska Peddler**   Online retailer.

   GO ALASKA

**California Forum**   Includes sections on major cities and regions.

   GO CALFORUM

**Caribbean Travel Forum** Discussions relevant to tourists.

GO CARIBFORUM

**City.Net** A comprehensive guide to cities around the world.

WEB http://www.city.net/

**Colorado Forum** For residents and tourists.

GO COLORADO

**Florida Forum** For residents and tourists.

GO FLORIDA

**Florida Today Forum** Online newspaper.

GO FLATODAY

**Hawaii Forum** For residents and tourists.

GO HAWAII

**Lycos Road Map** Instant Web-based mapping service; enter your information and a detailed map will be drawn.

WEB http://www.proximus.com/lycos/

**MAGELLAN Geographix** Online mapping.

GO MAGELLAN

**New York Magazine** Online magazine.

GO NYMAG

**New York NewsLink Forum** New York-area news and information from Gannett Suburban Newspapers.

GO NEWYORK

**Ohio Travel Forum** Discussions of interest to tourists.

GO OHIO

**State Travel Tourism Forum** Discussions of interest to tourists, organized by state.

GO USTOUR

**USA CityLink Project** A listing of Web pages for selected U.S. cities and states.

WEB http://www.NeoSoft.com:80/citylink/

**Virtual Tourist II** Map-based interface to City.Net. Highly recommended.

WEB http://wings.buffalo.edu/world/vt2/

**West Coast Travel** Travel guide to western U.S. destinations.

GO WESTCOAST

# Weather

**INTELLiCast** Local weather forecasts across the U.S., from NBC.

WEB http://www.intellicast.com/

**Jeppesen's Aviation Weather Graphics** Radar, Lifted Index, and Convective Outlook charts—more than 60 different maps in all.

GO JEPP

**NWS Aviation Weather** Official aviation weather reports from the National Weather Service (NWS).

GO AWX

**UK Weather** Weather from the British Isles.

    GO UKWEATHER

**Weather Channel** Online version of the popular cable channel.

    WEB http://www.weather.com/

**Weather Channel Forum** The cable weather channel online.

    GO TWCFORUM

**Weather Maps** Up-to-the-minute weather maps, including radar and satellite images.

    GO MAPS

**Weather Reports** Current weather forecasts.

    GO WEA

# Women's Issues

**Ninety Nines Forum** Private forum of The Ninety-Nines, Inc., the International Organization of Women Pilots.

    GO NINETYNINES

**Women in Aviation Forum** For women in all fields of aviation and space endeavors.

    GO WIAONLINE

**Women's Wire** Women's issues online.

    GO WOMEN

**Women's Wire Forum** Women's issues discussed.

    GO WWFORUM

# Writing & Journalism

**Journalism Forum** Targeting professional journalists, photographers, and freelance writers.

    GO JFORUM

**Literary Forum** For writers and readers.

    GO LITFORUM

**Time-Warner Authors Forum** A gathering place for famous and would-be authors.

    GO TWAUTHORS

**Working-From-Home Forum** Includes sections on taxes, equipment, consulting, writing, etc.

    GO WORK

# ZDNet

**Bendata Forum** Vendor forum; part of ZDNet.

    GO ZNT:BENDATA

**Cobb Applications Forum** Part of ZDNet.

    GO ZNT:COBAPP

**Cobb Programming Forum** Part of ZDNet.

    GO ZNT:COBBPR

**Computer Life** Online magazine.

    GO LIFE

**Computer Shopper Magazine** Online magazine; part of the ZDNet service.

    GO CSHOPPER

**Executives Online Forum**   Direct access to computer industry executives; part of ZDNet.

    GO ZNT:EXEC

**MacUser/MacWEEK Index**   Index of stories from *MacUser* and *MacWEEK* magazines, part of ZDNet.

    GO ZNT:ZMACINDEX

**Newsbytes**   Daily computer news; part of the ZDNet service.

    GO ZNT:NEWSBYTES

**PC Computing**   Online magazine; part of the ZDNet service.

    GO PCCOMP

**PC Contact Forum**   Part of ZDNet.

    GO PCCONTACT

**PC Direct UK Magazine Forum**   Online magazine; part of the ZDNet service.

    GO PCDUK

**PC Magazine**   Online magazine.

    GO PCMAGAZINE

**PC Magazine UK Forum**   Online magazine; part of the ZDNet service.

    GO PCUKFORUM

**PC Magazine UK Online**   Online magazine; part of the ZDNet service.

    GO PCUKONLINE

**PC MagNet Editorial Forum**   Part of ZDNet.

    GO EDITORIAL

**PC MagNet Programming Forum**   Part of ZDNet.

    GO PROGRAMMING

**PC MagNet Utilities/Tips Forum**   Part of ZDNet.

    GO TIPS

**PC Week Forum**   Online magazine; part of the ZDNet service.

    GO PCWEEK

**Public Brand Software Applications Forum**   Libraries full of shareware programs; part of the ZDNet service.

    GO PBSAPPS

**Public Brand Software Home Forum**   Libraries full of shareware programs; part of the ZDNet service.

    GO PBSHOME

**Software Center**   Libraries full of shareware and freeware programs; part of the ZDNet service.

    GO ZNT:CENTER

**Speakeasy Forum**   A relaxed online meeting place; part of the ZDNet service.

    GO SPEAKEASY

**ZDNet**   Ziff-Davis' online service accessible for CompuServe members.

    GO ZIFFNET

**ZDNet Designer Templates**   Downloadable spreadsheet and word processing templates; part of ZDNet.

    GO FORMS

**ZDNet Electronic Books**   Online retailer.

GO ZNT:EBOOKS

**ZDNet File Finder**   File Finder for files on the ZDNet service.

GO ZNT:ZFILEFINDER

**ZDNet FREE UTILS Forum**   Free downloadable software utilities; part of the ZDNet service.

GO ZNT:FREEUTIL

**ZDNet Membership and Benefits** Information about the ZDNet service.

GO ZNT:ZIFFMEM

**ZDNet Reviews Index**   Database of reviews from various Ziff-Davis computer magazines.

GO ZIFFINDEX

**ZDNet Support Forum**   Part of ZDNet.

GO ZIFFHELP

**ZDNet Surveys**   Part of ZDNet.

GO ZNT:SURVEY

**ZDNet/Mac**   ZDNet's Macintosh resources, also known as Zmac.

GO ZMAC

**ZDNet/Mac Download Forum**   Top Macintosh shareware and freeware programs from the editors of *MacWEEK* and *MacUser* magazines; part of ZDNet.

GO ZMC:DOWNTECH

**ZDNet/Mac File Finder**   File Finder for Macintosh-compatible files on the ZDNet service.

GO ZMC:FILEFINDER

**Ziff Editor's Choice**   Database of Editor's Choice awards; part of ZDNet.

GO ZNT:EDCHOICE

**Zshare Online Newsletter**   Monthly review of shareware programs; part of the ZDNet service.

GO ZNT:ZSHARE

# Index

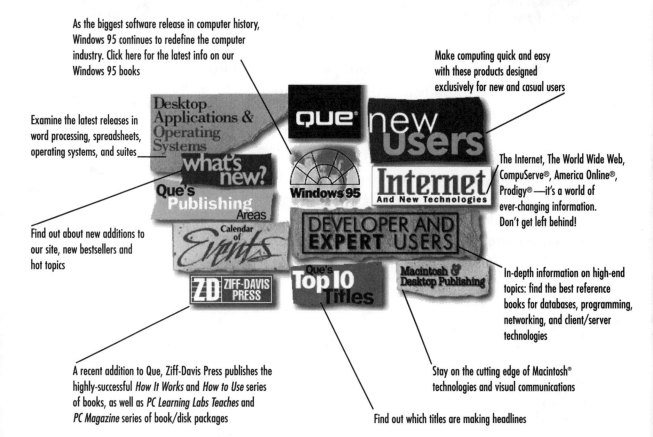